UNCHAINED

UNCHAINED

THE EDDIE VAN HALEN STORY

PAUL BRANNIGAN

PERMUTED
PRESS

A PERMUTED PRESS BOOK
ISBN: 978-1-63758-350-0
ISBN (eBook): 978-1-63758-351-7

Unchained:
The Eddie Van Halen Story
© 2021 by Paul Brannigan
All Rights Reserved

Cover design by Tiffani Shea
Cover photo by Paul Natkin via Getty Images

First published in the UK in 2021 by Faber & Faber Limited
Bloomsbury House
74–77 Great Russell Street London WC1B 3DA

PERMUTED
PRESS

Permuted Press, LLC
New York • Nashville
permutedpress.com

Published in the United States of America
1 2 3 4 5 6 7 8 9 10

CONTENTS

PRELUDE

Lost in music, Eddie Van Halen didn't initially hear his wife screaming at him as he repeatedly pounded out the keyboard riff which had been living rent-free in his head for the best part of two years. Only later, listening back to his first demo recording of that percussive chord vamp, instantly recognisable now as the introduction to his band's signature anthem 'Jump', could Eddie pick out the exasperated yells of 'Shut up!' coming from the couple's bedroom as he jabbed staccato triads on the synth on his living-room floor.

In the earliest months of his residency in America, constantly hearing those same two words – from bullying teachers, from racist classmates, from the stressed, exhausted, homesick parents in the two families who shared the three-bedroom property in the Pasadena suburbs in which his own family was housed upon emigrating to California – caused the previously confident, happy-go-lucky, inquisitive Dutch youngster to withdraw deep into his own imagination. It wasn't until he discovered rock 'n' roll, and the liberating potential of an over-amplified electric guitar, that the young Eddie Van Halen found his voice and began to reimagine the world around him. That process began soon after he reached the age of majority, when, dissatisfied with the mass-produced 'classic' guitars that had helped democratise rock 'n' roll for the generation which preceded him, he invented his own hybrid instrument, a bespoke 'Frankenstrat'. He then set about creating a whole new vocabulary for this misshapen mongrel as, alongside his elder brother Alex, he negotiated a life in music with the band that bore his surname. Still he was told to shut up: by club owners who wanted their patrons sedated with familiar pop standards; by buzz-kill cops who'd gate-crash the chaotic, over-subscribed backyard parties Van Halen played every weekend, barking dispersal orders at hundreds of high-school students flipping the bird skywards at the hovering Pasadena Police Department helicopter; even, with increasing regularity, by the needy, limelight-addicted, man-child singer by his side. But the guitarist would be silent no more.

The release of Van Halen's dazzling self-titled debut album in February 1978 shifted the course of rock 'n' roll history. As with debut sets from the Jimi Hendrix Experience, Led Zeppelin, Black Sabbath, Ramones, Public Enemy and N.W.A., it created a fresh, original, revitalising blueprint for music with attitude.

Let's be clear: while it emerged at a time when disco and new wave had captured the popular imagination, *Van Halen* didn't 'save' hard rock and heavy metal – no rock fan in 1978 listening to *Powerage* or *Live and Dangerous* or *Stained Class* or *Hemispheres* or *Tokyo Tapes* considered the genre on its knees, and the nascent New Wave of British Heavy Metal movement which would propel Iron Maiden and Def Leppard into US arenas within five years owed precisely nothing to the Pasadena party rockers – but Eddie's innovative, incandescent guitar-playing undoubtedly lit a new fire under the genre. And with 'Eruption', his jaw-dropping 102-second solo showcase, blending laser-guided hammer-ons and pull-offs, blur-speed neo-classical triplets, two-handed legato tapping and gravity-drop whammy-bar plunges, the twenty-three-year-old guitarist established a new Year Zero for his fellow players. On hearing it, guitarists inevitably had two questions: 'How the fuck is he doing that?' and 'How can I copy it?' The most iconic instrumental showcase since Jimi Hendrix's Woodstock savaging of 'The Star-Spangled Banner', 'Eruption' served to bisect hard rock's timeline into 'Pre-EVH' and 'Post-EVH', creating both a generation of inferior copycat technicians and, arguably of greater significance, a subculture of 'alternative rock' guitarists who, awed and daunted by Eddie's virtuosity, sought to focus instead on fashioning less technical, more individualistic approaches to playing the instrument. Eddie, of course, had his own influences – early Eric Clapton, Alvin Lee, Jimmy Page, Pete Townshend, Jeff Beck and Allan Holdsworth to name but a few – but in terms of a mindset and modus operandi underpinning his approach to the guitar, it may be instructive to remove any identification with England's rock aristocracy and, instead, recentre Eddie spiritually with California's Z-Boys skateboard crew of the mid-1970s – Tony Alva, Jay Adams, Stacy Peralta, Peggy Oki – fearless, questing, daredevil athletes who constantly pushed boundaries, both physical and psychological. Like Tony Alva with a wooden deck and polyurethane wheels beneath his feet, Eddie felt at his most weightless with wood and wires in his hands – uncontainable, unstoppable, unchained. As with the Z-Boys launching themselves into empty suburban Californian swimming pools, Eddie's approach to guitar solos was to leap into the unknown, with no preconceived idea of where, or indeed how, he might land and no fear of the descent. Like a skater, too, he viewed the bumps and dips of the landscape stretching before him as a space for free expression, and where others saw obstacles, he saw opportunities. 'Edward has a sense of adventure,' David Lee Roth once noted approvingly. 'He will dive headfirst. We'll see if there's water in the pool later.'

I met Eddie Van Halen only once, at his 5150 studio facility in the grounds of his Los Angeles home, in spring 1998. With its twin-seater SEGA *Daytona USA* racing game, *Twister* pinball machine, *Asteroids* arcade game, widescreen TV and racks of video cassettes and CDs, the studio's reception room resembled a teenage boy's idea of an adult male's home, but the juxta-position, in the kitchen, of a photograph of Eddie and Alex's childhood home in Nijmegen, Holland, with a huge, gleaming Recording Industry Association of America presentation plaque acknowledging their group's 60 million US record sales was a striking reminder of just how far Jan and Eugenia Van Halen's boys had come.

The man of the house could not have been more gracious or hospitable, proffering non-alcoholic beers before taking a seat on a black couch alongside his band's new vocalist, former Ex-treme frontman Gary Cherone, ready to talk up Van Halen's third act, which was being heralded by the St Patrick's Day re-lease of the quartet's eleventh studio album, *Van Halen III*. He spoke about his love for his six-year-old son Wolfie, telling how the pair would take trips together to the beach to collect stones to fashion into plectrums, and shared his regret at the demands of his job taking him away from his actress wife, Valerie Berti-nelli. Speaking of his pressing need for a hip replacement op-eration, he noted, 'I'm just a fucking old jerk like anyone else.' But when he picked up one of his signature series guitars and began tapping out the riff to 'Drop Dead Legs' on the fretboard, his well-lined face seemed to shed the wear and tear of the past fifteen years in an instant. Over the course of the next hour, as he shared war stories from his twenty-five years in the rock 'n' roll business, that guitar never left his hands. It sang, it roared, it squealed, it grumbled, it spat, and often it seemed to laugh aloud, with Eddie smiling and laughing too, seemingly scarcely able to believe the sounds he was making. Notoriously wary of journalists – 'No one really understands what I'm trying to say,' he once complained to *Guitar Player* magazine's Jas Obrecht, the writer who conducted Eddie's very first media interview in 1978 and became a trusted confidante – he placed his own Dictaphone on the table alongside mine as our interview began. It was only years later, as I read more about his working methods, that I realised that his tape recorder wasn't rolling to ensure that his words would not be misquoted in a publication he would surely never read, but rather to capture the riffs and musical motifs which streamed unselfconsciously from his fingers as he spoke, lest there might be gold buried in the deep.

In conversation with US writer, and avowed fan, Chuck Klosterman for *Billboard* magazine in 2015, Eddie confessed that he couldn't recall writing the iconic riffs to any of his band's biggest songs, having written the vast majority of them while drunk and wired on high-grade cocaine. When he shared with me his belief that, in the past, his excessive drinking was born from a desire to mask the fact that he considered himself 'the most insecure fuck you'll ever meet in your life', it was hard not to wonder whether his tried and trusted methodology of drinking in order to create hadn't contributed, over the years, to a debilitating sense of imposter syndrome. *Van Halen III*, he proudly declared, was the first album he'd written while completely sober. Somewhat cruelly, it was also, inarguably, the worst album ever released under the Van Halen name, and although Eddie spoke that afternoon of 'making music until I die', in his remaining twenty-two years on the planet he would never again release a full album of new songs, with Van Halen's final album, 2012's *A Different Kind of Truth*, being largely composed of reworkings of previously unreleased demo tracks originally recorded between 1974 and 1977. In quiet moments, the indignity must surely have stung the maestro. 'There's an old Russian saying: "There's no more lines in that guy's stomach,"' David

Lee Roth told the *LA Times* in 2012, as *A Different Kind of Truth* was released. 'It means somebody got fat and slow. There are still a lot of lines in Eddie's stomach.'

· · · · ·

Eddie Van Halen's death, aged sixty-five, on 6 October 2020, elicited a huge outpouring of grief and love from his fellow musicians, many of whom saluted him as 'the Mozart of the guitar'.

'He was the real deal,' said Led Zeppelin's Jimmy Page, 'he pioneered a dazzling technique on guitar with taste and panache that I felt always placed him above his imitators.'

'Eddie was a guitar wonder, his playing pure wizardry,' said AC/DC's Angus Young. 'To the world of music, he was a special gift.'

Queen's Brian May hailed his friend as 'probably the most original and dazzling rock guitarist in history', while the Who's Pete Townshend, another friend, simply called him '*the* Great American Guitar Player'.

Putting the finishing touches to this book in the spring of 2021, six months after Eddie's death, I dug out the copy of *Kerrang!* magazine in which my 1998 interview with the guitarist was published. The closing lines of the piece, perhaps inevitably, seemed to carry more gravitas and weight in the wake of his passing.

'Music is not a competition,' he told me, 'and hopefully when I'm gone, there'll be something that will stay with people, and move them. Whether that'll be ten people, or ten million people, that'll be my mission here accomplished.'

In the article's concluding paragraphs, I had referenced the fact that Eddie freely admitted that he had never attempted to keep up with trends in modern music. He had revealed that most recently he'd been listening to Bob Dylan's thirtieth studio album, 1997's *Time Out of Mind*, but that his CD of the album kept sticking on track three. Now, out of curiosity, I identified the song, 'Standing in the Doorway', and decided to listen to it as a way of paying my own respects to Eddie. A song about growing old and reflecting on days gone by, it's written from the perspective of an ageing narrator who smokes, strums a 'gay guitar' and recognises that, soon enough, he'll be meeting once more with the ghosts of his past.

That seems like a fitting elegy for Eddie Van Halen, an artist who'll forever be enshrined in the collective consciousness standing on a stage, smiling broadly, listening in wonderment to the sounds being conjured from his home-made guitar, hard rock's own Peter Pan, a free-spirited soul who never grew up but who learned how to fly.

1
LITTLE DREAMER

For passengers bound for the New World, the Holland America Line's sales and marketing team did a fine job of evoking the egalitarian spirit of the American Dream before they ever boarded one of the company's flagship vessels. Those in possession of Tourist Class tickets for the SS *Ryndam*'s Atlantic crossings, for instance, were informed that they would have unprecedented access to the ship's finest facilities – the stylish Palm Court on the Promenade Deck, the Card Room, the Library, the American Bar and Smoking Room, an enchanting children's playroom – rather than being restricted to the most basic below-deck quarters, as was standard industry practice. To European emigrants bound for New York in the 1950s and '60s – those 'huddled masses yearning to breathe free', to quote the poetic words of welcome cast on the bronze plaque beneath the Statue of Liberty – the ship represented a gilded gateway to the future.

In the hazy half-light of the early hours of 1 March 1962, Jan van Halen, his wife Eugenia and the couple's two sons, eight-year-old Alex and seven-year-old Edward, pulled the door of their apartment at Rozemarijnstraat 59, Nijmegen, firmly behind them and set off for the town's railway station, bound for the port of Rotterdam, a Tourist Class cabin aboard the SS *Ryndam* and, ultimately, America's distant shores.

In their possession the family had three large suitcases, 75 Dutch guilders and an upright Rippen piano. A professional musician since his late teens, equally gifted on clarinet and saxophone, Jan van Halen had spent much of his adult life in transit, boarding boats, trains and automobiles to bring music to the masses in a succession of highly regarded jazz bands, swing outfits and orchestras. Undertaking this voyage into the unknown, he hoped, would finally unlock opportunities allowing him to call his own tune.

Each evening of the first week of March 1962, to help subsidise his family's passage across the Atlantic the forty-two-year-old musician donned his sharpest suit and sat in with the house band to perform popular standards and ragtime and swing compositions above the soft burr of conversational babble and the delicate clinking of silvered cutlery on fine bone china in the ship's First Class restaurant. One night the van Halen children, too, were given the chance to show off their musical abilities on the family piano, and the youngsters delighted their audience with a recital of meticulously performed, melodious European waltzes, which so charmed the captain of the ship that the family were invited to join him at his table for dinner the following evening. As waiters flitted attentively around the SS *Ryndam*'s newest VIP guests, young Edward van Halen drank in the opulence of his new surroundings, tugged at his father's sleeve and asked one simple question:

'Can't we just live here?'

$$\bullet \quad \bullet \quad \bullet \quad \bullet \quad \bullet$$

'I have to hand it to my dad for having the balls, at the age of 42, to sell everything, pack his bags and come to a whole new country,' Eddie Van Halen noted in 2015, when reflecting upon his family's immigrant experience. In truth, though, it was Eugenia van Halen's decision to uproot her young children from Holland to America at the dawn of the 1960s. For all her husband's charm and confidence, those closest to the family knew it was always Eugenia who called the shots in matters of importance, a fact of which Jan's friends – and mischievous sons – were never slow to remind him.

The pair first met in Jakarta, Indonesia, in the late 1940s. For Jan van Halen, a six-week radio-orchestra booking in the Dutch colony had initially offered a chance to rid himself of painful memories of the war years, when as a member of a marching band he'd been coerced, sometimes literally at gunpoint, to perform propaganda tunes for the German military forces occupying his homeland. That six-week booking would subsequently stretch to a six-year stay when van Halen fell in love with a vivacious, elegant office worker, five years his senior. A sensible, level-headed girl from rural Rangkasbitung, Eugenia van Beers was, at first, somewhat wary of getting romantically entangled with a flighty, twinkle-eyed European musician, but Jan was funny and sweet, kind-hearted and attentive, and the two soon fell happily in step, marrying in the Indonesian capital on 11 August 1950.

Domestic upheaval on the islands would soon bring a measure of uncertainty to this blessed union, however. Following three years of wartime occupation by the Japanese military, Indonesia had declared independence in August 1945, just forty-eight hours after Emperor Hirohito's unconditional surrender to Allied forces in the wake of the devastating bombing of Hiroshima and Nagasaki. After four years of bitter fighting, during which almost 150,000 Indonesian and 5,000 Dutch lives were lost, the Dutch reluctantly acquiesced to international pressure to end the conflict and ceded to the nationalists' demands in 1949.

Though it would be a further eight years before President Sukarno formally nationalised all Dutch companies in Indonesia and expelled 40,000 Dutch citizens from the country, in the earliest days of their marriage Jan and Eugenia could already feel the winds of change. A decision was taken to relocate to Holland, and in the spring of 1953, with Eugenia heavily pregnant, the couple bade Indonesia farewell and set sail for Jan's native Amsterdam.

Starting afresh in Holland presented new challenges. With the 'Big Band' era drawing to a close, professional engagements for jazz musicians were vanishingly scarce, and the pursuit of fresh employment opportunities would often require Jan to be absent from the marital home for weeks, sometimes months, at a time. Indeed, he was on the road when, on 8 May 1953, Eugenia gave birth to the couple's first child, a son, whom they named Alexander Arthur van Halen. Jan would be absent, too, when the family was blessed by the arrival of a second son, Edward Lodewijk, on 26 January 1955, a fact Eugenia would often bring to her husband's attention during their frequent ill-tempered exchanges in the family home. Increasingly frustrated by the lack of support from her rather less-than-dependable spouse, Eugenia insisted, shortly after the birth of her second child, that the family relocate from Amsterdam to Nijmegen, the oldest city in the Netherlands, in the province of Gelderland, where Jan had relatives who were eager to assist with the parenting duties he so blithely neglected.

From the cradle, Edward and Alex were inseparable, 'two peas in a pod', as the younger of the two boys liked to recall. Jan's music would provide the soundtrack to their earliest years. The usually boisterous pair would sit becalmed, enrapt and captivated, while their father practised clarinet, and would gleefully stomp around their living room, bashing and thrashing pots and pans, when heavy black shellac 78s were placed on the family stereo and the house shook to the martial beats of up-tempo military marches. On the occasions when

Eugenia was compelled to work night shifts in one of the part-time service-industry jobs she had taken on, white-collar employment opportunities having been repeatedly closed off to her by businesses openly hostile to women of colour, the boys would be packed off to Jan's gigs, with their mother hoping that their presence might help curb her husband's predilection for extensive post-gig drinking marathons. In reality, to Eugenia's mounting irritation, it did nothing of the sort, serving only to bond the trio more tightly together, with Alex and Edward delighting in being transported to an alternative universe and returning from each excursion increasingly enthralled by their father's high-spirited, bohemian friends and their freewheeling, laissez-faire approach to discipline, regulations and responsibilities.

Though she never masked her distaste for her husband's nomadic lifestyle, Eugenia was quick to recognise and grudgingly accept that her sons shared with their father a genuine fascination and passion for music. And so, when Edward was five years old and Alex six, she enrolled her children in piano lessons with a Russian concert pianist who lived locally. The elderly maestro was a strict disciplinarian, much feared by his young charges – 'He would just sit there with a ruler ready to slap my face if I made a mistake,' Eddie recalled – but venerated by Eugenia, who told her boys, 'If you're going to follow in your dad's footsteps, it better be respectable.' On one occasion, when Alex dared to complain about having to practise his scales, his mother placed his hands flat on the kitchen table and rapped his fingers repeatedly with a heavy wooden spoon. For this particular lesson, no encore was required.

'It was important to her that we maximised our opportunities,' Alex recalled.

'She wore the pants in the family,' Eddie acknowledged, characterising his parents as 'the conservative' – Eugenia – and 'the screw-up' – Jan. 'I hate to say it, but I don't think my dad would have drank as much as he did if it wasn't for her. She had a heart of gold, and don't take this the wrong way, but Hitler on a bad day...'

In retrospect, it's easy to empathise with Eugenia's frustrations. Half the world away from family and friends, and treated, at best, as a second-class citizen in her adopted homeland due to her Indonesian heritage, she was required to balance whatever menial employment she could hold down alongside the commitment of raising her young family on a shoestring budget, with little assistance from her errant husband. It's no wonder that missives from relatives in California, extolling the delights of life in America, began to fire within her dreams of a fresh start. By the middle of 1961, with Jan scraping a living and scant indication of the family's prospects improving any time in the immediate future, Eugenia proposed the idea of emigrating to the US to her husband, not as a hypothetical notion up for extended discussion, but as a fait accompli. By this point in his marriage, Jan knew better than to argue.

• • • • •

The state of California has always been inextricably linked with the American Dream. In March 1848, the San Francisco-based newspaper *The Californian* broke the news that gold had been discovered along the American River at Coloma, near Sacramento. The following year – encouraged by above-the-fold newspaper editorials thundering 'Go West Young Man!' – tens of thousands of US citizens set off for California hoping to stake a claim to a glittering future, in a mass migration which became known as the 'Gold Rush'. More than a century on, in seeking a fresh start in the Golden State the van Halen family were traversing a well-signposted route. Upon docking in the port of New York on 9 March

1962, ahead of a four-day train journey to America's west coast, Jan van Halen opted to officially change the family name to Van Halen, a superficially minor alteration, but one laced with significance, symbolic as it was of a new beginning.

Though Jan had taken to jokingly telling friends that the family were moving to Beverly Hills, they were bound instead for Pasadena, where Eugenia's relatives had secured lodgings for the new arrivals in the city's south side at 486 South Oakland Avenue, a small three-bedroom, one-bathroom apartment they were to share with two other families. Truthfully, the location mattered little to Jan — in his mind, the idea of California was of greater significance than the actuality of where the family might settle — but the chastening reality of this new life impacted from the moment the quartet arrived in Los Angeles County.

'When we finally arrived in Pasadena, it was rough,' Eddie told an audience at Washington DC's National Museum of American History, during a February 2015 talk convened as part of the Smithsonian's 'What It Means to Be American' series. 'We lived in one room, slept in one bed. My father had to walk three miles to go wash dishes [at the Arcadia Methodist Hospital], he was a janitor at Masonic Temple, at Pacific Telephone, my mom was a maid . . . We used to go dumpster-diving for scrap metal, then go to the scrap yard and sell the metal we found.'

'For my dad, America was the land of opportunity,' Alex Van Halen noted. 'Then he found out differently, of course. The big-band thing wasn't happening here, either.'

The Van Halen boys had their own teething problems to contend with. Upon arriving in the US, Alex and Eddie could speak only four words of English — 'yes', 'no' and, somewhat randomly, 'motorcycle' and 'accident' — and their education in the mores of their new environment was swift and often brutish, with their earliest days at Alexander Hamilton Elementary School on Rose Villa Street marked by racist threats, bullying and random acts of violence.

'It was absolutely frightening,' Eddie recalled, 'beyond frightening. The school that we went to was still segregated at the time, and since we couldn't speak the language, we were considered a minority. My first friends in America were black. The white people were bullies: [they would] tear up my homework papers, make me eat playground sand. The black kids stuck up for me.'

One afternoon, Alex was walking in a local park when an older white boy strolled by carrying a Louisville Slugger. Keen to show off a recent addition to his limited vocabulary, Alex pointed to the bat and said, 'Baseball!' The teenager stopped and asked the youngster a question he couldn't understand, which the uncomprehending but unfailingly polite Dutch boy responded to with a smile and a nod of his head. Seconds later, he dropped to his knees in shock, clutching a bloodied, broken nose, as his assailant walked away laughing. It transpired that the question posed was, 'Do you want me to hit you in the face with this?'

Unsurprisingly, such frightening incidents drew the Van Halen boys together tighter than two coats of creosote.

'We were two outcasts that didn't speak the language and didn't know what was going on,' said Eddie. 'So, we became best friends and learned to stick together.'

Amid the turbulence of this transitional period, music provided a measure of continuity with more stable and settled times. To supplement the family's meagre income, Jan began gigging in wedding bands and oompah ensembles with musicians befriended in neighbourhood bars, and Alex and Eddie were re-enrolled in piano lessons by their mother as soon as funds permitted. Their elderly tutor was a fellow immigrant, Lithuanian-born Stasys 'Stanley' Kalvaitis, a graduate of Russia's elite Imperial Conservatory in St Petersburg who had studied alongside the world-famous Ukrainian composer Sergei Proko-fiev and the Lithuanian violin virtuoso Jascha Heifetz. The ac-complished Kalvaitis was a stern, demanding teacher, and Eddie chafed against his methodology, considering his rote-learning tuition tedious. Engaging in his own subtle, low-key form of rebellion, he refused to learn to read sheet music, feigning at-tentiveness while opting instead to play complicated recitals by ear. If the Lithuanian maestro was duped, he was nonetheless an astute judge of his pupil's abilities: when he entered Eddie into the third annual Southwestern Youth Music Festival at Long Beach City College in August 1964, he encouraged Eugenia and Jan to attend to watch their boy bring honour to the family. Eddie didn't disappoint, duly taking home first prize in his cat-egory, though his indifference to the accolade was every bit as pronounced as the pride felt by his parents.

'I didn't give a shit,' Eddie freely admitted. 'It wasn't like "Wow, I won, I'm good!" It wasn't a motivation of any kind. I guess the only thing it really did to me was make me more ner-vous for the next time. I actually won first place two years in a row. But I hated it.'

In truth, in his head the young prodigy was already march-ing to a different beat, a fresh, vibrant, exhilarating new sound imported from across the Atlantic.

· · · · ·

Bland, conservative and painfully well-mannered, the British music scene was of negligible interest to American consumers at the dawn of the 1960s. The only artist from the UK to score a number 1 US single in the 1950s was 'Forces Sweetheart' Vera

Lynn, while clean-cut British rock 'n' rollers such as Cliff Richard, Adam Faith and Billy Fury were rightly derided as pallid, flaccid and wholly irrelevant facsimiles of their Sun Records counterparts. Though Fury's backing band the Tornados scored the first *Billboard* Hot 100 chart-topper by a British group with their instrumental 'Telstar' in December 1962, British musicians remained largely invisible in the US during the Van Halen family's first year of residency in California.

The Beatles would change that. Though the group were not an immediate success in America – indeed, their first two UK number 1 singles ('Please Please Me' and 'From Me to You') failed to chart at all in the US – the release of the thrillingly effervescent 'I Want to Hold Your Hand' rammed an adrenaline spike squarely into the heart of the US music industry. Even before their historic 9 February 1964 appearance on CBS television's *The Ed Sullivan Show*, watched by an estimated 73 million viewers, demand for their 45 exceeded supply, with their record label, Capitol, forced to outsource a proportion of the pressing and production of the seven-inch vinyl disc to rival companies Columbia and RCA in order to fulfil unprecedented orders. On 1 February 1964, the song reached the top of the *Billboard* Hot 100 chart, where it would remain for seven weeks, the first of seven chart-topping singles the Liverpool quartet would release in that calendar year. By March, *Meet the Beatles!*, the quartet's first long-player for Capitol, had shipped 3.6 million copies, making it, at that point, the biggest-selling album in history. The Liverpool group's phenomenal success prompted US record labels and fans alike to look afresh at the previously moribund UK music scene, and a slew of UK chart hits were repackaged and rush-released for the American market.

Curiously, however, given their dominance of the airwaves, it was not the Beatles but their more mannered peers the Dave Clark Five who turned Eddie Van Halen on to rock 'n' roll. In April 1964, in the same history-making week which saw the

Beatles secure the top five placings on the Hot 100, the Londoners' 'Glad All Over', which had toppled 'I Want to Hold Your Hand' from the summit of the British singles chart earlier in the year, broke into the *Billboard* Top 10. Its success prompted the first murmurings of a potential 'British Invasion' of the US pop charts, and in the summer of 1964, its heavily accented *whomp* transformed the life of one young immigrant boy.

'Alex and I went to the local theatre to see [the Beatles' 1964 musical comedy] *A Hard Day's Night*, and the girls were screaming,' Eddie recalled. 'Alex loved that. For me it was "Glad All Over". To this day I listen to some of those old recordings, and they have a magic to them. They were badass. Every kid goes through the phase of building model cars and stuff. I would take boxes and paper and make something like a snare drum, and I'd play along with the Dave Clark Five stuff . . . I loved to beat on things.'

That same summer, the Van Halen boys decided to form their first band. The Broken Combs featured Eddie on piano and Alex on saxophone, Eddie's Hamilton Elementary School classmate Kevan Hill on guitar, Kevan's brother Brian on drums and neighbour Don Ferris on second saxophone. The quintet worked up two original songs, 'Rumpus' and the intriguingly titled 'Boogie Booger', and performed them alongside interpretations of British Invasion standards in the school's dining hall. Almost overnight, the brothers were transformed from distrusted outsiders to schoolyard heroes, a process which did wonders for both their confidence and their social skills, even as the pair retained a healthy wariness towards their former tormentors.

Delighted by his sons' growing immersion in the process of making music of their own, Jan offered to upgrade Eddie's rudimentary cardboard drum kits to rather more robust instrumentation, and duly procured a $125 Japanese-made St George kit for the boy, which Eddie promised to pay off with the proceeds from his morning newspaper delivery round. Having committed to this arrangement, the youngster was more than a little annoyed to find his hard labour being exploited by his elder brother, who – neglecting the flamenco guitar he himself had been gifted – could be found pounding upon the kit each morning as Eddie returned home exhausted from his dawn deliveries. Even more irritatingly for the younger boy, it quickly became all too apparent that Alex had a greater aptitude for the instrument: 'He could play [the Surfaris' 1963 instrumental hit] "Wipe Out" and I couldn't,' Eddie later recalled. 'I said, "OK, fuck you. I'll play your guitar."'

There was, said Eddie, 'no message from God' when he first held a guitar in his hands. But the challenge of decoding the sounds he heard on AM radio and transposing them to six vibrating strings proved both stimulating and addictive. 'I didn't even think about whether it was easy or hard,' he told *Guitar World* in 1985, 'it was something I wanted to do, to have fun and feel good about doing it. Whether it took me a week to learn half a song or one day to learn five songs, I never thought of it that way.

'The first song I ever learned was "Pipeline" by the Surfaris, and "Wipe Out". Then I heard this song on the radio – it was the "Blues Theme" [by Davie Allan and the Arrows] on the soundtrack to [Roger Corman's 1966 cult 'outlaw biker' movie] *The Wild Angels*. It was the first time I heard a distorted guitar, and I'm going, "God, what is that?"

'Fuck the piano, I don't want to sit down – I want to stand up and be crazy.'

However, to properly replicate the stinging, aggressive, reverb-drenched sound of California's surf-guitar heroes Eddie was aware that he needed a new weapon of choice. A visit to Sears department store duly yielded his first electric guitar, a $110 Japanese-made Teisco Del Rey model, chosen, Eddie remembered, purely on the basis of it having four pickups, one more than any other guitar in the store. Jan provided him with his first amplifier, home-made by a Pasadena neighbour, which Eddie modified using a Radio Shack adapter.

'I plugged my normal guitar cord into it and turned the thing all the way up,' he recalled. 'It made a lot of noise and I started playing it while it was making all that noise. I remember Al walking in and going, "That sounds neat, man, what is that?" It was right around the time of that song, "Blues Theme": Al said, "Play that," and it sounded identical. It was crappin' out, distorted, nasty. So, I guess that was my first exposure to that grungey noise.'

Soon enough, the Van Halen boys would be utterly spoiled for choice when it came to 'grungey noise'. 1967 was the year of *Sgt. Pepper's Lonely Hearts Club Band*, of *The Doors* and *The Velvet Underground & Nico*, of Pink Floyd's *The Piper at the Gates of Dawn*, the Rolling Stones' *Their Satanic Majesties Request* and the Jimi Hendrix Experience's *Are You Experienced* and *Axis: Bold as Love* albums. One long-player, above all, captured the imagination of the brothers, however: British rock 'supergroup' Cream's second album *Disraeli Gears*, which was a showcase for the prodigious talents of bassist Jack Bruce, drummer Ginger Baker and former Yardbirds/Bluesbreakers alumnus Eric Clapton, at twenty-two considered by peers, critics and music fans alike to be the most exciting young guitarist in the world.

'What attracted me to his playing and style and vibe was the basic simplicity in his approach and his tone, his sound,' Eddie noted. 'He just basically took a Gibson guitar and plugged it straight into a Marshall and that was it. The basics. The blues.

'I was just turned on by the sound and feel he got. I like phrasing; that's why I always liked Clapton. He would just play it with feeling. It's like someone talking, a question-and-answer trip.'

To Eddie, Clapton's tone and phrasing were reminiscent of a tenor sax, evoking, on a subconscious level at least, warm, nostalgic memories of his father's playing back in Holland in simpler times. In Cream's daring, uninhibited, virtuoso playing, Eddie also heard echoes of the late-night jazz sessions he and Alex had sat in upon as children.

The trio, he later told *Guitar World*, 'made music exciting in a way I don't think people really understood.

'It was almost as if the lyric and actual song structure were secondary. "Let's get this shit over with so we can make music and see where we land tonight."'

Inspired by the English group, the Van Halen brothers formed their own 'power trio' at their new school, Jefferson Elementary on East Villa Street, with Eddie's classmate Jim Wright on bass. Originally called the Sounds of Las Vegas, and later simply the Sounds, the group played surf music, hits by the Beatles and the Monkees and, inevitably, any Cream songs they could master.

The fledgling group's talents did not go unnoticed by Jan Van Halen, who began 'borrowing' first Alex and then Eddie (as a bassist) for his own gigs, playing 'weddings, bar mitzvahs, polkas, and all that other shit', as Eddie recalled.

'We would play at the La Mirada Country Club,' he said. 'My dad would play at the Continental Club every Sunday night and we would sit in with him. He'd play at a place called the Alpine Haus off of San Fernando Road in the Valley, and we'd wear the lederhosen.'

On occasion, the brothers would also serve as their father's opening act or as intermission entertainment – 'the little freak sideshow', as Eddie disparagingly remembered it. Not surprisingly, such engagements initially made the twelve-year-old boy anxious, a condition Jan sought to ease with his own tried-and-trusted, if unconventional, remedies.

'My dad got me into drinking and smoking when I was 12,'
Eddie remembered. 'I was nervous, so he said to me, "Here.
Have a shot of vodka." Boom – I wasn't nervous anymore.

'Al would be yelling at me, telling me basically what chords,
even though I didn't know the chords. [He] would just say, "I,
IV, V!" which is basically the three chords structure of any basic
song, basically everything from polkas to . . . wedding songs,
old standards. I had never heard any of these songs before, so I
didn't have a clue. That's when I kinda learned to smile a lot!'

At the end of one such evening, as was the tradition, Jan
Van Halen passed his fedora among the audience, asking them
to show their appreciation for the night's entertainment in a
tangible fashion. The hat returned from its circuit containing
$22. Dipping into the takings, Jan handed his side men Eddie
and Alex $5 apiece. The boys may not have been familiar with
American labour laws yet, but they weren't so green that they
couldn't see that this division of income was inequitable, and
they commented indignantly upon the fact. Their father simply
shrugged and offered a smile.

'Welcome to the music business, boys,' he said with a wink.

2
ERUPTION

On 31 December 1970, Paul McCartney filed a legal suit against John Lennon, George Harrison and Ringo Starr in a bid to formally dissolve the Beatles. Rumours of McCartney's desire to split the band had been circulating since 10 April that year, when the *Daily Mirror* spun quotes included in a press release for the twenty-eight-year-old Beatle's debut solo album into the front-page headline 'Paul Quits The Beatles'. 'The event is so momentous that historians may, one day, view it as a landmark in the decline of the British Empire,' a reporter from CBS News duly informed the American public with appropriate gravity. John Lennon initially dismissed the story, insisting to *Rolling Stone* magazine that the comments were merely born of his songwriting partner's mischievous inclination for 'causing chaos'. But in presenting his petition to wind up the quartet's contractual partnership at London's High Court of Justice on New Year's Eve, McCartney made his intentions a matter of public record. There was now, officially, a vacancy for the position of the biggest rock 'n' roll band in the world.

Into the void boldly strode Led Zeppelin. In truth, Jimmy Page's band already considered themselves peerless. In September 1970, having been made aware that advance orders for their third album, *Led Zeppelin III*, were nudging a million copies in the US alone, the hard-rock quartet had taken out a full-page advertisement in *Melody Maker* that read, 'Thank you for making us the world's number one band.' Released the following month (on 5 October in the US, 23 October in the UK), the ten-song set duly topped the album charts on either side of the Atlantic. But with radio programmers initially wrong-footed by the bucolic folk and blues stylings showcased on the largely acoustic collection, airplay, and consequently sales, soon tapered off sharply. Sensing blood, influential music critics who had dismissed the group as 'hype' from the outset began to devote column inches to their considered belief that the quartet had peaked both commercially and creatively, questioning whether the latest British superstars genuinely had anything new, significant or important to offer the world.

Zeppelin's sensitive but controlling bandleader Page took the criticisms personally. In December 1970, as he convened recording sessions for the group's fourth album – initially at London's Island Studios, then at Headley Grange, a supposedly haunted former Victorian poorhouse-turned-stately home in Hampshire – the guitarist was determined to make a statement to his detractors.

At Headley Grange, Page, vocalist Robert Plant, bassist John Paul Jones and drummer John Bonham lived and created together under the same residential roof for the first time, though Plant, Jones and Bonham would later decamp to more luxurious digs once Page pronounced himself satisfied with their input. With the rural setting affording the musicians both space and privacy, the writing sessions were relaxed but concentrated, with new songs being committed to tape in the Rolling Stones Mobile Studio by engineer Andy Johns within minutes of coming into focus. This spontaneous, liberating approach imbued Zeppelin's new material with palpable energy and swagger: here was a sure-footed, road-hardened unit who instinctively understood that their time had come. In February 1971, Page, Johns and Zeppelin's manager Peter Grant flew to Los Angeles to mix the record at Sunset Sound Recorders on Sunset Boulevard, but, unconvinced by the results achieved at the facility, the guitarist subsequently oversaw a new mix back in England at Island Studios.

As an arch statement of confidence, and a calculated, albeit slightly oblique, 'fuck you' to his critics, Page refused to allow Atlantic Records to include his band's name, much less a title, on the cover artwork of Zeppelin's fourth album. The focus, the guitarist insisted, was to be on the forty-two minutes of music cut into the grooves of the black vinyl disc, and on that music alone: 'I thought, "Okay, if it's a hype, we'll put out an album with not a reference to Led Zeppelin at all on it,"' he later explained. Though label executives privately considered Page's decision akin to professional suicide and the ensuing boardroom debate forced the album's scheduled release date to be pushed back from spring to winter, Zeppelin's past successes – coupled with Peter Grant's truly fearsome reputation – had earned the group the right to conduct their business by their own rules, and Atlantic eventually, if most reluctantly, acquiesced to Page's demands. Consequently, on 8 November 1971, the album emerged with just four mysterious runic symbols adorning its label and inner sleeve.

When the stylus dropped upon the vinyl, however, there was no confusion as to the identity of the album's creators.

From the cocksure amphetamine blues strut of 'Black Dog' and 'Rock and Roll' through to the open-hearted Laurel Canyon folk stylings of 'Going to California' – a dedication to 'the days when things were really nice and simple, and everything was far out all the time', according to Robert Plant – and the ominous southern Gothic stomp of 'When the Levee Breaks', the kaleidoscopic collection had Zeppelin's unmistakable sonic fingerprints all over it.

As the closing track on side one of the disc, Jimmy Page's signature composition 'Stairway to Heaven' dominates the album. From its delicately finger-picked arpeggiated opening through to its thunderous John Bonham-driven denouement, the eight-minute track is a masterclass in mood, colour, pacing and dynamics, with Page imperiously directing the light and magic like an orchestra conductor.

The rescheduling of the album's release meant that 'Stairway . . .', along with 'Black Dog', 'Going to California' and 'Rock and Roll', was given its live US premiere on the night of 21 August 1971 – a full ten weeks before the studio version would grace the turntables of expectant fans – at the first of two sold-out Led Zeppelin shows at the 17,505-capacity arena the Forum, in Inglewood, California. In the bleachers to hear it that evening, witnessing the elemental force of Zeppelin in full flight for the first time, were Eddie and Alex Van Halen. The brothers had been confirmed Led Zeppelin fans since the day a neighbourhood friend brought a copy of the quartet's self-titled 1969 debut album into their home at 1881 Las Lunas Street, a two-bedroom bungalow Jan and Eugenia purchased for the family in the spring of 1966.

'I tripped on it,' Eddie remembered. 'Page is a genius. When you hear a Page solo, he speaks.'

Studying the English guitarist's every move from the arena's cheapest seats, Eddie was struck by one particular moment of virtuoso showboating from his hero. During his solo on 'Heartbreaker', the rollicking, raunchy introduction to side two of *Led*

Zeppelin II, Page raised his right hand high in the air, holding his plectrum above his head, while simultaneously conjuring a rapid-fire cascade of notes from his Les Paul, utilising only his left hand, tapping a succession of hammer-ons and pull-offs on the fretboard. Impressed by both the theatre and sound of Page's playing, the watching sixteen-year-old guitarist mentally filed away the flashy technique as one he himself could employ in future gigs alongside his brother.

By the summer of 1971, the Van Halen boys considered themselves grizzled music-industry veterans, adept at negotiating the choppy waters of the rock 'n' roll game. Their current project, Genesis, was their fourth group, following on from the Broken Combs, the Sounds and blues-rock power trio the Trojan Rubber Company, which featured bassist Dennis Travis, who had hooked up with the brothers after overhearing them play flawless instrumental versions of Cream songs in the gymnasium at Marshall Junior High School. Mindful not to cause offence, TRC had tactfully used the pseudonym the Space Brothers when chasing bookings at Catholic high-school dances, so it was a touch ironic that they were ultimately silenced when Travis's church minister father moved his family out of the state in early 1971. With bassist Mark Stone stepping into the breach, the group was born again as Genesis, and their note-perfect covers of songs by Grand Funk Railroad, Black Sabbath, Deep Purple, Led Zeppelin, the Who, Cactus and Cream quickly established them as a popular draw for students from Pasadena's three senior high schools who were looking to cut loose at weekends.

'When you wanted to go out and look for girls, you asked where Genesis was playing,' Robin 'Rudy' Leiren, who would become Eddie's guitar tech from 1974 onwards, recalled to writer Steven Rosen. 'The first time I saw them they were playing at an assembly at Marshall Junior High School. I was blown away.

They were playing Cream and all the stuff on the radio. Edward stuck out in particular. I remember thinking to myself, "This guy is going to become famous." Here he was, a kid my age, up there on stage, playing everything note-for-note, playing the Clapton riffs note-for-note. I was awed.'

'Playing guitar was my sanctuary,' Eddie remembered. 'It was the one place I could go to if I got fucked around by a girl-friend, or anyone else for that matter.

'Everybody goes through teenage growing up, getting fucked around by a chick or not fitting in with the jocks at school. I just basically locked myself up in a room for four or five years and said to myself, "Hey, this guitar's never gonna fuck me in the ass. What I put into it, it gives me back."

'My brother would go out at 7pm to party and get laid, and when he'd come back at 3am, I would be sitting in the same place, playing guitar.

'When we began playing high school dances, and parties, we had a hell of a reputation. We used to play backyard parties down in San Marino, the real rich part of Pasadena. The parents were away for the weekend, the kids would have a party and hire us. We'd get a little Abbey Rents stage, cheap lights and charge a buck. We'd play until the helicopters would come at 10pm and shut us down.'

It was on one such evening that another Pasadena teenager harbouring dreams of rock 'n' roll stardom first encountered the Van Halen brothers. Watching Genesis steamroller through covers by the Who, Deep Purple and Ten Years After, David Lee Roth was captivated by the group's prodigious, assured mu-sicality – 'It was amazing stuff,' he recalled – but not so over-whelmed by the presentation that the preternaturally confident seventeen-year-old couldn't see scope for improvement. One Sunday afternoon in spring 1971, Roth presented himself at 1881 Las Lunas Street and informed Alex Van Halen that he wished to sing for Genesis. Mindful that his younger brother, never comfortable with his singing voice, was only fronting the group under duress, the drummer graciously decided to give the brash, ballsy teenager a shot.

'We asked him to learn a few songs like "Crossroads", by Cream, and something by Grand Funk Railroad, then come back and see us the next week,' Eddie later told *Rolling Stone*. 'And he came back the next week, and it was terrible . . . I put my guitar down and said, "Al, I'll be right back."'

'The guy couldn't sing for shit,' Alex said bluntly. 'I was completely and thoroughly appalled. Ed and Mark left the room, and I had to tell Dave this was no good.'

Embarrassed by his face-plant of an audition, but conscious that the kid looked the part and didn't lack for confidence, the drummer didn't immediately show Roth the door. Instead, he thoughtfully selected a handful of staples from the trio's repertoire for the singer to work on and invited him to return to Las Lunas Street the following week. If anything, though, Roth's second try-out for Genesis would prove to be even worse.

'It sounded like pure hell,' Alex recalled. 'The intonation was completely out of whack, the timing was completely off, and it was an abysmal failure. I remember one song was "Still Alive And Well" by the old [Johnny] Winter boys, and it was bad. I told him he didn't make the audition, and he walked off in a huff and a puff.'

Soon enough, however, Genesis were to meet with a rude awakening of their own. On this occasion, for all their capacity to disrupt the serenity of the Pasadena suburbs, it wasn't cops or religious elders who would muzzle the trio, but a group of well-mannered ex-public schoolboys from England who were wholly unaware of the Californian band's existence. Having met as pupils at the prestigious Charterhouse School, Peter Gabriel,

Mike Rutherford and Tony Banks had been making music under the name of Genesis since 1967, signing to Charisma Records in 1970, ahead of the release of their second album, *Trespass*. In November 1971, the group released their third long-player, the acclaimed *Nursery Cryme*, and it was this album that Eddie Van Halen subsequently found in a Pasadena record shop while rifling through the bins in search of new music. 'Hey, we've got a record out, Alex!' the amused guitarist shouted across the shop to his brother. However, once their laughter abated the pair recognised that, sooner or later, their band would be required to change its name. Exit Genesis; enter, in early 1972, Mammoth.

By this time, another band name was appearing with increasing frequency on the handbills and flyers wheat-pasted on the walls and streetlights around the John Muir, Blair and Pasadena High Schools. Formed in the summer of 1971, Red Ball Jet, a nimble, colourful, razzle-dazzle dance band, was conceived as nothing less than David Lee Roth's revenge upon the Van Halen brothers. Though Red Ball Jet would never claim to possess musicianship on a par with Mammoth – even the cocky Roth only rated their musicality as 'a solid five [out of 10] . . . six on a good night' – their preening peacock of a frontman, all teeth and tits and dangerously over-stuffed trousers, was determined to ensure that they always made an impression, whatever it took. If the Van Halens were publicly dismissive of Roth's new vehicle – in Eddie's opinion, Red Ball Jet were 'totally into showmanship . . . [but] couldn't play a note', while Roth was a 'clown' – they were not blind to the fact that the band were drawing increasingly bigger, wilder crowds on the local backyard circuit on the strength of the singer's lightning-fast wit, pretty-boy looks and complete absence of self-awareness, restraint or shame.

'Playing at those parties', Roth would later state with some relish, 'got competitive fast.'

'All the girls would go down and see Dave, and all the guys would go down there and hate Dave,' noted Rudy Leiren.

'It was never about the music for him,' Eddie insisted. 'It was about the show. We kinda became rival bands. People who liked us at one party would go to the next party, and I guess they'd throw stuff at him.'

'At that time, Roth was a very cocky guy,' observed Alex. 'Ed and I couldn't stand the motherfucker – couldn't stand the band, couldn't stand the music.'

It was somewhat awkward then, initially at least, when in 1972, Roth and Eddie enrolled in the same music classes at Pasadena City College, where Alex was already studying composition and music theory.

'When you graduate high school and can't afford to go to a university, you go to your local junior college, which happened to be PCC,' Eddie explained in 2015. 'All I took were music courses; my most memorable was Truman Fischer's class. He was a wonderful teacher.'

A devotee of the Austrian composer and music theorist Arnold Schoenberg, who is hailed by many as the father of modern music, Dr Truman Fischer was a firm believer in learning musical rules in order that one might be able to completely disregard their existence. In his classes, one simple, singular precept applied: if it sounds good, it is good.

'Dr Fischer was very avant-garde and the one thing he taught me was, Fuck the rules,' Eddie recalled.

'My first encounter with Dave was in Truman Fischer's Scoring and Arranging class. From the outside looking in, it might have appeared to be a very odd pairing . . . He looked like David Bowie, with platform shoes and spiked hair. I was just a jeans and tee-shirt guy. People would say to me, "Why are you hanging out with that weird faggot?" and I'd say, "He's not a fag, it's just what he's into." He was the only guy we knew in Pasadena who was as serious as we were about music.

'We would stumble into class very tired from having played clubs the night before. Other students would make fun of us, calling us musical prostitutes because we were not, in their mind, being true to whatever it meant to be a musician according to their principles. We were just trying to make a living. At that age, you're either serious about pursuing a music career or it just becomes a hobby. Dave, Alex, and I were very serious when it came to music being our profession.'

• • • • •

Asked to nominate his heroes during his formative adolescent years, David Lee Roth once cautioned that 'they didn't have much to do with the frontman in Led Zeppelin, much as you might expect.

'They had more to do with Miles Davis, [Akira] Kurosa-wa, and P. T. Barnum,' he stated. 'Let's start there – that's a power trio!'

Identifying with an iconic musical maverick, a visionary master storyteller and America's greatest showman was a typically 'on-brand' answer from Roth, a man well versed in the art of centring himself in home-spun mythological narratives. 'Everything with me has to be dramatic,' the singer would write in the closing coda to his best-selling 1997 autobiography *Crazy from the Heat*. 'Everything with me has to be full of emotion and drive and tragedy and catastrophe, valor and victory.' Nowhere in the book's 359 pages is mention made of the singer's two failed auditions with Genesis, of course, or, indeed, the fact that Roth's mother once bluntly told him to his face that his very existence was 'an accident'. Discussing his approach to music, Miles Davis once famously said, 'It's not the notes you play. It's the notes you don't play,' and long before he enrolled for Dr Truman Fischer's tuition, Roth adopted a similar stance to his personal biography, understanding that when opening himself up to the scrutiny of his peers, inconvenient truths were best left unspoken.

Roth was born on 10 October 1954 in Bloomington, Indiana, where his father, Nathan, the son of Russian immigrants, had attended medical school upon exiting the US Air Force, and his mother, Sibyl, taught art and language classes. His was not always a happy home. 'I remember my parents always fighting,' the singer once said. 'They fought even before they were married . . . Coming from a supremely dysfunctional family, I can see why I am the way I am.' Upon graduating, Dr Roth relocated his family several times, first to a small ranch in Newcastle, Indiana, next to Swampscott, Massachusetts, then to Brookline, a suburb of Greater Boston. In his earliest years, young David was plagued by health issues, suffering from food allergies and requiring correctional braces on his legs, which naturally impeded his movement, causing considerable frustration for the naturally curious, energetic child. Roth was sent to see a psychiatrist for the first time at the age of six – 'my mom had no idea what to do with me', he admitted – and, having been diagnosed as hyperactive, was prescribed the ADHD medication Ritalin from the age of eight.

'Every night at dinner when I'd get the blood sugars up, I'd start ticky-tacking with the knives and forks on the table, and I'd start telling jokes and singing commercials from television and everything,' he later relayed on *Entertainment Tonight*. 'And the folks would say to the company, "Now don't worry about David, he's just doing what we call Monkey Hour."'

Considering himself starved of attention and validation by his parents, who by then had a second child, Lisa, to attend to, Roth took to immersing himself in popular culture – television, movies, books, records. In 1961, he discovered *Playboy* and *Mad* magazine, two publications offering an alternative vision of the prevailing societal mores, and was mesmerised by the libertine lifestyles they promoted and documented. In the summer of 1962, the youngster was offered glimpses of this world first-hand when visiting New York for the first time, at the invitation of his Uncle Manny and Aunt Judy, who lived in Greenwich Village. Three years earlier, Manny Roth had opened a club in the Village, at the intersection of MacDougal Street and Minetta Lane, called Café Wha?. It soon became a popular hang-out for the neighbourhood's freewheeling, bohemian poets, writers, artists and musicians, with Jack Kerouac, Allen Ginsberg, Bob Dylan and Peter, Paul and Mary among its patrons, and it fascinated Manny's seven-year-old nephew from out of state. 'It was even better than the magazines,' he marvelled in *Crazy from the Heat*.

'I saw lesbians . . . the transvestite crowd . . . uptown socialites . . . royalty . . . junkies . . . prostitutes . . . senators,' Roth recalled. 'I developed an appreciation – not just a tolerance, but an appreciation – for all types of people.'

In 1963, the family moved to California, settling in Altadena, north of Pasadena, where Dr Roth, who was training to be an ophthalmologist, set up his own medical practice. This was the year of 'Surfin' U.S.A.' and 'Wipe Out', Martha and the Vandellas' 'Heat Wave', the Ronettes' 'Be My Baby'... and the first batch of US newspaper articles and network television reports documenting a new teen craze sweeping England: Beatlemania.

'Music got cool,' Roth noted. 'You could watch *The Ed Sullivan Show* and one week see the Beatles and the next week see the Rolling Stones . . . There were quite a few school-yard fistfights over who were better, the Beatles or the Beach Boys.'

By the time Roth entered Eliot Junior High School in autumn 1966, he was telling anyone who'd listen that he was destined to become a pop star. Three years on, and still undiscovered, he could regularly be found strumming his acoustic guitar in the sunshine on the campus of John Muir High, seemingly untroubled by the notion that the class schedule might apply to him just as much as to his fellow students. In recognition of his hunger for the limelight, friends teasingly took to calling the teenager 'Superstar'.

'I just wanted to be in showbiz,' said Roth. 'I wanted to make music and sing and dance, tell jokes and stories, make you smile, make you cry . . . and charge you $8.50.

'I used to love to take my guitar to school and just sit under a tree and play. I'd always forget what time it was, and I'd always miss class, but I found out very quickly that you could meet a lot more girls sitting under a tree with a guitar than you could in chemistry class.'

While the regular high-school curriculum was of scant interest to Roth, attending John Muir provided an invaluable education in other ways. The student body was largely Black, with a significant Hispanic and Asian minority, and Roth revelled in, and embraced, its diversity, acquiring a taste for the music of James Brown, Sly and the Family Stone and Marvin Gaye via classmates. 'I started to see myself as a black person,' he wrote blithely in *Crazy from the Heat*, before the concept of cultural appropriation became a hot-button topic.

'I picked up all kinds of dancing, dress, and musical styles from the black and Hispanic kids there,' he admitted. 'My pals from the all-white school across town would look at me in wonderment and say, "There goes Diamond Dave. Very shiny. Very colorful kid."'

One night in 1971, Roth watched Pasadena's teenage power trio Genesis light up the sky at a backyard party and saw a vision of the future.

'Eddie was kind of a mentor,' he later enthused. 'I saw what he did with his fingers, and I knew that's what I wanted to do with my feet, and with my voice.'

Knocked back by the Van Halen brothers after his brace of disastrous auditions at Las Lunas Street, Roth began to obsess over the idea of fronting a band capable of providing 'belligerent competition' to Genesis/Mammoth. As he later acknowledged, his prime motivations in fighting for a share of the local spotlight were 'fear and revenge'.

'Every time we go out and play,' he said, 'yeah, I'm having a great time, but I'm also dancing somebody else into the dirt.'

If enmity simmered between the Mammoth and Red Ball Jet camps throughout 1972, both bands' dance cards were sufficiently busy to permit an uneasy truce to hold. In the year of Deep Purple's *Machine Head*, David Bowie's *The Rise and Fall of Ziggy Stardust and the Spiders from Mars*, Black Sabbath's *Vol. 4*, ZZ Top's *Rio Grande Mud* and the Rolling Stones' *Exile on Main Street*, the Van Halens worked hard to update and overhaul Mammoth's repertoire, recruiting keyboard player Jim Pewsey to add Farfisa organ and Wurlitzer electric piano on their versions of 'Highway Star', 'Maybe I'm a Leo', 'Tomorrow's Dream', 'Chevrolet', Santana's 'Soul Sacrifice', the Zombies' 'Time of the Season' and more. Meanwhile, in the basement of Dr Nathan Roth's ten-bedroom Spanish-style mansion on 455 Bradford Street, Red Ball Jet added James Brown, Ohio Players and Motown songs to their own live arsenal.

Seeking, perhaps, to atone for his inattention to his son's development during his adolescence, Roth Sr began to increasingly involve himself in the group's affairs, putting down a security deposit to buy David a PA, pulling in professional favours

to secure gigs, voicing his opinions on stage clothes and live presentation, and even going so far as to hire a choreographer to work with the band on synchronised dance routines they could incorporate into their shows. Within the group, his well-intentioned meddling was initially met with bemused suspicion, then outright resistance, and at the tail end of 1972, after father and son attempted an internal power grab by arguing that Dr Roth should be given an equal vote on all of the band's decisions, the other four members of Red Ball Jet simply quit, much to their singer's intense irritation.

If news of the demise of Roth's band initially delighted friends of the Van Halen brothers who wished to see the arrogant teenager humbled, this *Schadenfreude* would soon dissolve into howls of outrage for some, when, approximately six months later, the singer was installed as the new frontman of Mammoth.

On one level, the union between the Van Halen brothers and their nemesis was undeniably a marriage of convenience. With Red Ball Jet inoperative, Mammoth had taken to renting Roth's PA with increasing frequency, a transaction that cut deep into their profit margin, so Roth's assimilation into the group, as Alex and Eddie repeatedly explained to bemused friends, made sense from an economic perspective. 'We were renting his PA every weekend for $35 and getting $50 for the gigs,' Eddie said. 'We figured if we got him in the band, we wouldn't have to rent it anymore.'

Whether or not the Van Halens were wise to the fact, Roth was never a passive agent in this merger, however. Though he would perform solo gigs on the coffee-house singer/songwriter circuit in the wake of Red Ball Jet's demise, the astute, ambitious Roth never wavered from his initial evaluation of the Dutch brothers as the local musicians with the most potential, and beyond the welcome income stream which their PA hire provided, his long tail game involved insistently marketing himself to the brothers. While Mark Stone and Jim Pewsey became increasingly wary about Roth's presence at Mammoth rehearsals – talking to writer Greg Renoff, author of the definitive early-years biography *Van Halen Rising*, the bassist remembered Roth being 'difficult and weird', while Pewsey, who wouldn't stick around much longer, offered the blunt assessment that the oleaginous, exhausting rich kid was 'a punk' – the Van Halen brothers would listen patiently as Roth reeled off his practised, and subtly persuasive, spiels about Mammoth's capacity to transcend the backyard circuit and the minor aesthetic tweaks which could – and would, in his humble opinion – be pivotal in supercharging their appeal far beyond the Pasadena city limits. Central to this vision, Roth maintained, would be a conscious shift away from technically demanding progressive-rock epics in favour of songs with groove and soul and primal energy, music to dance, fight and fuck to.

'You play all 20 minutes of "I'm So Glad" by Cream, complete with drum solo, live, note for note, and it's very impressive, but you can't dance to it,' he explained patiently to the brothers, as if addressing slow-on-the-uptake children. 'That's not "Excuse me, do you come here often?" music.

'Now *I* can dance,' Roth continued. 'And since you're always renting my PA system and coming back frustrated, I'm in a position to assist. I will personally check every song for danceability. We'll play rock tunes, but ones you can dance to.'

Reading the room, Roth wisely refrained from advocating for synchronised dance routines.

Under Roth's direction, Mammoth reworked their core set list to include hits by Aerosmith, ZZ Top, James Brown, David Bowie, Bad Company, Kiss and Queen. Their mission statement, Roth insisted, should be to make every gig seem like the wildest, most outrageous out-of-control Saturday-night party.

The new-look Mammoth's first backyard party with Roth in the summer of 1973 proved to be a faltering reboot. The audience, as the singer recalled, hated it. 'So unanimously, in fact, that I knew I was onto something big.

'It was the first time I really became aware of how possessive an audience could really be about a given artist or a given band,' he noted. 'Way beyond "This is great music," it was almost as if it was football team time. "Hey, this is our band, they represent us." I came from another side of town, so to speak.'

Aware that he faced a challenge to win over hearts and minds, and determined to make himself indispensable to his new band, Roth secured a new practice space in which he could drill the unit. A fellow student at Pasadena City College, Linda Estrada, had managed Red Ball Jet for a time before Dr Roth's fateful intervention in the band's affairs, and she and her younger sister Liz Wiley regularly accompanied David to his solo acoustic gigs at open-mic nights – 'to boost his confidence', Wiley recalls. When she purchased a former Hells Angels clubhouse on Maiden Lane in Altadena at a foreclosure sale, Wiley offered Roth and his new group the use of the garage for rehearsals, if they assisted her in renovating the run-down property. Watching Mammoth run through their repertoire, Liz and Linda quickly recognised that with the gifted Van Halen brothers backing Roth, their fame-obsessed friend might actually have a group capable of matching his vaunting ambition.

'The first time I saw Eddie play was at a high school, when Dave had asked us to come and see other bands with him,' Liz Wiley remembers. 'I was always awed by his ability to hear music and instantly play it. My sister Linda used to call Ed "the Little Shy Boy", but he was an artist. One day I went into Dave's father's house and thought he must be at home listening to classical music on the house-wide stereo system, and then realised that it was a real person playing the piano – Eddie.'

When the sisters began accompanying Mammoth to back-yard parties, Linda realised that the band were outgrowing her modest management set-up and offered to introduce them to a full-time manager with connections to the Los Angeles music industry.

Formerly the manager of British rhythm-and-blues band the Glorious 39th, Catherine Hutchin-Harris, known to friends as English Cathy, or 'E.C.', had relocated from London to Los Angeles in 1967, and established Transatlantic Management to promote and manage LA area rock 'n' roll acts, including Sorcery, Yankee Rose and Sudden Death, who featured her future husband, guitarist Joey Dunlop, in their ranks. After Linda Estrada passed along Hutchin-Harris's number to David Lee Roth, the singer invited the vivacious Londoner to check out the band at a party in the grounds of his father's mansion.

'When we got to the house, which was in San Marino, there were cars parked everywhere, and my assistant Lynore and I had to park quite a way away and walk over in our platform shoes,' 'English Cathy' recalls. 'We could hear the music from streets away, and when we got into the party it was crazy, absolutely crazy. The first thing that hit me was Edward. He was unbelievable. He was playing with his fingers over the frets, which nobody did then, and I was absolutely blown away. Lynore and I looked at each other, and I said, "Oh. My. Goodness. This kid is a virtuoso." They were kinda just another rock band, until Edward cut loose. David was brilliant on stage, but it was Edward who really grabbed us.

'After they finished playing, I introduced David to Lynore. When he heard her name, he said, "How poetic!" and proceeded to quote Edgar Allan Poe's "The Raven" to her, as Poe had written a poem called "Lenore". Lynore was wearing this beautiful antique negligee as a dress, and when Edward was introduced to her, he accidentally spilled his drink all over her, turning her dress see-through: that appealed to David in particular, I remember. Edward used to drink Singapore Slings – vodka was his drug of choice then – and he drank a lot. The party got so rowdy: I remember kids were throwing beer bottles and they were smashing on the rocks beside the pool. I looked at Lynore and said, "We have to leave." I mean, some of these kids were only fourteen or fifteen, and the band were all under twenty-one, so I was concerned that if the police came, I'd be the oldest one there, and I'd be the one to get busted! David called me afterwards, and he sounded a bit disappointed when he said, "Oh, you guys left . . ." I told him that I didn't want to get a night in jail for drinking with under-age kids, but I'd be interested in helping out and getting them gigs.'

As is often the case in the music business, this surge of forward momentum for Mammoth was tempered somewhat by an unforeseen setback; specifically, in this instance, another name change being forced upon the band. Roth barely had time to unbutton his satin and velvet stage clothes under the glare of a hovering police helicopter spotlight before a 'cease and desist' notice was passed along to the band from an established San Fernando Valley hard-rock act who had been using the name Mammoth for years. The brothers toyed with rebranding as Rat Salad, a tip of the hat to the penultimate track on Black Sabbath's *Paranoid* album, but Roth argued against it. Mammoth's early success, he pointed out, quite correctly, was built around recognition of the precocious talent of the group's guitarist and drummer, so why not go route one and simply title this latest upgrade after the family name?

With this kink in the steel hammered out, Van Halen the band threw all their energies into spreading Van Halen the brand state-wide. A demo tape featuring a selection of fan-favourite covers and two original songs – the harsh-riffing boogie of 'Gentleman of Leisure' and the more progressive-rock-influenced 'Glitter' – was recorded at Dr Roth's house and distributed to club bookers. While English Cathy timetabled future dates in the Los Angeles area, the quartet blitzed Pasadena to snaffle up every engagement that might conceivably require a live music soundtrack, from backyard keg parties and wet T-shirt contests through to BDSM conventions and high-school carnivals. It seemed as if no Pasadena area high-school student could open their school locker without a fistful of xeroxed flyers for the latest Van Halen gigs fluttering to the floor.

'They had an amazing work ethic, it seemed like they were playing all the time,' says Mark Kendall, who would later find fame as the guitarist of hard-rock band Great White, but back then was a high-school student in Huntington Beach, California. 'A friend of mine kept telling me that I had to see this band, and then they played in someone's backyard right up the street from where I was living, three blocks from my house, so my friend was like, "OK, now you have no excuse!"

'If I remember correctly, Eddie was playing a Les Paul Junior – no tremolo bar, no tapping – and they were playing all covers. This was 1974. David Lee Roth had just joined, and he was jumping around like he just owned the place. When I walked in, Alex was doing a drum solo and Roth was blowing into a tube connected to the drums to make the pitch go up and down. That was my very first view of them. I was shocked by how good Eddie was. It seemed like he was pretty special. I don't think anybody had seen anybody playing outside of the box like that.

'I started following them all over the place. I remember that once, on the day on which one of the Zeppelin albums came out, they were already playing a song from it. I was thinking, "Wow!" And their shows were pretty out of control: I remember someone getting shot one night. The cops would be around by the fourth or fifth song, every time. They really tried to discourage it. There'd be cars parked a mile away, people standing in other people's front yards, throwing beer cans everywhere. So the neighbours would complain, and then the helicopters would come in . . .

'It seemed like every time I went to see them, Eddie was better than the time before. I'd be practising guitar in my bedroom for hours on end, and then I'd go to see Van Halen, and he'd have improved too. It was a little discouraging! I don't remember anyone from that era that had a bigger musician following than Eddie. I'd look into the crowd at their shows and I could see the guitar player from every band I knew watching him. He made us all want to try harder.

'There's always a lot of local bands and one musician that stands above them all, and where we grew up Eddie was the Man, he was the King. It was unquestioned.'

Though the buzz surrounding Van Halen was getting louder across southern California, the quartet were still struggling to lock down regular club bookings in Los Angeles. 'There was no room for a bunch of long-haired, platformed, goofy-looking fools!' Eddie would later explain in *Guitar World*.

'When we used to play clubs we learned just enough Top 40 songs to get hired,' he recalled. 'At the gig you had to play five 45-minute sets, but most pop songs are three or four minutes long, so that's a lot of tunes to learn. We figured we could play our own stuff, and no one would care as long as the beat was there. One day we were playing at this club in Covina called Posh. We ran out of Top 40 tunes, so we started playing our own music. The owner of the club walks up to us while we were playing a song and goes, "Stop! I hired you to play Top 40. What is this shit?" He told us to get the fuck out of there, and he wouldn't let us take our equipment. We had to come back the next week to pick up our equipment. It was always that way. It was either "the guitarist is too loud" or "plays too psychedelic." They always complained about me.'

'The best club they ever played was a teenage nightclub [the Rock Corporation] in Van Nuys, in the Valley,' remembers English Cathy. 'They loved them there. They'd also play Barnacle Bill's, which was kinda a dump. And I remember once we played a gig at a club called the Topanga Canyon Corral, a hippy club in the mountains, totally unsuited to Van Halen, but I talked them into letting them play. Before the show Edward said, "Hey, EC, come and look at this!" He opened his guitar case, and I said, "Wow, how cool, a copy of a Flying V!" He was so devastated, because he knew that it was a copy, but he was so bummed that I knew it too. I said, "It's a cool guitar, Edward, and one of these days you'll be able to buy a real one."'

Occasionally, the Van Halen brothers would arrive back at 1881 Las Lunas Street late, just as their father would be returning from playing a bar mitzvah or wedding in Oxnard. The three of them would pile into the back of Eddie's van, knocking back beers until their laughter and raised voices would waken and enrage Eugenia. 'My mom's just going fucking crazy,' laughed Eddie later. '"Get your ass in here!" She'd lock us out and we'd have to break a window to get in. She hated the fact that we were into music.'

In the spring of 1974, English Cathy pulled off a coup in securing the band an audition at Gazzarri's nightclub, on the Sunset Strip, via her friendship with the West Hollywood club's flamboyant owner, Bill Gazzarri. In the late '60s, the club had hosted gigs by the Doors, Buffalo Springfield, ? and the Mysterians and the Walker Brothers, but its reputation had taken a hit as competitor clubs such as the Whisky a Go Go, the Starwood and the Troubadour gained popularity and kudos. Van Halen had blown previous auditions at the club, and the memories rankled.

'The first time we auditioned at Gazzarri's, they said, "Man, you guys look like you're out of Hicksville!" because I was wearing a T-shirt and jeans,' Alex recalled. 'I was like, "So what? You don't like it? Fuck you!" They told us to turn down five times, and then they kicked us out!'

This time, the quartet were determined to finally land the gig. Their charm offensive not only involved learning a set of FM radio-friendly covers to woo Bill Gazzarri, Eddie even bought a new pair of platform shoes for the occasion, for that added touch of showbiz glamour. The gambit worked: Van Halen were handed a contract to perform at the club on 4, 5, 6 and 7 April, and then again on 11, 12, 13 and 14 April. The residency wasn't an immediate success – 'The first time we ever played there, there were only four people in the audience,' Alex revealed. 'And those four people were our friends. And we paid to get them in! Gazzarri wouldn't even let us park in the parking lot' – but word spread quickly. The numbers coming through the doors increased, and the quartet were booked in for two more weekends in May . . . then fourteen nights in June . . . then twelve in August, with Gazzarri now declaring himself their biggest fan.

'We'd have meetings every night and I'd say, "You are gonna be the biggest rock and roll band to come out of Gazzarri's,"' the club owner recalled. 'And they would say, "Well, are you sure? How come there are five of us here and you're the only one who knows that?"'

'We did everything for him,' Eddie said. 'We'd play the dance contests. They had a Coca-Cola telethon, and we MC'd that and played. The highest pay we ever got was $125 for a night. We started off at $75 a night for the band, then we moved up to $100 . . . then for a while we were paid $125. Then he might slip us $20 extra on a Sunday when we were packing up. But that wasn't enough to pay for equipment, strings, gasoline, oil, transportation . . .'

'Eddie was the quiet one, but he was the most popular,' Gazzarri observed. 'Every week that we played 'em here, there were at least 50 girls who would come and pay and sit on Eddie's side [of the stage] all night long.'

'They were blowing the doors down,' recalled Lizzie Grey, the guitarist in LA rockers Sister, alongside future W.A.S.P. frontman Blackie Lawless (Steven Duren) and future Mötley Crüe leader Nikki Sixx (Frank Ferrano). 'You'd hear stories about them in Hollywood all the time, there was so much hype around them. When I first saw them, they were just mindblowing. I remember thinking that Roth was totally ripping off Black Oak Arkansas singer Jim Dandy, but Eddie was a revelation. My guitar heroes were people like Ariel Bender and Mick Ronson, but Eddie was doing something new: there were shades of Jeff Beck there for me, but he was definitely putting the pedal to the metal.'

'Edward was never cocky about his talents,' says English Cathy. 'He never came across like he thought he was God's gift; he just played his music. But people were definitely starting to pay attention.'

'I had older friends who were going into Hollywood, and you'd hear them saying, "Shit, this guy is better than [Deep Purple guitarist Ritchie] Blackmore!" or "This guy is better than [UFO guitarist Michael] Schenker!"' says Los Angeles-based music writer/podcaster/film director Bob Nalbandian. 'I used to think, "But how could a local guy be that good?" There were other great bands playing Los Angeles at that time – A La Carte, Stormer, Wolfgang – but Eddie began to dominate the conversation, especially among guitarists.'

'We were jealous, and we were all trying to play catch-up,' admits future Dokken/Lynch Mob guitarist George Lynch, then playing in the Boyz. 'We thought, "Oh boy . . . this guy's going to change the world." I had been hearing about this guy with the weird European name . . . I saw him and it blew my mind. They were still doing covers at the time – Rainbow, Montrose – and their original stuff was as good or better than their cover stuff, which was pretty exceptional. After their show, I went back to our band room and played my guitar until the sun came up.'

Though the residency at Gazzarri's was a huge boost for Van Halen's profile, the demanding nature of the booking, with the quartet required to be onstage for multiple sets each night, soon exposed a flaw in the unit: Mark Stone. Unlike his bandmates, the bassist was a straight 'A' student studying to be a pharmacist, and could not devote his every waking hour to the group. On those nights when he swapped his white lab coat for a tie-dyed Zeppelin or Hendrix T-shirt to get onstage with Van Halen, Stone understandably wanted to get a little loose, which meant downing a few cans of Schlitz Malt Liquor pre-show and smoking a little weed. As relaxing as this customary ritual was, it probably wasn't the ideal preparation for rattling through fifty to sixty cover songs onstage under hot lights, in a booking stretching into the wee small hours. 'We were playing parties with a repertoire of a hundred songs, and he wouldn't remember stuff,' Eddie recalled. As their popularity spread, Van Halen demanded ever higher standards, and Mark Stone was slipping just at the wrong time.

Even the best-drilled bands could face unexpected challenges, of course. On the afternoon of 3 May 1974, as Van Halen soundchecked for a headline show in the Pasadena High School auditorium, David Lee Roth's PA blew up. Securing a new rig on a Friday evening wasn't really an option, so Eddie approached Michael Sobolewski, the vocalist/bassist of support band Snake, and politely asked if it might be possible for Van Halen to share their PA for the night.

'I knew of Ed and Alex from school, because I was taking some music classes at Pasadena College and Ed and Alex were taking basically a lot of the same classes, but we were taking them at different times,' recalled Sobolewski, now much better known to the world as Michael Anthony. 'Before they even got Roth in the band, I remember going to a carnival that our school had, and I heard this band playing Grand Funk Railroad's "Inside Looking Out" . . . and it's Edward and Alex. Everything they played, Edward sounded exactly like the guitarist he was copying. It was like, "Wow, this band is heavy competition here in the area . . . these guys are really happening."'

With Van Halen using his PA at Pasadena High School, Snake's frontman had no option but to stick around for the headliners' set. Watching the quartet storm through covers by Grand Funk Railroad, ZZ Top and Captain Beyond, alongside a fistful of original compositions, Anthony was once again struck by their energy and ability.

'I remember standing on the side of the stage watching Edward and Alex play and thinking, "Wow, these guys are good!"' he said. 'Then Dave came up the side of the stage, and I forget what he was dressed in, some kind of a tux vest, but that was it, with a cane and a hat. He had long hair. I don't remember if he had it colored, but I know he'd done something weird to it. And he said, "How do you like my boys?" And I just went [horrified], "Jesus Christ, get this guy away from me!"'

Post-show, the Van Halen brothers thanked Anthony again for the PA loan and chatted about their shared musical interests. 'It might be kind of cool to jam sometime,' the bassist said casually, before the two parties headed for their respective rides. Within two weeks, he received a phone call at home from one of the brothers, asking if he'd fancy coming over to Liz Wiley's house on Maiden Lane for that jam they'd talked about.

'I was nervous,' Anthony remembered. 'I was playing backyard parties and these guys were playing in Gazzarri's in Hollywood. So, I brought my brother along with me for kind of moral support.

'It was just Edward and Alex, and we played all night and it was really neat. Al had a case of Schlitz Malt there and we had a few beers and kept playing and playing . . . And Ed asked me, "Hey, would you like to join the band?" I looked at my brother and he was really blown away, and I'm just going, "Well, yeah!"'

A few weeks later, Eddie handed the bassist a demo cassette that Van Halen had taped at Cherokee Studios in Chatsworth, featuring four original songs: the funky, swinging, cowbell-accented 'Take Your Whiskey Home'; 'In a Simple Rhyme', something of a guitar masterclass, with its chunky palm-muted runs, Pete Townshend-style open chords and ringing arpeggios; the hard-riffing, Zeppelin-esque 'Believe Me'; and the acoustic 'Angel Eyes', a holdover from Roth's short-lived singer/songwriter phase bearing the influence of James Taylor and Crosby, Stills, Nash and Young. The demo would represent Mark Stone's final contribution to Van Halen.

'We met one day, and they actually asked me to leave,' Stone later recalled. 'For a long time, it really hurt. It was tough leaving that band because I knew they were destined for greatness. They say, "Don't leave before the miracle happens." And I did.'

· · · · ·

Like his three new bandmates, Michael Anthony Sobolewski wasn't a native Californian. The bassist was born on 20 June 1954 to Polish immigrant parents in Chicago, Illinois, and came to the Golden State in 1966, when his father Walter moved the family to Arcadia, north of Los Angeles, in the San Gabriel Valley. Walter Sobolewski played trumpet in polka bands and passed on his love of the instrument to his eldest son, who joined Dana Junior High School's marching band upon settling in Arcadia. Thanks to his older sister Nancy's record collection, soon enough Michael was exposed to Cream, Blue Cheer, Led Zeppelin and Electric Flag, and at the age of fifteen, with his younger brother Steve on drums and neighbour Mike Hershey on guitar, he formed his first band, Poverty's Children. After stints with garage rockers Balls, and the Black Opel, upon transitioning to Arcadia High School the bassist recruited guitarist Tony Codgen and drummer Steve Hapner to form Snake – 'your basic three-man power trio type thing' – covering Foghat, ZZ Top, Lynyrd Skynyrd and Johnny Winter songs. Joining Van Halen, the bassist remembered, was 'really challenging' initially, with Anthony being required to learn three or four new covers at every band rehearsal, but he settled fast. Which was fortunate, because Van Halen had a huge list of upcoming shows booked.

English Cathy's booking calendar for the early months of 1975 makes for interesting reading. In addition to their regular gig at Gazzarri's, Van Halen had engagements at Monrovia High, St Frances High and Pasadena High, a $100 cash booking for a wedding, backyard parties, and dates at Myron's Ballroom and the Duarte International Casino. In April, she secured her boys five consecutive nights at Barnacle Bill's, which paid $125 a night: 'That was the big time!' she laughs. But while the money was obviously welcome – particularly at a time when, to keep the band afloat, Eddie and Alex were knocking on front doors throughout Pasadena, offering homeowners the opportunity to have their house numbers painted on the kerb outside their property for just $5 – the quartet were increasingly mindful that becoming reliant on income from the covers circuit carried with it a risk of getting stuck in a rut, not least because, as Eddie understood, they were being tasked to 'make sure people got into the bar, not into the band'.

'We knew we had to do something to get us out of the bars where all we could do was play other people's hits,' David Lee Roth told the *LA Times*. 'We had to develop a following: people who'd realize that we could do more than play Aerosmith songs well.

'We only had a small kit: one guitar, bass and drums, so we really had to work on the singing to fill out the choruses without brass or keyboards,' Roth explained, shedding light on the band's early approach to songwriting. 'So, we dignified those choruses with glorious harmonies, all four of us singing. My contribution, because of the black influence, owed a lot to old Motown records. Weight the backgrounds on the second verse, glorious chorus, Beatles-esque middle-eight. I didn't know any other way to write.'

If the young musicians needed a sign that the covers circuit ultimately might not be the healthiest environment in which to operate, an incident during one of their shows at Walter Mitty's Rock & Roll Emporium, a rowdy, 300-capacity club in Pomona, in the spring of 1976 would have sharpened their focus. Van Halen were playing their final set of the night when they spotted a 'fracas' unfolding between rival biker gang members, as an argument over who had the fastest 'hog' escalated.

'It got rough,' Eddie recalled, 'and one of them pulls out a knife, and a minute later the other guy is lying there with his intestines hanging out. That was pretty shocking. There was blood gushing everywhere, and the guy actually died.'

'We didn't play anymore that night,' David Lee Roth noted.

It was Rodney Bingenheimer, the self-styled 'Mayor of the Sunset Strip' and charismatic owner of the notoriously hedonistic, glam rock-friendly West Hollywood nightclub Rodney Bingenheimer's English Disco, who proposed that Van Halen should switch their allegiances from Gazzarri's to the Starwood, in order to find an audience that was supportive of fledgling acts showcasing original material. In the early months of 1976, the Santa Monica Boulevard club had hosted gigs by emerging Los Angeles area talent (the Runaways, the Quick), fast-rising international acts (Slade, Rush) and established Californian rockers (Sammy Hagar, Journey), and Bingenheimer suggested that this was the sort of company a local hard-rock act with genuine ambition should be keeping. He also suggested that maybe Van Halen might want to enquire about the possibility of opening a show he was due to MC in May at the Golden West Ballroom in Norwalk. English rockers UFO had been booked to headline the gig, but no local supports had been confirmed yet. If Van Halen wanted to prove their mettle, here was a gilt-edged opportunity.

In the summer of 1973, when stand-in guitarist Bernie Marsden had failed to show up for a series of UFO club shows in Germany, the Londoners had been forced to borrow teenage guitar prodigy Michael Schenker from their support band Scorpions in order to fulfil the contracted dates. One month later, UFO frontman Phil Mogg phoned Schenker and invited him to come to London to join the band. Just seventeen years old when he relocated to England, Schenker's incendiary playing transformed UFO and, jettisoning their original bluesy 'space-rock' sound, the Londoners were reborn as a stylish hard-rock band with *Phenomenon*, their debut album for Chrysalis Records, gaining a whole new audience thanks to the Schenker co-penned singles 'Doctor Doctor' and 'Rock Bottom'. UFO's 1975 album *Force It* reached number 71 on the *Billboard* 200, and bigger things were expected in the US for *No Heavy Petting*, which was set for release in May 1976. When three scheduled nights at the Starwood in early May quickly sold out, the band's agent booked them into the 2,000-capacity Golden West Ballroom on 9 May. The chance to go head-to-head with the hotly tipped Londoners and their mercurial German guitar virtuoso appealed to Van Halen's sense of adventure and their competitive instincts.

If the band were expecting red-carpet treatment at their most high-profile gig to date, they would be swiftly disabused of the notion: when they arrived at the venue and asked for directions to their dressing room, UFO's brusque British road manager pointed them towards the venue's public bathroom. If the intention was to put the young Californians in their place, the tactic backfired, for it served only to galvanise Van Halen. The quartet hit the stage without nerves, tearing through punchy originals 'On Fire', 'Somebody Get Me a Doctor', 'Show Your Love' and 'Runnin' with the Devil' in quick succession, as the local audience roared their approval. Back in the venue's toilets post-show, changing out of their sweaty stage gear, the group were congratulated by scores of well-wishers. Eddie remembered one of their number as a drug dealer from Los Angeles and nodded across the room in recognition.

'I'm changing my clothes in the toilet stall,' he recalled, 'and the guy next to me goes, "Hey, Eddie. Great show. Want some dynamite blow?" I said, "Yeah, sure." So he hands me this paper, and I took my guitar pick and went to town. I didn't taste it first to see what it was. Ten minutes later, I barely made it 50 feet. Alex saw me collapse from across the ballroom and ran to me. I had overdosed on PCP . . .'

With his muscles spasming, the stricken guitarist was loaded into Michael Anthony's station wagon and hurriedly driven across town to Norwalk Hospital. Inside the emergency room, his wrists and ankles were bound tightly to the operating table and an oxygen tube was forced down his throat.

'I actually died on the table in the hospital,' Eddie revealed. 'When I woke up the doctor said, "Your heart stopped. If it was thirty seconds later, we couldn't have brought you back."

'The doctor even said to me, "It's funny, your fingers wouldn't stop moving."'

Outside the operating theatre, a panic-stricken Jan, Eugenia and Alex Van Halen were informed that Eddie was out of danger. For Eugenia, the near-tragedy was the starkest of reminders that she needed to steer her boys away from the soul-ruining music industry, and she offered to underwrite Eddie's tuition fees if he called time on the band in favour of taking up a course in computing at DeVry University in Phoenix, Arizona. In her heart, though, she must have known her entreaties would go unheard.

On 1 June 1976, Van Halen played the Starwood for the first time. For much of the rest of the year, the quartet would alternate between their new adopted home and Gazzarri's, enhancing their reputation, honing their chops and bolstering their self-confidence with every show.

'The Starwood had a great, nasty rock 'n' roll vibe,' recalls photographer Neil Zlozower, a native Los Angeleno. 'It had a lot of rooms. You could go there and get lost, do drugs, play with chicks. It was fucking great, a lot of fun. You'd have Elvis Costello or Blondie or X at the Whisky, but the Starwood was for the rockers.'

'Van Halen would come round to my house at about two in the morning after they played, two or three times a week,' recalls Lynore Grace, then English Cathy's twenty-four-year-old assistant, 'and I'd fix them dinner. They were always buzzing with excitement from the shows. I remember making them spaghetti once, and they were hanging it out of their nostrils and mouths, pretending they were zombies with worms crawling out of them, while David ran around shouting, "We're gonna be rock stars! We're gonna be superstars!" Once they started playing in Hollywood, they were so positive that they were going to make it.'

'I was living with Cathy and her husband Joey,' says Grace's brother Greg Magie, formerly the lead vocalist with Sorcery, 'whom I knew as the guitar player from Sudden Death. I remember Cathy showing off photos of Van Halen, and she was super-excited about them. We actually had Van Halen open up for us a couple of times, and they were undeniably a powerful band, with Eddie as the real star, a fantastic guitar player even then.

'I remember being at the Starwood one night when the Runaways were playing, because [manager] Kim Fowley managed another band I was playing in, Sleepy Hollow, and Ed and Dave were there. Dave was super-friendly, and Eddie was more shy, but they were both real high. I knocked on the Runaways' dressing-room door before the show, just to wish them well with their gig, and at that exact moment Eddie threw up right in the doorway and had to be dragged away by Dave. We used to tease him about that a lot.'

In October 1976, while Kiss were in Los Angeles to film a segment for ABC television's *Paul Lynde Halloween Special*, a three-song performance that would instantly make the New Yorkers the most recognisable rock band in the country, vocalist/guitarist Paul Stanley and bassist/vocalist Gene Simmons asked Rodney Bingenheimer to nominate a couple of local bands they might wish to check out when they hit the town. They were pointed in the direction of Van Halen and George Lynch's band the Boyz. Informed that the two bands were sharing equal billing at the Starwood on 2 November, the pair promised to drop by for a look.

'I'd actually gone to the Starwood the night before with [Runaways guitarist] Lita Ford and saw both bands,' recalls Paul Stanley. 'I remember the Boyz covering "Detroit Rock City", and I was thinking, "Boy, this a great song . . ." and then realised it was mine! But Van Halen were just a powerhouse – Eddie was something completely different, and Dave was already on his way to becoming the ultimate frontman. So we came back the next night, and Gene came too.'

Though the Demon and the Starchild weren't sporting their stage make-up, their presence in the Starwood's VIP area with Ford, her Runaways bandmate Jackie Fox, Simmons's model girlfriend Bebe Buell, Bingenheimer and his friend Hernando Courtright caused a stir. As they took the stage, the Boyz knew that they were effectively competing with Van Halen for Stanley and Simmons's attention. And when Simmons and Buell came backstage to introduce themselves after his group's performance, Lynch felt sure that the Boyz had made a genuine impression. But, unable to carry on their conversation above the sound of Van Halen warming up on stage, Simmons and Buell returned to their balcony seats, as the Pasadena quartet began their set. Within five minutes, Simmons had effectively forgotten that the Boyz even existed.

'I was thinking, My fucking God, listen to *these* guys,' Simmons remembered. 'As soon as Eddie started playing, the thing that struck me right away was that the guy was amazingly fast and light on touch . . . Eddie was just swimming over that fretboard, and I couldn't believe the control he had.

'Everybody's head just turned around like Linda Blair in *The Exorcist*: what is *that*? When the solo came up, you couldn't believe your ears because all this music was symphonic, the melodies and the runs and the speed, all coming out of one guitar.'

Rodney Bingenheimer took Simmons backstage after the show to introduce him to the band members, and the bassist immediately expressed a desire to work with the quartet. 'I think you guys can make it,' he told the wide-eyed musicians. 'I'm not stroking you, I'm not interested in doing anything for myself, but I love your band and I'd like to help you.' The bassist proposed signing the band to his management label, Man of 1,000 Faces, and promised that he would produce a demo for them to shop around the major labels. Eddie Van Halen was given Simmons's phone number at the Sunset Marquis hotel and was told to call the bassist when he got back to Pasadena. The bleary-eyed musicians were subsequently instructed to be at Village Recorders Studio in Santa Monica at 6 a.m., where Simmons would be ready to commit a selection of their best songs to tape.

'I remember Gene coming into Studio B with no make-up, shoes with high platforms and a gorgeous girl who'd been a centrefold, saying that he was producing the next guitar god,' recalls Hernan Rojas, who was employed as an engineer on the 3 November session and remembers being 'totally impressed' by the band's musicality. Simmons selected thirteen Van Halen originals to work on – 'On Fire', 'Runnin' with the Devil', 'Somebody Get Me a Doctor', 'Babe, Don't Leave Me Alone' and 'House of Pain' among them. At the end of the session, he informed the stunned quartet that he was flying them to New York to finish the recording at Jimi Hendrix's Electric Lady Studios and to introduce them to his manager, Bill Aucoin. To Simmons's genuine astonishment, however, upon being played the Van Halen demo tape both Aucoin and Paul Stanley claimed they were unable to hear what the bassist was getting so excited about.

'Everybody shrugged their shoulders and went, "So what?"' Simmons recalled. 'And I'm going, "You're killing me! Whaddya mean, so what? Listen to that!" But everybody was too busy with their life.'

Displaying the sort of stubborn tenacity that serves him so well in driving Kiss forward year after year, Simmons convinced his manager to allow his protégés to play a live showcase for him at SIR Studios, where the New Yorkers' backline was already set up for their tour rehearsals. Playing borrowed instruments on a sterile sound stage for an industry giant they instinctively knew wasn't buying Simmons's increasingly desperate sales patter, Van Halen's nerve, for once, deserted them, with Roth, starved of the wide-eyed female adulation he'd come to view as a default setting each time he stepped on a stage, particularly cavalier in his phrasing and note selection.

In *Crazy from the Heat*, Roth offers a vivid snapshot of the group being summoned to Bill Aucoin's Madison Avenue office to hear his decision. 'We sat in front of his mahogany desk, and he had his shoes polished by a little Italian man while he spoke to us,' Roth wrote. 'And he said to us, "Guys, I think the music is great, but I don't think the vocals hold up. I just don't hear the melodies, the hits that are required in this day and age." He said, "Dave, maybe there are a couple other acts that I handle that we could get you to work with. Guys, you and the band, maybe another vocalist would work. But otherwise, Gene has his own career, he's in Kiss, and barring any other permutations I don't think I can work with you."'

'I tore up the contract and said, "You guys are free,"' says Simmons. 'I said, "We're going out on tour, and when I get back, if you don't have a deal, I'll come back and I'll try to help you. But right now, I don't feel ethical in shopping your tape, because the rest of the guys don't get it."'

'It was really depressing, we were totally bummed,' Eddie recalled. 'Bill Aucoin was saying basically what everyone else said at the time: "Too much uncontrolled energy and no commercial potential."'

This assessment, admits Kiss frontman Paul Stanley now, was nothing to do with Van Halen and everything to do with Aucoin's canny management of Gene Simmons.

'We didn't want to take Van Halen on because we were trying to hold Gene in check,' he says simply. 'Gene is often more concerned – and this is just part of his personality – with Gene, and it wasn't going to be to our benefit for him to run off and get involved with something else. Were Van Halen undeniable? Absolutely. Were they fabulous? Yeah. Did they have what it took? Absolutely. But we had to take care of Kiss, and the way to protect Kiss at that time was to pull the reins in on Gene. It's that simple.'

Their confidence dented, Van Halen returned to California with their collective tail between their legs. Even Roth, their loudest, most voluble cheerleader, was deflated, and troubled by unfamiliar feelings of vulnerability and self-doubt, having been singled out as the unit's weakest link by Aucoin. 'I didn't know what the Van Halens were thinking at the time,' he admitted. 'Perhaps they were buying this load of horseshit.'

There was little time, however, for the group to indulge in self-pity or navel-gazing. And a sold-out homecoming show at the Pasadena Civic on 19 November would prove to be just the restorative confidence boost the quartet needed.

While Van Halen soundchecked at the Civic, Marshall Berle, the nephew of celebrated Hollywood entertainer Milton Berle, was battling with traffic en route to the venue. A former booking agent at the William Morris Agency, Berle was now the man responsible for procuring talent for the legendary Whisky a Go Go club, which had recently reopened on Sunset Boulevard after being shuttered for several years. Berle had been tipped off about Van Halen by Hollywood scenester Kim Fowley, and though he privately questioned why any sane promoter would book an unsigned local band into a 3,000-seat venue, as he drew closer to the auditorium Berle was impressed by the sheer numbers of teenage rock fans streaming towards the entrances. Impressed, that is, until ushers at the venue began closing the doors, refusing to admit anyone else into the building.

'I went around back to the stage entrance and identified myself to security, and they let me in,' Berle recalled. 'I went out front into the audience, where the place was so packed that I couldn't move. All of a sudden, the lights went out, the audience started screaming as the band was introduced, and the place went nuts! I could not believe my eyes and ears. There have been many times in my music career that I saw something for the first time that blew my mind, but I was not prepared for what was unfolding right in front of me. The hair on the back of my neck stood out, and for the next 45 minutes I saw the guitar-playing shredding of Edward Van Halen backed by the best rhythm section I'd ever heard. Dave Roth was the most amazing frontman/singer I had ever seen. His showmanship, coupled with the baddest-ass trio of musicians, was a formula that had success written all over it.'

After the show, Berle went backstage, introduced himself to Roth, Anthony and the Van Halen brothers, and made them an instant offer for a three-night stand at the Whisky, to take place on 3, 4 and 5 December.

'As I gave Dave a contract for the band to play the Whisky I said, "You guys should have a record deal,"' Berle recalled. 'My statement probably seemed like bullshit to them, but I told them that I would help them get one and they said, "Sure, go ahead."'

Berle's enthusiastic championing of the band persuaded the *LA Times* to send a reviewer, Richard Cromelin, to check out their debut at the Whisky.

'If the term punk-rock implies a musical primitivism and an attitude of street-bred defiance, the Pasadena-based quartet Van Halen falls into an entirely different category,' wrote Cromelin in his review, published in the 24 December 1976 edition of the newspaper. 'Even through the group is associated with the local punk-rock scene, its highly developed musical attack and conventional image give it a good chance of moving from the L.A. circuit into national popularity.

'It was apparent', the review continued, that 'Edwin [*sic*] Van Halen is the heart of the group. In addition to some flashy solo spots, he does a superb job (as the group's only lead instrument) of establishing, guiding and adorning the sound. The material itself is pretty fundamental, but Van Halen's resourcefulness keeps things interesting and steers the music clear of formulized heavy-metal monotony. Add to that a solid rhythm section and a rampaging vocalist of the Robert Plant/Jim Dandy school, and you have a package that's certain to do the trick for the Kiss–Aerosmith crowd. With just a bit more melody in the songs, and expressiveness in the singing, Van Halen could probably win over some stodgier listeners as well.'

His confidence restored, on 14 December David Lee Roth helped further exorcise the memories of Van Halen's dispiriting meeting with Bill Aucoin by securing the band their first radio airplay, on Rodney Bingenheimer's KROQ show, with the fiery version of 'Runnin' with the Devil' from the Gene Simmons-produced demo. 'Tell us about this tune we're going to play . . .' said Bingenheimer by way of an introduction, offering Roth a platform for his sales pitch.

'Well, we were playing one night,' drawled Roth, 'and some of the fellas from Kiss came down to see the band, who you brought along, and they came by and...a couple of days later we were in New York City doing a little tape recording down Electric Lady Land [sic] Studios. So what we have here is one hell of a demo tape...'

Marshall Berle, meanwhile, was fulfilling his promise to the band by talking Van Halen up to his contacts at record labels. One afternoon in January 1977, he placed a call to Ted Templeman's Burbank office. Formerly a member of 'sunshine pop' band Harpers Bizarre, Templeman was now a hotshot producer (having worked with Van Morrison, Little Feat and Californian hard-rock band Montrose) and a trusted A&R executive at Warner Bros.

By his own admission, Templeman rarely accepted or returned calls in relation to local bands, but he'd known Berle from his time at William Morris and liked the agent's energy and drive, so he took the call.

'Ted, I've got a band for you,' Berle enthused. 'Their name is Van Halen, they're from Pasadena, and next month they're going to be playing two shows on back-to-back nights at the Starwood.'

As he recalled, Templeman's A&R instincts at this point in his career were informed by one simple criterion: he wanted to find 'somebody with nuts'. As he slipped quietly into the Starwood on the night of 2 February, the fact that the club was almost empty didn't immediately fill him with confidence, and deciding against taking a seat at the table Berle had reserved for him, he made instead for the balcony, figuring it would afford him an easier escape route should the band suck.

'When Van Halen came onstage it was like they were shot out of a cannon,' Templeman remembered in his engrossing autobiography *A Platinum Producer's Life in Music*. 'Their energy wowed me, especially because they performed like they were playing an arena and not a small Hollywood club. So my interest was piqued, even though their singer didn't impress me. At that moment, that didn't matter much, because their guitar player blew my mind.

'Right out of the gate, I was just knocked out by Ed Van Halen. It's weird to say this, but encountering him was almost like falling head-over-heels with a girl on a first date. I was so dazzled. I had never been as impressed with a musician as I was with him that night. I'd seen Miles Davis, Dave Brubeck, Dizzy Gillespie, all of these transcendent artists, but Ed was one of the best musicians I'd ever seen live . . . So, right away, I knew I wanted him on Warner Bros.

'When I think back on that night, it wasn't just one thing about him that grabbed me. It was his whole persona. This guy, when he played, looked completely natural and unaffected; he was so nonchalant in his greatness. Here he was, playing the most incredible shit, acting as if it were no more challenging than snapping his fingers.'

When he returned to the Starwood twenty-four hours later, Templeman had Warner Bros. chairman/CEO Mo Ostin in tow. Ostin had signed the Kinks and the Jimi Hendrix Experience to Reprise, so he had previous form in spotting talent. That Van Halen included a Kinks cover – a supercharged version of Ray Davies's 'You Really Got Me' – in their set didn't escape Ostin's attention. When the quartet finished playing, Berle took the two label executives to the Starwood's dressing room.

'[Ostin] asked us if were signed,' Eddie recalled. 'We said no. He then asked us if we had a manager. We said no. Finally, he asked us if we had an agent, and we said no again.'

Ostin took down the brothers' home phone number and told the pair, 'Don't sign with anybody else.'

'Do they have a manager?' he asked Berle. Informed that the group were self-managed, Ostin declared, 'You're their manager.'

Templeman immediately booked out three days in April at Hollywood's Sunset Sound Recorders for the band. Having worked with Montrose, Little Feat and, most recently, the Doobie Brothers at the facility, the producer knew the rooms, the desks and – just as importantly in terms of impressing his new charges – the building's rich history. The Rolling Stones had recorded tracks for *Exile on Main Street* in Studio 1, he explained; Jimmy Page had mixed *Led Zeppelin IV* here; the Doors, Brian Wilson and Janis Joplin had created magic here. As a younger man, he revealed, he himself had cut tracks in this studio, when, in March 1967, Harpers Bizarre recorded two Leon Russell songs, 'Raspberry Rug' and 'I Can Hear the Darkness', for their debut album *Feelin' Groovy*.

On 13 April, between 11 a.m. and 4 p.m., the quartet rolled through twenty-five songs for Templeman and his trusted engineer Donn Landee in Sunset Sound's Studio 2. 'That's when we knew we had a band that could play,' noted an approving Landee.

The tape showcased a band as diverse as they were musically daring. Though the perfectionist Van Halen brothers had some misgivings about the quality of the production – 'We popped it [the demo cassette] into the player in my van and expected to hear Led Zeppelin coming out,' Eddie later confessed, 'but we were kind of appalled by what we heard. It just didn't sound the way we wanted it to sound' – they were not about to question Templeman's authority or tear up their golden ticket. As far as Templeman was concerned, Van Halen were good to go.

'Within a week we were signed up,' Eddie later marvelled. 'It was right out of the movies.'

Bounding into 1881 Las Lunas Street to deliver the good news to their parents, the duo were embraced by their father Jan, who was utterly delighted. Eugenia, who constantly warned her boys against becoming 'nothing nuts' like their father, was distinctly less impressed.

'My mom just hated it,' Eddie laughed. 'You know what she said? "Yeah? How long will it last?"'

3
ON FIRE

Guitar Player magazine editor Don Menn threw open his office door and beckoned writers Jas Obrecht and Tom Wheeler, plus *Keyboard* magazine editor Tom Darter, to join him in his sanctum. Anticipating either a dressing-down or a business update, the trio waited expectantly as Menn strode across the room to his record deck, carefully raised the tonearm and dropped the stylus on the run-in groove introducing the second track on the red vinyl EP spinning on the turntable. 'What is that?' he asked his silent colleagues, as an over-distorted cascading flurry of rapid-fire triads and squealing pinch harmonics filled the air. 'What *is* that?' he repeated.

Though he'd spent countless long hours meticulously poring over the twenty-five-song demo tracked at Sunset Sound in April 1977 in order to collate the strongest possible song selection for Van Halen's debut album and isolate specific verses, bridges and choruses from weaker cuts that could potentially be cleaved, grafted or repurposed elsewhere during pre-production, Ted Templeman hadn't identified 'Eruption' as a potential cornerstone of the recording. This was no sloppy oversight: Eddie Van Halen's technically dazzling guitar instrumental wasn't on the original tape reel. In fact, the very first time the producer heard what would become the album's defining musical motif was towards the business end of the studio sessions, when Templeman nipped out from the control booth at Sunset Sound to grab a coffee and overheard the guitarist extemporising variations on a classical theme.

'What is that?' Templeman enquired.

'Ah, nothing,' came Van Halen's reply. 'Just something I warm up on.'

'Let's hear it again,' the producer said. 'We gotta record it. Right away.'

Templeman walked into the control booth and instructed Donn Landee to turn on the monitors.

'We've got to record this,' Templeman recalls telling the engineer.

'Already rolling,' Landee assured him.

Eddie Van Halen had been finessing his solo showcase onstage in Hollywood clubs for the best part of three years. As often as not, he would perform the dramatic instrumental with his back to the audience, so that no one could pinpoint exactly what he was doing. The secret technique the guitarist was shielding involved using both his hands on the fretboard to tap out notes at light speed – not in itself a revolutionary innovation, with ukulele-playing 'Wizard of the Strings' Roy Smeck, country legend Jimmie Webster, 'Touch' guitar inventor Dave Bunker, jazz maestro Barney Kessel, Genesis guitarist Steve Hackett and Canned Heat's Harvey Mandel, a player Eddie admired, all owed recognition for their own pioneering contributions to expanding the instrument's vocabulary in this way, but Van Halen's tumbling arpeggiated torrents elevated the technique into an art form.

'It's like having a sixth finger on your left hand,' Van Halen would tell Steven Rosen for *Guitar World*. 'Instead of picking, you're hitting a note on the fretboard. Nobody was really doing more than just one stretch and one note, real quick. So, I started dicking around . . .'

Word travels fast on Hollywood's gossip grapevines. The echoes of Ted Templeman and Mo Ostin's footsteps had barely stopped reverberating in the Starwood's corridors when, on 11 February 1977, the *Los Angeles Free Press* reported: 'Local favorites Van Halen have signed to Warner Bros., marking them as the first band of the new wave of young groups to work their way through the local clubs onto a major label.' And the ink of the signatures scrawled on the contracts negotiated by Marshall Berle and Dr Roth-appointed attorney Dennis Bond had barely dried when, in May, LA music-scene hype man Kim Fowley penned the group's first print feature in *Phonograph Record*.

'One doesn't need to write any introduction on the general rock history and geographical relevance of Hollywood,' Fowley wrote. 'Hollywood is Los Angeles, Los Angeles is California and thus, Hollywood is the big time! This year there is only one choice for new aspiring and worthy new talent: Van Halen!

'Van Halen, newly signed to Warner Brothers Records, are a modern-day Black Oak Arkansas and are just a few steps removed from the level of rock greatness attained by Led Zeppelin during their "Squeeze My Lemon" period. Lead singer Dave Roth is rock authority and lead guitar genius Ed Van Halen is going to change a lot of lives around the world in the next 12 months.'

No pressure there, then.

Already committed to working on the Doobie Brothers' seventh studio album at Sunset Sound in the spring and summer of 1977, Ted Templeman wasn't able to reserve the facility for Van Halen until late August. Much to his own surprise, as the appointed hour drew ever closer, it was the hugely experienced producer, not his rookie protégés, who began to feel nervous about the upcoming collaboration. By his own admission, as relayed to his biographer Greg Renoff, Templeman became 'obsessed' with getting everything on the Californian quartet's debut right. 'I was crazed,' he reflected. 'I wanted it to be perfect.'

For all the acclaim heaped upon his work with Van Morrison, Little Feat and Captain Beefheart, Templeman's inability to deliver mainstream commercial success for Californian hard-rockers Montrose still stung on both a personal and professional level. In Van Halen, he saw not only another Golden State hard-rock outfit with even greater potential and reach, but also a shot at personal redemption. Though he would share his concerns only with his trusted and discreet wingman Landee, Templeman's misgivings about Roth's vocal abilities actually led him to speculate as to what this powerhouse of a band might achieve with a more 'traditional' singer front and centre, a more traditional singer such as, say . . . former Montrose frontman Sammy Hagar. But in the weeks between the group's blitzkrieg demo session in April and their 29 August return to Sunset Sound, the producer grew to appreciate Roth's unique phrasing, his outrageous tongue-in-cheek ad libs and his irreverent, off-kilter perspectives on familiar lyrical tropes. He was impressed, too, that with Bill Aucoin's stinging criticisms still lodged rent-free in his head, Roth took it upon himself to sign up for singing lessons ahead of his return to the studio – an indication that he was prepared to put in hard yards for the greater good.

Once installed at Sunset Sound, Templeman outlined to his charges his vision for how the sessions would unfold. Aware of the quartet's discomfort with Gene Simmons's fussy and fastidious working practices at Electric Lady, he promised that he and

Landee would keep things simple and organic and aim to cut virtually every track live off the floor, without overdubs, so as to faithfully replicate the pure, bombastic energy of the band's live shows.

'They'd barely had any studio experience,' reasoned Landee. 'It was obvious that in time they would become proficient at making records, but at that point, we really wanted to get them before they really knew what they were doing – just have them come in and play and then get them out.'

This proposed bare-bones approach was music to Eddie's ears, as Simmons's carefully layered multitracking in New York had sucked much of the joy and spontaneity out of the process for the guitarist.

'Gene said, "Here's what you do in the studio – you play your rhythm parts on one track, and your solo parts on another,"' Eddie recalled. 'I remember feeling very uncomfortable with separating my lead and fill parts from my rhythm parts. Onstage, I'd gotten used to doing both simultaneously. I'd just noodle in between chord lines. Because it was my first time in a recording studio, it didn't occur to me to say, "Can't I play just the way I play live?"

'Van Halen is three instruments and voices with very few overdubs. I hate overdubbing because it's just not the same as playing with the guys. There's no feeling there to work off of.'

It's Templeman's recollection that the group set up first in Studio 2 at Sunset Sound, though the studio's own contemporaneous paperwork suggests Studio 1 was employed first, with Templeman and Landee later bouncing the group between the two rooms, depending on their availability. And while the received wisdom is that the quartet cut the entire album in just twenty-one days, Sunset Sound Recorders' original invoices for the sessions reveal that the team actually racked up a total of thirty-three days at the facility, working from noon to 6 p.m. each day.

With Roth isolated in the vocal booth but able to maintain eye contact with his bandmates at all times, Michael Anthony and the Van Halen brothers set up as if playing a club gig or jamming in Roth's basement. Each day, morning beers were sunk, surreptitious lines of 'krell' (band code for cocaine) hoovered out of sight of the adults, and then the tapes started rolling. Simple. The session started in earnest with 'Atomic Punk', tracked on 30 August, with 'Feel Your Love Tonight', 'Runnin' with the Devil', 'Ain't Talkin' 'Bout Love' and the Kinks' 'You Really Got Me' laid down on tape the following day. After two or three runs at each song, Templeman and Landee would select their favourite take, dismiss the Van Halen boys and Anthony for the day, and then begin the often time-consuming business of coaxing a usable vocal take from Roth. 'It took forever, sometimes, to get Dave on point,' Templeman admitted long after the fact, but the Van Halen brothers didn't need to know that at the time. Each evening, the producer would listen back to rough desk mixes, utterly convinced that something special was happening.

'People always ask me how I got such an incredible sound from Ed,' Templeman said. 'The answer is simple: I put the right microphone in front of the right speaker and stood back. It's really all Ed. My strategy was just to take the guitar and blow it up all over the face of the damn map, because I thought it was the most amazing thing I'd heard.

'Donn Landee is such a great engineer, he really took a major part in capturing that raw guitar sound,' Templeman acknowledged. 'But Edward pretty much had that sound of his at the Starwood.'

'What Ted managed to do was put our live sound on a record,' Eddie agreed.

'Sunset Sound's just a big room – it's like our basement actually,' he explained to *Guitar World*'s Steven Rosen. 'The guys who ran the studio and maintain the place would walk in after we were done, boy, and there were beer cans all over the floor and Pink's hot dog smears all over the place.

'It was a party. We played the way we played onstage, and it was great. It didn't feel like we were making a record. We just went in, poured back a few beers and played.'

This nonchalant, modest and understated depiction of the album sessions was very Eddie. Templeman's autobiography *A Platinum Producer's Life in Music* offers a more 360-degree view of proceedings, with Templeman utterly charmed by the young man's attention to detail, openness to fresh ideas, respectful manners and genuinely astonishing improvisational skills. Rather touchingly, despite his obvious talent Eddie would get nervous before takes and would seek regular reassurance from Templeman that he'd delivered as required. The producer, who would later hail Eddie as one of the finest musicians in history, sometimes found himself slipping into 'awed fanboy' mode, feeling privileged to be sharing the same creative space as the guitarist.

'I knew he was a guitar genius from the first rehearsal,' Templeman told *Rolling Stone*. 'Actually, when I saw him play at the Starwood, I had never seen anything quite like that . . . There's Art Tatum, there's Charlie Parker, and then there's this kid.

'I had a good reference because I worked with guitarists in so many bands: Montrose, the Doobie Brothers, Van Morrison. Ronnie Montrose was pretty goddamn good. So when I saw Ed, I thought, He's way above all that shit. This is something from another world.'

By mid-October, the album was in the bag, recorded, mixed and mastered for a bargain outlay of between $46,000 and $54,000, depending on whose accountancy skills you trust. Whatever, when the stylus dropped onto its grooves, *Van Halen* undeniably sounded like a million dollars. Warners were thrilled, though the group decidedly less so when they saw the album artwork the label's art director planned to foist upon them. Shot after sunset in the grounds of Dr Roth's Pasadena mansion, the proposed cover image presented the quartet as moody, sullen punks, a look that was very much *en vogue* in 1977, but hardly an accurate representation of this band or their Big Rock sound.

'They tried to make us look like The Clash,' Eddie recalled. 'We said, "Fuck this shit!" and came up with the Van Halen logo and made them put it on the album . . . It was our way of saying "Hey, we're just a rock 'n' roll band, don't try and slot us with the Sex Pistols thing just because it's becoming popular."'

Warners' art director Dave Bhang commissioned German-born, Los Angeles-based photographer Elliot Gilbert for a reshoot and, careful not to repeat past mistakes, invited him to meet the band at the label's Burbank office ahead of the shoot so that he could get a genuine feel for their personalities, aesthetic and sound.

'Ted Templeman was there, and the four guys in the band, and they gave me a cassette of the album,' Gilbert recalls. 'The guys didn't say anything, but David gave me a big jar of marijuana and said, "Make me look like cock and balls." I never did quite understand what that meant!'

The new shoot took place, not at the Whisky a Go Go, as has often been erroneously reported, but at Gilbert's photo studio on Curson Avenue in Los Angeles, in what the photographer calls 'the rock 'n' roll hours'.

'It was three in the morning, and they were all smoking and having a good time,' he remembers. 'They kinda did a show for me in my studio, and I'd just rotate them in, asking them to step in front of my camera. David was jumping in and out of the frame; Eddie just smoked his cigarettes and smiled. They looked cool, like a band with something worth saying.'

No sooner had one pre-release crisis been averted than another drama lurched over the horizon . . . and this time the blame lay squarely at the feet of a certain loose-lipped Dutch guitarist. With the album sessions wrapped, Eddie and Alex spent much of the closing months of 1977 redistributing every red cent of their weekly $83.83 pay cheque from Warners to the proprietors of Sunset Strip's loudest bars and nightclubs. One winter evening, the guitarist found himself at the infamous Rainbow Bar and Grill with the members of Angel, a flamboyant glam-rock troupe from Washington DC signed to Casablanca Records following another hot A&R tip from Gene Simmons. After hours, the party continued at drummer Barry Brandt's house, where a relaxed and refreshed Eddie offered his new best friends an exclusive premiere of his band's forthcoming debut album. Days later, a furious Ted Templeman phoned Eddie and informed him that Angel were now in the studio hurriedly taping their own take on 'You Really Got Me', with the express intention of rush-releasing it to radio to gazump Van Halen. As a consequence, Warners hurriedly pressed up a five-track album sampler on twelve-inch vinyl (A1 'Runnin' with the Devil', A2 'Eruption' and A3 'Ice Cream Man', backed up by B1 'You Really Got Me' and B2 'Jamie's Cryin'") and forced the promo EP into the hands of as many of the nation's radio pluggers as they could locate.

Van Halen rounded off a memorable year with a brace of club shows at the Whisky a Go Go on 30 and 31 December. Previewing the gigs in the *LA Times*, after alerting readers to the fact that the band's forthcoming debut long-player was set to receive 'a big push' from their record label in 1978, music critic Robert Hilburn's distaste for the group was barely disguised when he wrote, 'If you're still into the heavy metal sound, this is your chance to see what it looks like up close.'

Interviewed around the same time by *Raw Power*, David Lee Roth made a bullish prediction. 'We started in the little bathroom places,' the singer said, 'and now we're at the Whisky and we're probably gonna take over the world as soon as our record comes out.'

On 10 February 1978, *Van Halen*, the Pasadena quartet's debut album, appeared in record shops across America. As all good things should, it begins with chaos, specifically with a jarring, clashing blare and whirr of car horns, conjuring up the claustrophobic tension of a smog-heavy mid-afternoon LA freeway traffic jam. Mixed deep in the cacophony are the horns of Eddie's 1958 Volvo and Alex's Opel Kadett. But when Michael Anthony's 'Runnin' with the Devil' bass line stomps in like a Toho Studios *Daikaiju* kicking automobiles over left and right, it's as if a path has been cleared right through to the Pacific Coast Highway, clear blue skies and a world of glittering promises. Not once in the thirty-five minutes and thirty-four seconds of music that follows is there a single glance in the rear-view mirror.

From the seductive 'Runnin' with the Devil' via the dazzling 'Eruption' and the muscular cover of 'You Really Got Me' (Templeman's banker for ensuring that Van Halen, unlike his former charges Montrose, would secure a hit single), through to the raucous 'Ain't Talkin' 'Bout Love' – a song Eddie wrote as a joke to take the piss out of punk rock, overdubbed with electric sitar – the irresistible, harmony-drenched 'I'm the One' and 'Feel Your Love Tonight', and on to David Lee Roth's long-time party piece, bluesman John Brim's raunchy 'Ice Cream Man', and the aptly titled rocker 'On Fire', the album is the purest distillation of hedonistic, liberated, sun-kissed Californian rock music ever committed to tape. It's fast cars and loose morals, cheerleaders, cheeseburgers and cocaine, Daisy Dukes and bikini tops, bongs, breaking surf and broken curfews; a soundtrack to teenage rebellion, with every trace of self-doubt and self-restraint eradicated. Just as the Beach Boys supplied the soundtrack to American adolescence with their surf symphonies in the 1960s, and the Eagles owned the '70s with their tales of Laurel Canyon misadventures, with their stunning debut Van Halen boldly declared that the 1980s would be their playground.

'We celebrate all the sex and violence of the television, all the rockin' on the radio, the movies, the cars and everything about being young or semi-young or young at heart,' David Lee Roth told Phast Phreddie Patterson in an interview for LA underground sheet *Waxpaper*. 'That's Van Halen.'

If Roth was out there pimping an all-new American Dream to a generation ready to over-indulge, it was Eddie Van Halen's jaw-dropping virtuosity that lit up the sky, his sweet, seemingly effortless and utterly electrifying playing making his band's debut album truly sing. From the moment the needle hit the wax on *Van Halen*, every bedroom guitarist had a new gold standard to aspire to.

'Mark my words: in three years, Van Halen is going to be fat and self-indulgent and disgusting, and they'll follow Deep Purple and Led Zeppelin right into the toilet,' noted *Rolling Stone* in their review of the album. 'In the meantime, they are likely to be a big deal . . . Van Halen's secret is not doing anything that's original while having the hormones to do it better than all those bands who have become fat and self-indulgent and disgusting. Edward Van Halen has mastered the art of lead/rhythm guitar in the tradition of Jimmy Page and Joe Walsh; several riffs on this record beat anything Aerosmith has come up with in years.'

'All we're trying to do is put some excitement back into rock 'n' roll,' Eddie told Steven Rosen. 'It seems like a lot of people are old enough to be our daddies and they sound like it, or they act like it. It seems like they forgot what rock 'n' roll is all about.'

Just a matter of weeks later, audiences across America would discover exactly how this played out, when Van Halen hit the road with Journey and Ronnie Montrose. Warners appointed Noel Monk – fresh, if that's the correct word, from overseeing the Sex Pistols' chaotic and ill-fated January 1978 US tour – as the quartet's road manager. Those in possession of a ticket for the Journey/Ronnie Montrose/Van Halen show at Chicago's Aragon Ballroom on 3 March 1978 can lay claim to have been among the first outside California to see the Golden State's new golden boys in full flight. Journey guitarist Neal Schon, for one, was intrigued to see whether the group's young hotshot guitarist was worthy of the hype already building around him.

'Three months prior to the tour starting, I had received a little red [vinyl] promotional EP,' Schon recalled. 'It had "Eruption" on it and "You Really Got Me". So, I proceeded to put it on my turntable in my bedroom, with my guitar and amp, and I'm sitting there listening to "Eruption" and I'm going, "What the fuck is this guy doing, for real?" I could not figure it out. I had been listening to Mahavishnu [Orchestra], all kinds of people, and breaking things down, but I could just not figure out what he was doing. It drove me nuts. And we finally got out there, and I got to know Ed, and watched him night to night just *kill* it. And all I can say is I was very happy not to be following him . . . Eddie was just so on fire and doing new things that nobody had seen before. Everybody was just kind of, like, "What is going on?"

'Ed was the new kid on the block, a gunslinger.'

The tour would prove to be an eye-opening education for the Californian rookies. Less than one week in, as the caravan rolled into Madison, Wisconsin, Monk was informed that his boys would have to sit out the scheduled gig at the Orpheum Theater, as the stage couldn't accommodate all three bands' equipment. Thinking on their feet, Marshall Berle and Monk

obtained permission for their charges to find alternative arrangements for this newly open slot in their itinerary and began phoning around local venues to see whether anyone might be able to accommodate the boys for a special one-night-only headline performance. With the quartet's rambunctious cover of 'You Really Got Me' worming its way up the *Billboard* Hot 100, the managers of Madison's Shuffle Inn regarded booking the fresh-faced Californians as a fairly low-risk gamble, even for a last-minute gig. Author and journalist Susan Masino, then the associate editor of local newspaper the *Emerald City Chronicle*, was among those in attendance.

'The Shuffle had about a six-hundred capacity and there had to have been a thousand people in the sold-out club that night,' she recalls. 'It was insane. Once the band hit the stage, you couldn't move. You couldn't go to the bar for a drink; you couldn't go to the restroom. You literally couldn't move from where you were standing.

'Seeing Eddie for the first time . . . I heard him on the record, and I was like, "This is unbelievable." I wondered if he could play like that on stage. And he was amazing. I'll never forget it. I can still see it in my head.'

Understandably elated by the reception they'd received at their very first out-of-state headline show, the four young musicians celebrated in time-honoured rock 'n' roll fashion by laying waste to their accommodation on the seventh floor of the Madison Sheraton hotel. They hosted fire-extinguisher battles in the corridors, taped frozen fish to the ceilings and reduced the in-room furnishings to match wood. At one point, Berle looked out of his bedroom window three floors down to see a large wooden table obeying the laws of gravity.

'Alex was going to throw a TV out the window, but somebody from Journey stopped him because he said it was going to come right out of his pay cheque,' recalls Masino.

'They were kids having a good time,' said Berle.

As the tour progressed, it was blindingly obvious to all in the party that Van Halen were stealing the show night after night. Journey's road crew pulled the standard sabotage tricks to try to knock the newcomers off their stride – limiting the PA volume, shortening set times arbitrarily – and Monk and Berle were warned more than once by Journey's 'people' that the group would be removed from the tour, citing their offstage behaviour as justification. The pair might have taken the threats more seriously were they not able to see, daily, that it was Van Halen, not the headline act, who were driving an upturn in ticket sales.

'We're kicking some ass,' Eddie cheerily related to his friend Steven Rosen, as he received word that Van Halen would breach the *Billboard* Top 30 the following week. 'When we started out . . . we were brand new; I think our album was only out a week at the start of the tour. And now we're almost passing up Journey on the charts and stuff. So, they're freaking out. I think they might be happy to get rid of us.'

In the end, Van Halen stayed on through to the closing night of the tour, playing New York's Palladium on 28 April. For the quartet, there would be little time to reflect on the lessons learned over the previous six weeks: they were expected in Belgium within the week, to begin a tour with Black Sabbath.

Operating at such intensity, it was, perhaps, inevitable that this highly calibrated machine would develop a glitch sooner rather than later. Yet no one in the band anticipated Eddie cracking first. The band had played a triumphant headline show in Paris and were enjoying some downtime in the French capital when Noel Monk was alerted to the fact that Eddie wanted to go home. Monk found the guitarist crying in his hotel room.

'I don't want to be a rock star,' Eddie explained between sobs. 'I hate this bullshit. I just want to go home.'

Scarcely able to believe what he was hearing, Monk consoled the guitarist, but pointed out that the best thing that Eddie could do, for himself, for Alex, for Jan and Eugenia, was to follow through on his dreams and chase the success that would change his parents' lives for ever. The gamble worked. Eddie stayed.

• • • • •

The godfathers of heavy metal were starting to feel their age. Black Sabbath had earmarked 1978, their tenth anniversary as a band, as a year of celebration, but in reality the group was coming apart at the seams.

'The fun of being in a rock band was dwindling for me,' frontman Ozzy Osbourne admitted. 'I don't think anyone's heart was in it anymore.'

Osbourne had taken a leave of absence from Sabbath in autumn 1977, officially to spend time with his father Jack, who was dying of cancer. But when the *New Musical Express* interviewed the twenty-eight-year-old singer at his home in Staffordshire in November '77, his disillusionment and frustration with the music business were all too apparent, and he was adamant he would not be returning.

'I realise I've let a lot of people down,' he said, '[but] people don't really know how black my Sabbath was over the years.

'The business is fucked. There are too many people sitting on their arseholes and doing nothing for vast amounts of money. There's so much talent out there who're so frightened to get involved, because they think they're going to end up floating down the River Thames in a pair of concrete wellingtons.

'We all thought we were tin gods. But at the end of the day, it just turned round and kicked us in the teeth. I just want a simple life for a while. I just want to be an ordinary, everyday, run-of-the-mill guy. I ain't a tin of beans walking around. And that's what I began to feel like: a product. I won't ever let myself be prostituted again.'

When Sabbath started the new year with an appearance on BBC TV's *Look! Hear!* programme on 16 January 1978, ex-Savoy Brown/Fleetwood Mac frontman Dave Walker stood between guitarist Tony Iommi and bassist Terry 'Geezer' Butler to sing the anti-war anthem 'War Pigs' and the newly written, as yet unrecorded 'Junior's Eyes'. It was, then, a genuine surprise when Osbourne quietly shuffled back into the fold ahead of the Birmingham band's departure to Canada to record their eighth studio album at Toronto's Sounds Interchange Studios. In the heart of a brutally cold winter, familiar tensions resurfaced constantly during fraught studio sessions – 'We were all fucked-up with drugs and alcohol,' is Osbourne's prime recollection of his time at the facility – but the prospect of returning to the UK for a sold-out springtime tenth-anniversary tour offered succour in sufficient quantity that the four musicians could convince themselves that their new album title, *Never Say Die!*, was a genuine mission statement. Still, Sabbath were wary of putting too much strain on their internal engines, and having taken AC/DC on the road as support on their last run of European gigs, when they struggled nightly to match the energy levels of Malcolm and Angus Young's feral, livewire Aussies, Osbourne instructed Sabbath's booking agency Premier Talent to find 'a bar band from LA' to open the show on their homecoming dates.

Though Van Halen shared a record label with Sabbath in the US, the young American band were not yet on the English quartet's radar. Out of curiosity, then, ahead of their scheduled stage time on the tour's opening night at Sheffield City Hall on 16 May, Osbourne, Iommi, Butler and drummer Bill Ward crept out of their dressing room to catch the tail end of the Californian quartet's set. They arrived at the side of the stage just as the group's boyish, smiling guitarist completed his solo showcase 'Eruption', his fingers dancing and darting along the fretboard, and their swaggering bare-chested blond frontman signalled the rhythm section to slam into 'You Really Got Me'. Sabbath filed back into their dressing room in slack-jawed silence.

'We sat there going, "That was incredible . . ."' Ozzy Osbourne recalled, 'and then it finished, and we were just too stunned to speak.'

'I didn't know very much about Van Halen at all,' admits Tony Iommi, 'but when I first heard them, it was like, "Bloody hell!" They were so energetic, such great players, and they had good songs. We were just like, "Wow, blimey, these are really good!"'

By Eddie Van Halen's own admission, the prospect of touring with Black Sabbath initially 'scared the shit' out of his band; Noel Monk remembers the group being 'practically awestruck' in their presence. The Van Halen brothers had been playing Sabbath covers since they were gigging as Genesis, with Eddie on vocals, and the guitarist considered Tony Iommi 'the master of riffs'. Eddie's nerves were hardly eased when his fumbling first attempt to break the ice backstage with Iommi, referencing 'the second song on side two of [Sabbath's 1971 album] *Master of Reality*', was met with a cold stare from the imposing guitarist and the bemused retort, 'What the fuck, mate?' But the UK music press had lavished praise on Van Halen's debut album – *Sounds* writer Geoff Barton judged it to be a 'magnificent debut' and hailed the band as 'brand new heavy metal heroes', while even the snotty, pseudo-intellectual *NME* considered it 'vaguely bearable', a rave review by their traditional hard-rock-hating standards – and Sabbath's audience were warm and welcoming from the off. Van Halen's confidence grew with every show.

'They were unbelievably good,' recalls Ozzy Osbourne. 'We'd never heard that kind of finger-tapping playing that Eddie did. He was a remarkable guitar player.'

'They went down incredibly well,' agrees Geezer Butler. 'The only thing that pissed me off was that at the beginning of the tour they seemed like a really raw band, but as the tour went on, they were sorta ripping us off. Eddie's guitar solos were getting longer, David Lee Roth was copying everything that Ozzy would do, and the bass player even started using a wah pedal, at a time when I was the only bass player that had ever used a wah pedal. By the time we went onstage, people were like, "Oh, I've already seen all this." It was like we were our own tribute act. They were all really good blokes, so we weren't really that bothered about it, but Tony had to have a few words with Eddie, in a "behave yourself" kind of way.'

'They watched us almost every night from the side of the stage,' says Iommi, 'and obviously they'd pick things up from us, seeing what worked and what got the crowd going. But it was just a bit awkward when we'd come onstage and it felt like we were just doing what they were doing.

'One night I said to Eddie, "Hey, Eddie, are you gonna play a couple of tracks off our new album tomorrow?" And I took him in my room and said, "You can't be doing the same sort of thing on the same show."

'Eddie had obviously listened to other guitarists growing up, but he'd come up with his own thing and he was just a fabulous guitar player. Most nights he'd come around to my room or I'd go to his room and we'd do a bit of coke and talk all night. He became a really good friend and I really respected him as a player. I'm really glad we had them with us, because it led me to make a friend for life.'

Four dates into the tour, on 19 May, ahead of their show at Aberdeen's Capitol Theatre, Van Halen received the news that their album had passed the 500,000 sales mark in the US, earning the group their first gold record. They celebrated by getting thoroughly shit-faced on Glenmorangie whisky and, in time-honoured fashion, applying their patented interior decorating skills to their accommodation.

'We took shoe polish and wrote our logo all over the walls,' admitted Eddie, with a touch of shame. 'The next morning the cops came and escorted us out of the country, not because we wasted their hotel, but because one of our crew stole a pillow! They escorted us right to the border and said, "Don't ever come back." We were all scared shitless!'

'A gold record was only division finals,' Roth soberly reflected later. 'Even if you had a gold record, was that success if you weren't on the radio or television? We had no real way to calibrate our success. We weren't accepted by the cognoscenti. Those in the know, and particularly the UK press, were enthusiastic at that time about Elvis Costello and The Clash, worthy opponents. [But] it was a reason to have a blow-out in a quiet little hotel.'

When the tour reached London's Hammersmith Odeon, Tony Iommi collared his good friend Brian May from Queen to join him at the side of the stage to watch the hotshot Californians at play.

'The pair of us watched Eddie Van Halen do his stuff, and it was just glorious,' recalled May, 'almost too glorious to take in. To see this guy romping around a guitar like a kitten, just running and taking it to places undreamed of . . . There hadn't been anything so shocking since Jimi Hendrix.'

Also in attendance that night was photographer Ross Halfin, a contributor to *Sounds* who'd come to the storied west London venue intending to shoot the show.

'Before the Hammersmith gig, I went to see them in [unfashionable south London borough] Lewisham, and David Lee Roth shook up two champagne bottles at the end of their set and screamed, "Lewisham, this is the rock 'n' roll capital of the fucking world, man!" which was just hilarious,' Halfin recalls. 'Back then, as a photographer, you could usually shoot whatever you wanted, especially when it came to opening bands, but when we turned up at Hammersmith, Van Halen had a PR girl from Warners in LA with them, Heidi Robinson, and she demanded that she had to clear every photographer who was going to shoot them. We all just started laughing and refused to shoot, though I did take some pictures from the balcony. Looking back, that was quite a smart way of selling them. They seemed a bit special, and hard to get to.'

'The place was packed for Van Halen,' recalls music writer Malcolm Dome, then a journalist for *Record Mirror*. 'Everyone wanted to see them, because they'd already got a real buzz around them from the metal cognoscenti, the people who regularly bought rock records on import. They were definitely better than Sabbath that night. Sabbath were sloppy, but Van Halen were so exciting, vibrant, lively and new. They made Sabbath look old. There was a genuine feeling of "This is amazing." They sounded like the future.'

This, in fact, was the message that Van Halen began to hammer home in every interview. On the afternoon of their appearance at the Hammersmith Odeon, the group conducted their first-ever TV interview, for the Australia Broadcasting Corporation's long-running *Countdown* programme, in London's Soho Square. When the interviewer suggested that hard rock was enjoying an unexpected revival, Eddie looked straight into the camera and confidently stated, 'The '60s are over, so are the '70s. We're the new thing.'

The following week, making their first bow on Japanese TV, during a whirlwind eight-date tour of the country, Roth informed those watching that Van Halen were going to be 'the future of rock 'n' roll for the United States and for the world'. That mission statement was amplified in a full-page advert, booked by Warners, in the 3 June issue of US trade magazine *Billboard*: 'This is the start of something big,' the text ran, flagging up the album's Top 30 success in France, Australia and Japan. 'Clearly, the planet cannot get enough of Van Halen.'

For now, however, domestic concerns took precedence. Following their final Japanese show, held at Osaka's Cultural Hall on 27 June, the band flew – via Tokyo's newly built Narita airport and Los Angeles – to Dallas, Texas, for what was going to be the biggest gig of their career to date, the inaugural Texxas Jam. Almost 100,000 people had paid $12.50 per head for a line-up featuring Aerosmith, Ted Nugent, Heart, Journey, Frank Marino and Mahogany Rush, and more . . . and Van Halen arrived on site to learn that almost all of their equipment had gone missing somewhere between Osaka and Texas. Unsurprisingly, the news left Noel Monk incandescent with rage, as photographer Neil Zlozower, hired by the promoter to document the day, was to discover to his cost.

'Me and another photographer got hired by the promoter to shoot the festival,' he recalls, 'and we had access to shoot all the bands, for their whole set; back then they didn't have that "first three songs only" bullshit that they have now. I was onstage waiting for them to come on, and this little guy dressed in black leather pants, black leather gloves, a black leather coat and Peter Fonda *Easy Rider* sunglasses – probably the most intimidating guy I'd ever seen – comes over and goes, "What the fuck are you doing on my stage?" It was Noel Monk. I'm like, "I'm shooting Van Halen." And he said, "No, you aren't, get off my stage right now." I said, "But we're doing it for the promoter!" And he said, "Yeah, you're doing everybody else for the promoter but Van Halen." He was pretty brutal, and I thought to myself, "I don't want to argue with this fucking guy, he looks like he means business." So I was like, "OK, I'll go out and watch this band

and see if they deliver the goods." And, shit, Van Halen were fucking amazing, they were phenomenal. I think a lot of people walked away from that festival with a new favourite band.'

On 9 July, Van Halen returned home to California for what was to be their biggest headline show to date, at Long Beach Arena. Robert Hilburn, the chief music writer at the *LA Times*, who'd been so dismissive of the band's prospects when they closed out 1977 with their sold-out two-night stand at the Whisky a Go Go, was dispatched to cover the quartet's honorary homecoming.

'David Roth was excited,' Hilburn wrote in his report, published in the newspaper on 11 July. 'The 22-year-old lead singer with the Pasadena-based group wouldn't go on stage at the Long Beach Arena for another three hours, but the adrenaline was already pumping. This was a show he had been looking forward to for years.

'After a lengthy apprenticeship in the bars, small clubs and other stops on the local rock back streets, Van Halen has finally graduated to the big time.

'"This is really special," the slender, long-haired Roth said, sitting backstage after the sound check. "We haven't played LA since New Year's Eve at the Whisky. It's like our homecoming. We've been on the road since February, and now we've got our first gold record. What better place to celebrate?

'"From the minute we started, we thought we could make it. We thought, 'We're cool now, and we're going to be cooler.'"'

Post-gig, the celebratory vibe was sullied somewhat for Eddie by a fracas with security at the venue. The guitarist had bought gifts back from Japan for his family, and post-show he enlisted the help of his friend Wally Olney to take the presents from the band's tour bus to his father's car. Strolling back to the auditorium, Eddie was surrounded by well-wishers, some begging the guitarist for passes so that they might be admitted into the venue to join the after-show party. Seeing the commotion, one of the venue's security guards intervened and demanded that the throng vacate the area with immediate effect.

'I'm in the band and I'm going back in,' Eddie protested.

'No, you aren't.'

The guard attempted to manhandle the guitarist away from the backstage area, and punches were exchanged.

'Fuck you! You're in deep shit, man!' Eddie spat, breaking away and pushing his way into the arena. Minutes later, Marshall Berle accompanied his guitarist back into the parking lot, with the show's promoter in tow. When Eddie identified the security goon who'd sought to have him ejected, the guard's employment was terminated on the spot.

Van Halen's tour itinerary for the rest of the year reads like a hard-rock fan's wet dream. On 13 July, the band supported the Doobie Brothers and the Rolling Stones at the Superdome in New Orleans. Forty-eight hours later, the quartet joined Eddie Money, Kansas and the Steve Miller Band for the Summer Jam in the Royals Stadium in Kansas City, Missouri. Two days after that, they opened up once more for the Doobie Brothers, the Atlanta Rhythm Section and old pals Journey on Credit Island, outside Davenport, Iowa, at the Mississippi River Jam, in front of an estimated 25,000-strong crowd. One week on, on 23 July, they returned to California, and San Francisco's Bay Area, for the sixth annual staging of Bill Graham's Day on the Green festival at the Oakland Coliseum. The third of five single-day festivals promoted under the Day on the Green banner that summer, the event was co-headlined by Aerosmith and Foreigner, with AC/DC taking the day's opening slot and Van Halen billed to appear between the Australian group and Canadian guitar hero Pat Travers. Ahead of his band's set, Eddie ventured to the side of the stage to check out Malcolm and Angus Young's band.

'AC/DC was probably one of the most powerful live bands I've ever seen in my life,' he remembered. 'I was standing on the edge of the stage thinking, "We have to follow these motherfuckers?"'

If the guitarist was daunted, his apprehension didn't show in his performance. Watching Van Halen from side stage, Aerosmith guitarist Joe Perry was impressed.

'We got there early because we wanted to see all those bands, because it was an amazing bill,' says Perry. 'I thought the first Van Halen album was great: when I heard the record I just thought, "Wow, these guys are streamrolling, man!" It was the kind of music you knew would go over well in an arena. And playing live they definitely lived up to it. Eddie changed the way people thought about playing guitar, and David Lee Roth was one of the best live frontmen I've ever seen. I consider myself a fan of rock 'n' roll, and I remember that was one of the shows that lived up to its billing.'

Winding down after the show, Eddie decided to shoot some hoops in the backstage area. The guy he challenged to a one-on-one game turned out to be *Guitar Player* journalist Jas Obrecht.

'This kid walks up to me, really buffed and muscular, and goes, "Hey, man, can I shoot baskets with you?"' recalls Obrecht. 'I said, "Sure." So we played one-on-one for maybe fifteen minutes, and he was really good; in fact, he beat me. He had a hook shot that I just couldn't stop, and he was very fast. We sat down at the edge of the little court to cool off, and he said, "Hey, what band are you in?" I go, "I'm not in a band." And he goes, "Well, what are you doing here?" I said, "I'm here from *Guitar Player* magazine to interview Pat Travers, but Travers blew me off." He said, "Travers blew you off? I can't fucking believe that. Why don't you interview me? No one has ever interviewed me before . . ." And I go, "Well, who are you?" And he said, "I'm Edward Van Halen." And a light went on, like, "Of course!"'

As the pair spoke, the young guitarist noodled on his guitar, a model Obrecht couldn't place. Van Halen explained that it was his own home-made creation: a copy of a Fender Stratocaster, assembled with reject parts purchased from emergent Californian guitar manufacturer Charvel.

'I bought the body for $50 and the neck for $80, and put in an old Gibson PAF pickup that was rewound to my specifications,' he explained. 'I like the one-pickup sound, and I've experimented with it a lot. If you put the pickup really close to the bridge, it sounds trebly, if you put it too far forward, you get a sound that isn't good for rhythm. I like it towards the back – it gives the sound a little sharper edge and bite. I also put my own frets in, using large Gibsons. There is only one volume knob – that's all there is to it. I don't use any fancy tone knobs. I see so many people who have these space-age guitars with a lot of switches and equalizers and treble boosters – give me one knob, that's it. It's simple and it sounds cool.'

'I held his guitar and I noticed three things immediately,' says Obrecht. 'One was that the neck was wider than usual; it was almost like a classical-guitar width. The second was that the nut by the headstock, Eddie had filed that extra wide, so that you could actually grab the A-string or D-string and wiggle it around inside the space; he did that because he was so aggressive with the whammy bar that he needed to do something to stop it from going out of tune. And the third thing was how home-made it looked. It looked like what it was: a body that a kid had used wood tools on, and a paint job done with bicycle spray paint that he had painted in his mom and dad's garage. It was an inexpensive-looking instrument but, man, the sound he got out of that was otherworldly.'

As *Rolling Stone* writer Brian Hiatt would later comment, the 'Frankenstrat . . . looked like Van Halen sounded: barely controlled chaos'.

As Obrecht and Van Halen parted company, the writer gave props to the young guitarist for helping light a fire under contemporary rock music.

'I have never given up on rock,' Van Halen insisted. 'There are people out there who used to say that rock is dead and gone – bullshit.'

On 22 August, the quartet rejoined their friends in Black Sabbath for their US tour. The promoters should also have hired a crime-scene investigator to document the tour and draw chalk outlines around Ozzy, Tony, Geezer and Bill onstage, for it was clear to all in attendance that Sabbath were being murdered, night after night.

'The record company was all over Van Halen,' recalls Geezer Butler. 'They already thought we were old-hat and over the hill, so Van Halen were getting all the star treatment from the record company, and we were getting nothing. When the *Never Say Die!* album came out, we went to a reception for it at Warner Brothers, and they were playing Bob Marley's album and they didn't know who we were! Our sales had dipped, and I guess they were on the verge of dropping us.'

'I remember being in a hotel room in San Diego with Geezer and one of the reps from the record company,' says Osbourne, 'and we'd had a few drinks, and one of us said to this guy, "Be honest, you're only using us on this tour to promote Van Halen, aren't you?" And he said, "You're right." And if you're with a record company that won't back you . . . When a band goes on stage before you and goes down better than you, you either say, "Right, we're going to go out there and fucking show them how to do it," or you just fold up. And they had years on us, and we'd been fighting this lawsuit with our old manager for fucking years, and I was just fucking tired of fighting. We never joined a band to become lawyers or fucking accountants, and that's how it ended up. We didn't have a clue.'

With a few days off during a short Midwest club run with AC/DC, Thin Lizzy's Phil Lynott, Scott Gorham and Gary Moore went along to the 14 September show at Detroit's Cobo Hall to check out the Pasadena band.

'We were on the same label in America, Warners, and whenever we hooked up with anyone from the label, you always heard, "Wow, man, I was just out with Van Halen – what a fucking band!"' California-born guitarist Gorham recalls. 'It got to the point where Phil would tell them, "Look, if you get into this fucking car, you're not going to talk about Van Halen, all right?" So we were interested in this band we'd heard so much about. And these boys came on and just shredded everybody a brand-new asshole. They were *amazing*. When Eddie started doing his tapping thing, I turned around to Gary and said, "What the fuck is that? What is he doing there?" Gary was just staring at him, and he said, "I don't know." Ten minutes later, I went to ask Gary another question, and he was gone. The next day, I was standing in his hotel room, and he said, "Hey, check this out . . ." and he started tapping away. He'd gone back to the hotel the night before to teach himself how to do it.'

UK music journalist Sylvie Simmons caught up with the tour in Fresno, California, on 22 September and was equally smitten by the energetic young Californians.

'For sheer crowd-pleasing, Sabbath are hard to beat,' Simmons wrote in *Sounds*, 'or they would be if it weren't for a band like Van Halen. In some respects, they're like a young version of Sabbath, fresher, without that embalmed-from-ten-years-ago look. Dave Lee Roth must be the most energetic front man on the rock circuit today, but louder, bigger. Even the flares on his pants are bigger. His jack-knife leaps from the drum kit have to be seen to be believed. His singing is peppered with wows and pings and squeals. His between-song spiels are shameless –

"Fresno, the rock 'n' roll capital of the world?" C'mon! Women just flock to him. All the girls in this mostly-male crowd seem to have made their way to the front of the stage and are grabbing his legs. The rest of the band are rock heroes of the old mould and they really know how to play.'

Songs Simmons picked out as highlights included 'Runnin' with the Devil', 'Jamie's Cryin'', 'Feel Your Love', 'Ain't Talkin' 'Bout Love' and the quartet's set-closing cover, 'You Really Got Me' – 'a really macho, suggestive version of the Kinks' classic that has the audience going wild'.

'Any other band but the confident Sabs', she concluded, 'would refuse to follow this group. They're that good live.'

Later that night, in a hotel bar in the city, to the soundtrack of a jazz trio playing Barry Manilow hits, Ozzy Osbourne told Simmons, 'Van Halen are one of the most high-energy trips I've seen in America for years. They're fucking great. It's like watching an early me when I see that David up there. When I was 21, you know? I only hope that they last as long as we've lasted.'

Van Halen's biggest and boldest move of the year was to come twenty-four hours later, when they appeared alongside Sammy Hagar, Sabbath and headliners Boston at Summerfest at Anaheim Stadium. As opening act Hagar quit the stage, a plane began circling above the stadium and four parachutists spilled out. As they neared the ground, audience members realised that each parachute was emblazoned with the Van Halen logo. 'From out of the sky', the venue PA announced, 'Van Halen is coming into the stadium!' No sooner had the skydivers touched down in the backstage compound than Roth, Anthony and the Van Halen brothers ran onto the stage in identical jumpsuits, to explosive applause. They do say you only get one chance to make a first impression . . .

Filing for the *LA Times*, Robert Hilburn had to acknowledge that the quartet were 'hard to resist for anyone with a tolerance for hard-driving, assaulting rock', and concluded that the local heroes 'could well be the heir apparent to Aerosmith's hard-rock American crown'.

The band were back in Europe on a first headlining run when their debut album passed the one-million sales mark in the US, on 10 October 1978. Marshall Berle made up a VH platinum necklace for each band member . . . and later billed them individually for the manufacturing costs.

Van Halen's first world tour concluded in San Diego on 3 December, after which the quartet enjoyed a five-day break at the Club Med resort in Cancún, Mexico. Back in Los Angeles, the band received an invitation to a party hosted by their record label. Warners wanted to present the quartet with platinum discs, as their debut album had now racked up two million sales in the US. Held at the Body Shop on Sunset Boulevard, LA's only all-nude strip joint, with Marshall Berle's uncle Milton MC-ing and Stevie Nicks and Bonnie Raitt among the guests, the shindig was a suitably raucous affair. The next day, however, the hungover band were back in Sunset Sound with Ted Templeman, as their contract demanded the delivery of a second album within twelve months of the release of their debut . . . and the settling of a considerable debt.

'I went to Ted and said, "Let me get this straight. We sold two million records, we toured for a year, and we owe you $2 million?"' an incredulous Alex Van Halen asked. Templeman just shrugged and pointed the drummer back towards the live room.

Welcome to the music business, boys . . .

4
DANCE THE NIGHT AWAY

For the greatest rock bands of the 1970s, a sneering, patronising review from *Rolling Stone* was considered something of a badge of honour. Led Zeppelin's self-titled debut album was dismissed as 'dull', 'redundant' and 'prissy' by Jann Wenner's baby-boomer culture bible. The 'clubfooted' riffs on Deep Purple's *In Rock* were seen as evidence that these 'quiet nonentities' lacked 'both expertise and intuition'. Black Sabbath's self-titled 1970 debut was labelled 'inane', 'wooden' and 'plodding', the most influential band in the history of heavy metal written off as 'Just like Cream! But worse.' Six years on, assessing AC/DC's international debut *High Voltage*, reviewer Billy Altman stated: 'Those concerned with the future of hard rock may take solace in knowing that with the release of the first U.S. album by these Australian gross-out champions, the genre has unquestionably hit its all-time low.'

With the snarky review bestowed upon their second album, then, Van Halen could consider themselves in illustrious company.

'Van Halen is the latest rock act to fall out of a family tree of deadbeats whose ancestry includes slave drummers on Roman galleys, Ginger Baker's Air Force and the street crews of the New York City Department of Sanitation,' writer Timothy White declared, somewhat obliquely, before explicitly referencing 'the stilted instrumental blarings of guitarist Edward Van Halen' with distaste.

'I've had this amazing thirty-one-minute artifact on my turntable for hours,' White continued, 'and after almost one careful listening, I'm utterly convinced that the members of Van Halen must have been up half the night creating it. What an effort.'

To be fair, White wasn't wildly wide of the mark when quantifying the quartet's time in residence at Sunset Sound in December 1978. Where the official line on the making of *Van Halen* held that proceedings were wrapped up in three weeks, this time around Eddie nonchalantly told anyone who cared to listen that his group's second album was tracked within a single week.

'It's getting easier now,' the guitarist explained. 'Remember, the last album was the first we ever did. We're getting more used to the studio now.'

'This time', David Lee Roth told *Sounds'* LA stringer Sylvie Simmons, 'we decided to really take it to the edge and go in totally unprepared, and this way we'd get a totally spontaneous sound. It's like, "Bang, stick it on the plastic, next please!" That's the Van Halen attitude and lifestyle.

'The manager's getting lines in his forehead, and the record company's getting lines in their foreheads, and we're going [real blasé], "Hey, it's alright, the studio's alright, no pressure at all!"'

As ever, Roth's spiel was persuasive, carefully calibrated in line with Van Halen brand values, and roughly within winking distance of the truth.

'I was feeling a lot of pressure,' Eddie admitted to *Guitar*

World. 'We were in England touring in support of the first album, and for the first time in my life I called a meeting and said, "Goddammit, we have another album to do. Let's start getting together after shows or whenever we have time on the road, and I'll show you what I've got." I was really starting to worry. We weren't really working on any new material, and I was afraid if we didn't have enough strong songs our second album would flop.'

Given the intensity with which Van Halen promoted their debut album globally, and the mere hiccup of time they were afforded in which to recuperate upon fulfilling their touring schedule, it's entirely understandable that fear of the dreaded 'sophomore slump' – a decline in quality and performance following a successful debut – could have cast dark shadows upon the group's return to Sunset Sound in December 1978. But to claim that the quartet were 'totally unprepared' for round two was typical showboating on Roth's part. The group, after all, had fistfuls of unreleased, professionally recorded, high-quality material to draw upon, and Eddie had already revealed to Jas Obrecht, backstage at the Oakland Coliseum in July 1978, that he and Ted Templeman were meeting up in August to revisit the original Warners demos and 'figure out which songs off that tape we're gonna do for the next one'.

'Ted seems pretty sure that he's got some hit action or whatever just out of those songs,' Eddie said. 'A little polish here and there, but the basic ideas are there.'

Sticking to the prearranged party line, when the guitarist and vocalist offered up a track-by-track breakdown of *Van Halen II* for the readers of *Sounds*, Sylvie Simmons was informed that all but three of the ten compositions on the album were 'brand new', written 'in the studio or immediately prior to going into the studio – like, in the dressing rooms of the studio', with only newly established live favourites 'D.O.A.' and

'Bottoms Up!' ('our encore song . . . everywhere from Japan to Texas they love it', Eddie claimed), plus 'Outta Love Again', pre-dating the sessions.

Here, once more, the pair were being economical with the truth, for two further *Van Halen II* tracks were already firmly embedded in the group's muscle memory. The infectious, hooky 'Somebody Get Me a Doctor', written around the same time as 'Runnin' with the Devil', was on the set list for the quartet's memorable outing backing UFO at the Golden Ballroom in May 1976, and appeared as track seven on the twenty-five-song April '77 demo, with its lyrics tweaked to reference Eddie's near-death experience that same night. Similarly, sunshine-streaked, lust-driven album closer 'Beautiful Girls' could be found on that same 3M audio reel in the Warners vaults, albeit in a marginally different, sleazier form, under its original wet-T-shirt-contest-soundtracking title 'Bring on the Girls'. Additionally, album opener 'You're No Good', written by Clint Ballard Jr and taken to the peak of the *Billboard* Hot 100 by Linda Ronstadt in February 1975, had in its original form been part of the group's expansive repertoire at Gazzarri's, with Roth nominating it to Templeman for a filthy Van Halen-ising.

Among the freshly minted material on *Van Halen II*, Eddie declared the urgent, metallic, shape-shifting 'Light Up the Sky' a personal favourite, admitting to Steven Rosen that he initially thought that Templeman might veto its inclusion: 'The changes are a little bit more bent than the commercial and simple stuff, so I was surprised that he liked that.' Templeman could afford to indulge his gifted prodigy, though, for he had already witnessed the album's irresistible hit-single-in-waiting come together spontaneously at Sunset Sound.

Originally titled 'Dance Lolita Dance', and featuring an instantly memorable chorus inspired by Fleetwood Mac's 'Go Your Own Way', the upbeat, shimmering, Latin-flavoured 'Dance the Night Away' was based around a shared band memory from their club-gig days, when they realised that a young lady dancing enthusiastically in the front row at Walter Mitty's, oblivious to the fact that she was wearing her jeans back-to-front, was the female half of a young couple they'd observed, pre-show, having sex in the venue's parking lot. As with 'Eruption' on the band's debut album, Eddie's gorgeous, rippling acoustic guitar instrumental 'Spanish Fly' wasn't originally listed for selection on album two: the producer heard it first at a New Year's Eve party at his Pasadena home, when Eddie was fooling around with an aged Ramirez acoustic guitar his host had brought back from a trip to Spain in the early '60s.

'It was as jaw-dropping as when I heard "Eruption" on the electric,' Templeman told his biographer Greg Renoff. 'What he played that night wasn't exactly "Spanish Fly", but he played all of these wonderful runs and chord patterns on acoustic that sounded like a complete left turn from what he'd done on "Eruption". That night just reinforced my belief in Ed's musical brilliance. He played these unbelievable, innovative things on the Ramirez that we never put on the record. These were things, I would have thought, before I met Ed, that a guitarist would not have been able to do on an acoustic.'

To add further flavour to the album, the quartet also taped a version of Roth's wholesome Laurel Canyon whimsy 'Angel Eyes' and considered resurrecting demo favourite 'Big Trouble', but ultimately decided to hold both tracks back for potential future use, wary of appending additional minutes to the set's carefully weighted, streamlined running time.

'It's a fine line between enough and too much,' Roth later explained. 'On vinyl, there was also the question of bass response. The further apart the grooves were, the more bass you could load into it. And the further apart the grooves are, the less music you can put on the plastic. The quality of tone was always of paramount importance. If your ears can't differentiate between noise and what I call "girl-friendly tone", then all is lost. If you can turn it up blistering loud and nobody wearing high-heels covers up their ears, it's a win–win situation. Zeppelin had it. [The] Stones got it. The list is long. But the list of those that don't have it is a lot longer.

'To me, anything over 20 minutes is boring,' the singer blithely told Sylvie Simmons. 'I don't think people have long attention spans in the '80s – there's so much to listen to and do and touch and taste and smell and fuck or whatever. If you settle down for longer than 20 minutes, you're missing out on something.'

Curiously, parallels to the creation of the group's debut album extended to issues with the art and design process. Elliot Gilbert was once again approached to photograph the band members, but in contrast to the laidback, relaxed feel of his first session with the quartet, the photographer recalls the *Van Halen II* shoot being 'a huge production'. His discomfort with the set-up was intensified by the fact that he'd been asked to shoot using an unfamiliar panoramic camera in order to capture a series of images of a twinkle-toed Roth in full flight.

'The goal was to get David to dance across the panorama, to do one of his signature moves across the screen,' Gilbert recalls. 'But he wasn't into it, he just didn't really have it together that particular morning. The others did good, but David had some problems . . .'

Watching in the wings, observing the tensions and frustrations swell, was fellow photographer Neil Zlozower. As confident and charismatic a character as any of the rock stars he shot, 'Zloz' had quickly become a trusted confidante of the band – 'We were all buds, one big family, with the same likes...partying and boning chicks' – and his boisterous, larger-than-life presence can't have done much to becalm the atmosphere on set.

'They did it at Zoetrope Studios,' Zlozower recalls, 'on a huge sound stage, with six or seven assistants running around. It was ridiculous. They had Dave doing his jumps off the drum riser, maybe like eight or nine times, but on the last one he came down heavily and broke a bone in his foot, so they had to call the day quits.

'Later, I got a call from Warners, and they said, "We've canned the first guy. We need someone to shoot Eddie and Dave and Michael, and we want to know if you want to take over the project?"

'I definitely saw David as the leader of the band then, he was the spokesman,' says Zlozower, who effectively became Van Halen's in-house photographer from this point onwards. 'Between him and Pete Angelus, their lighting guy, they were the creative guys, they were innovators. Eddie was pretty quiet and low-key, but then once he went onstage and got that guitar in his hands . . .'

As Warners collated the various assets to ready the album for a spring release, Eddie and Alex took the opportunity to take care of some pressing admin duties. The first item of housekeeping on their list was firing their manager.

The appointment of Marshall Berle as Van Halen's manager was presented to the quartet as something of a fait accompli by Mo Ostin when he and Ted Templeman offered the group a record deal backstage at the Starwood. Given that Berle's long-standing relationships with the heavy hitters at Warners long pre-dated his connection with the four musicians nominally in his charge, a neutral observer may have queried whether his elevation to handle their business affairs might not have represented a conflict of interest. While there is no suggestion that Berle executed his duties as manager with anything but due diligence, the four musicians felt blindsided upon learning the full extent of their debt to the label, and aggrieved by Berle's stewardship of their finances, not least upon discovering that his first-class travel and extravagant entertainment expenses were effectively being drawn from their pockets. Serious questions were raised about Berle's professional judgement, too, when the quartet learned that their manager had staged a private screening for Warners staff of 8 mm camera footage extensively documenting the high and lows of the band's first world tour, including graphic, X-rated, home-made pornography featuring the band members and enthusiastic female fans. Whatever bizarre logic had informed Berle's wildly inappropriate cinematic premiere, this was understandably viewed as a grave betrayal of trust. The enraged musicians elected to exact vengeful retaliation by breaking into Berle's Hollywood office with Noel Monk and stripping the room of everything bearing the Van Halen name – gold discs, memorabilia, promotional items and more. Inarguably, this was not their finest hour or smartest decision, but a point was made, honour was somewhat satisfied, and a marker was laid down. The dispute would ultimately be resolved in a Californian courtroom.

'He had a heavy ego problem,' Eddie later stated of Berle. 'He wanted to be the big manager, in control of everything. We'd say, "Hey, don't do that. For better or worse, we want it our way," and he couldn't handle it. Went through a big lawsuit. It's just fucked. This is all stuff that I never imagined I'd get into. I just figured, "Hey, I can make my music – period." But I'm handling it. I've learned things you can't learn in any book or any school.'

When tempers cooled, Monk was asked to step up and become the quartet's full-time manager, on a subject-to-review, rolling thirty-day contract.

In a rather more satisfying and rewarding piece of business, Eddie and Alex's next task was to 'retire' their father Jan. In an early interview with *Guitar Player* magazine, Eddie promised that, as soon as the first royalty cheques dropped through the letter box at 1881 Las Lunas, he and Alex would remove Jan from the labour market: 'He's been working seven days a week ever since we came to this country and we're gonna buy him a boat and retire him so he can go fishing.' True to his word, on 18 January 1979, Jan's fifty-ninth birthday, Eddie handed his father the ignition key for his very own small craft. 'I want to make my people happy,' the guitarist said.

The following day, the US District Court in Los Angeles sat to address Petition No. 410016 pertaining to an application for naturalisation made by alien registration number A13 073 252, and ruled that, in accordance with his request, Edward Lodewijk Van Halen should be granted US citizenship.

With the scheduled release date of *Van Halen II* still two months away, Eddie dropped by the Weepah Way home of his friend, and *Guitar World* writer, Steven Rosen to play him an (out-of-sequence) cassette of the band's new songs. When Rosen asked whether the guitarist had imagined that his band's debut album would be as successful as it turned out to be, Eddie replied, 'Hell, no!'

'Who knows,' he laughed, 'the next one might bomb!'

Van Halen II was released on 23 March 1979, just two days before the band returned to the road, launching their World Vacation tour in front of a sell-out 7,333 crowd at the Selland Arena in Fresno, California, where they'd supported Black Sabbath just six months earlier. The album debuted on the *Billboard* 200 at number 46 and was certified gold (for 500,000 sales) on 3 April; it would peak, on 19 May, at number 6, a week after passing the one-million sales mark.

With no disrespect intended to the good people of Redding, Central Point, Missoula, Caldwell, Logan, Tacoma, San Rafael and San Jose, Van Halen's first worldwide headline tour truly began in earnest on 8 April, when, alongside Aerosmith, the

quartet co-headlined the second night of the California World Music Festival at the Los Angeles Memorial Coliseum, above a supporting cast which included UFO, the Boomtown Rats, Eddie Money and April Wine. Still touring in support of 1977's hit-and-miss *Draw the Line* album, America's 'Greatest Rock 'n' Roll Band' was falling apart at the seams – 'We were drug addicts dabbling in music, rather than musicians dabbling in drugs,' guitarist Joe Perry recalled dryly, while his fellow Toxic Twin Steven Tyler admitted to this writer that the Boston band had 'toured ourselves into oblivion' – and the ever-competitive Californians sensed blood, and an opportunity to upstage their former heroes.

As with their hugely successful bait-and-switch parachute stunt in Anaheim in September '78, Van Halen's plan was to make a first impression so vivid that it would be etched for ever in the mind of each of the 65,000 fans in attendance. To this end, they scripted an elaborate piece of theatre ahead of the weekend: early in the day, someone from Team VH would park a yellow Volkswagen Beetle on site in a prominent location visible to the crowd, drawing attention to it periodically throughout the afternoon and early evening by staging PA announcements requesting that 'someone in the Aerosmith organisation please move their car'. Having laid this groundwork, the idea was that when the stadium lights went down, Van Halen's imminent arrival onstage would be announced, and spotlights would pick out the four musicians rumbling into view atop a World War II-era Sherman tank. In a symbolic display of alpha-male dick-swinging, the VH tank would then crush the Volkswagen beneath its treads, at which point the four musicians would leap clear and sprint for the stage.

It would have made for an audacious and original entrance, but the prank was scrapped when word filtered through to the VH camp that Aerosmith had got wind of their scheming and intended to fire a metaphorical shot across their bows by screening a film showing airplanes blowing up tanks right before the mischievous Californians were scheduled to take to the stage. 'We didn't want to be one-upped on our one-upmanship,' Roth later admitted, not least because *Rolling Stone* had embedded writer Terry Atkinson with the group that day to conduct a first major feature with the band. Fortunately, with the sun setting upon a pumped-up and partisan local crowd desperate to renew their acquaintance with the group, and a clutch of ultra-accessible, stadium-friendly new songs, Van Halen would not need to lean upon decommissioned military hardware or showbiz gimmickry to make a positive impact, as Atkinson's celebratory article would later outline.

'Their set explodes with energy and moves along briskly,' he noted. 'Alex and Michael provide solid rhythms. Roth, though he still seems too much like a cross between Black Oak's Jim Dandy, Black Sabbath's Ozzy Osbourne and Led Zeppelin's Robert Plant, is beginning to develop his own personality and vocal style. As always, he's a consummate showman . . .

'But it's Eddie's guitar that forms the red-hot core of Van Halen's sound,' wrote Atkinson. 'He's right in there with Hendrix, Beck, Page, early Clapton, Blackmore and others of the let's-see-what-a-little-more-feedback-here-might-do tradition.'

Watching in the audience that evening was thirteen-year-old Aerosmith fan Saul Hudson, now better known worldwide as Guns N' Roses guitarist Slash.

'They were really powerful and alive,' Slash recalled, 'and there was a palpable rush of excitement the moment they hit the stage. Seeing Eddie live was unbelievable. It was loud and aggressive, melodic, rhythmic and fluid, with a boatload of charisma and showmanship on top of all that.'

Interviewed backstage by Atkinson, Eddie came across as self-effacing, humble and genuinely appreciative of those who'd stuck around to watch his band.

'Hey, I'm a kid just as much as the kids who come to see us,' he said. 'Not long ago, I was out there, watching Aerosmith. I like loud guitar, I like to play real loud on stage. And I play what I would like to hear. Sometimes I can't play what I'd like to hear, but I'm always trying.'

By the time Atkinson's article, published in the 14 June 1979 issue of *Rolling Stone* under the headline 'Van Halen's Big Rock', hit news-stands, the group were back in Europe – specifically, in Belgium – to kick off a twelve-date, five-nation headline tour that would close with two performances at London's 2,800-capacity Rainbow Theatre. In recognition of the quartet's burgeoning profile and popularity in the UK, where *Van Halen II* peaked at number 23 on the national album chart, eleven places higher than its predecessor, both *Sounds* and the *NME* dispatched writers to interview the fast-rising Californian collective. Catching up with the band in Newcastle on 26 June, ahead of their show at Newcastle City Hall, *Sounds* journalist David Hepworth appeared awed and horrified in equal measure by the slick and professional American invaders.

'This is not really rock and roll,' he wrote. 'This is a hybrid somewhere between a multinational promo exercise and a military campaign; just a vast, metal machine running on greased parts and total control, on enormous, frightening trucks that roll through the motorway night.

'In terms of power and energy,' Hepworth grudgingly acknowledged, '[Van Halen] could render most bands, from Led Zeppelin to The Skids (and definitely such stumblebums as Judas Priest), to fine powder.' But, he cautioned, 'Rock and Roll on this scale is pure power, ego expressed as sound, emotional terrorism.'

David Lee Roth was quick to remind the writer, however, that the group's current status had been hard won, pointing to early gigs where the audience could be counted on the fingers of one hand, and 'three of them were waitresses and one of them was the owner'.

'We never got terribly discouraged,' Roth insisted. 'There's always setbacks but you never plug into that . . . There's always a faith, always a spirit. See, we wanted to travel, we wanted to make records, we wanted to get into those magazines that we'd always read.

'Van Halen is definitely escape,' the singer summarised. 'It's a positive attitude. Straight up, number one, CHARGE! It's not the politics of despair. It's just WOW! INSTANT! No matter what it is, The Day Goes Away. Whatever it is; your boss, your wife, your girlfriend, your teacher, your probation officer . . . it all goes away. We drive out the evil spirits.'

If Roth found the chin-stroking Hepworth hard work, he would need to draw upon every last scintilla of his positive mental energy when he faced off against the *NME*'s self-appointed punk-rock conscience Nick Kent in London later that same week. A member of the Sex Pistols for about ten minutes, friends with Led Zeppelin and the Rolling Stones, and possibly the only music journalist in Britain who could credibly accessorise black leather trousers, a biker jacket and eyeliner with a raging heroin habit, Kent's doomy fascination with 'The Dark Stuff' was every bit as pronounced as 'Diamond' Dave's relentless championing of unabashed hedonism. Kent's commissioning editors at the *NME* were doubtless hoping that the two men's contrasting outlooks would make for a memorably spiky encounter.

As one of his generation's most perceptive music writers, Kent's description of Van Halen as 'Yank Zep clones' was, frankly, beneath him, a conclusion he could only conceivably have reached by reviewing the quartet with his eyes rather than his ears. This impression was furthered by the writer's description of Eddie as looking like 'a dimmer, non-elegant approximation of Jimmy Page' and his damningly reductive critique of the guitarist's musicianship as 'all fingers at a million miles a minute, blaring out but saying absolutely nothing'. For all that his words dripped with undisguised disdain, however, Kent's evocation of the chaotic scenes inside the Rainbow offer a snapshot of the night so vivid that the heat, the noise and the stench of stale lager, cigarette smoke and unwashed flesh is almost tangible.

'For two nights, the Rainbow is squeezed tight with rabid heavy metal fanatics bent on getting their brain plates bespattered into microbic smithereens by this gauche Yank pumphose gang,' Kent wrote. 'This audience are virtually all one of a kind: predominantly male, hair at varying lengths over the collar and down the back, while the most striking characteristic is the jacket–either leather, or more usually denim, often with the arms sliced off, upon which are scrawled or else emblazoned via a mass of patches the names of V.H.'s kindred spirits–namely "Rush", "Kiss", "Quo", "Zep", "Ted", right through to the more obscure likes of "Angel" and "Godz". These lads take their music seriously...

'When the lights go down . . . I turn back and notice the seating behind being totally demolished and the crowd blitz-krieging forward. I have to literally dash off to one side to avoid being trampled underfoot by the salivating hordes – a mass of arms and legs and dandruff doing the kamikaze bone-crusher waltz.

'They are crazed, they are "gone", out to lunch in a display of all-out frenzy that would make for a very real rock 'n roll dementia scenario, were it not for one spurious shortcoming. Van Halen, the object of all this delirium, have patented their act into a display of mock frenzy that is the very epitome of calculated hysteria mongering.'

For Kent, a zealous defender of rock 'n' roll authenticity, Van Halen's professionalism and poise marked the group out as poseurs and con artists, a Hollywood approximation of 'real' rock, cynically manufactured fakers. It was a testament then, surely, to Eddie's easy charm that when invited back-stage, Kent couldn't bring himself to level such accusations to the 'subdued, almost shy, timidly amiable' guitarist's face. He may, perhaps, have felt more comfortable engaging in some verbal sparring with Roth, had the verbose, loquacious vocalist actually given the *NME* man an opportunity to establish a di-alogue: 'a more overt exhibitionist it would be nigh impossible to locate, either in rock 'n' roll or used car salesmanship', Kent would later conclude.

'What we're doing is getting down to the roots of high en-ergy hard, heavy rock and roll,' Roth proselytised. 'We're out to establish Van Halen as *the* number one, *the* most energised, *the* most dependable rock and roll outfit on this planet. And we're working our fucking butts off – from playing biker clubs, surfer clubs...man, when we started, L.A. was all punk rock, but we still busted through.

'Rock 'n' roll is just pure fucking energy,' the unstoppable singer gushed. 'It's just the greatest high when you and that au-dience are just comin' together and gettin' down. Gettin' fuckin' down and getting' crazy. And that's Van Halen, man, that is what it's all about.'

Fully aware that Kent was here to bury, not praise, his band, Roth exited with a knowing wink to the writer.

'Hey, if you're gonna write a good thing about us, then make sure it's real good,' he said. 'But if it's gonna be bad, then make sure it's *real* bad, real shitty put down, OK!'

By his own admission, the *NME*'s star writer was left 'tem-porarily disorientated' by the Roth Effect. Later, when filing his copy, Kent would recall 'just how horrendous Van Halen were, what a dimensional cod sham, what a mindless howl of unmitigated bilge' – words which absolutely delighted the band when they eventually got around to reading the scathing reviews in their UK press file.

'It's great, man,' a laughing Eddie would later tell *Creem*'s Dave DiMartino. 'They're collector's items . . .'

Back in front of friendly faces on home soil, Van Halen closed out the World Vacation tour on 7 October 1979 with a sold-out show at the Forum in Inglewood, California, the same venue where an awestruck Alex and Eddie had watched Led Zeppelin perform eight years earlier. With their proud parents Jan and Eugenia watching on, the night should have been a huge celebration for the Van Halen brothers, as it represented 'a dream come true' in Eddie's eyes, but their triumph was marred when the family returned home to discover that 1881 Las Lunas had been burgled while the boys were on-stage, with the thieves making off with around twenty gold or platinum discs.

'It was a hell of an event for me,' Eddie told Jas Obrecht, 'and I come home and the back door is smashed in, and all the records are gone. It's such a drag . . . I'm not into the star bullshit at all.

'They were begging us to do another show at the Forum – we sold it out in an hour and a half – and we just said, no way. All these promoters are trying to take advantage . . . they're just thinking bucks, right now. There's got to be a little bit of mystique there. You gotta leave 'em wanting more.'

As the Van Halen family took stock of their losses, Eddie and Alex had the opportunity to look back upon what had been another remarkable year. Domestically, their group had scored a first Top 10 album and a Top 20 single (with 'Dance the Night Away' peaking at number 15 on the *Billboard* Hot 100 in mid-July), and while the album's second single, 'Beautiful Girls', under-performed against expectations (stalling at number 84 in October), both long-players were still in the Top 100 as the World Vacation tour wound up. One might imagine, then, that Eddie would have been somewhat bemused to see his likeness on the cover of the October issue of *Creem*, sandwiched between photos of Queen frontman Freddie Mercury and Boston guitarist Tom Scholz, beneath the stark cover line 'Is Heavy Metal Dead?'

The timing of this issue seemed peculiar. Led Zeppelin, another act gracing the magazine cover, had scored a number 1 album in August with *In Through the Out Door*, which went on to sell three million copies by the end of September; Queen, UFO and Judas Priest had consolidated their burgeoning reputations with the release, respectively, of their classic live sets *Live Killers*, *Strangers in the Night* and *Unleashed in the East*; AC/DC had delivered their most commercial album yet with *Highway to Hell*; Ted Nugent had a gold album with *State of Shock*; and the incorruptible Motörhead had served advance notice of an emerging grass-roots metal scene in Britain with the release of not one but two classic albums, *Overkill* and *Bomber*. Granted, fans of mainstream US hard rock may have been surprised by Joe Perry's departure from a weakening Aerosmith and shocked at Kiss embracing disco on 'I Was Made for Lovin' You', but for 'America's Only Rock 'N' Roll Magazine' to sound the death knell for metal seemed alarmist and defeatist.

And *Creem* could hardly have been more wrong. In arguably the single most significant year in hard-rock history, 1980 would see the release of *British Steel*, *Back in Black*, *Iron Maiden*, *Heaven and Hell*, *Ace of Spades*, *Blizzard of Ozz*, *Wheels of Steel*, *Permanent Waves*, *Animal Magnetism*, *On Through the Night* and, from Pasadena, California, *Women and Children First*.

'Heavy Metal: Back from the Dead' *Creem* thundered on the cover of its October 1980 issue, alongside a photo of Judas Priest's studs-and-leather-encased frontman Rob Halford.

As *Creem* backtracked furiously, *Rolling Stone* offered rock fans a more clear-headed state-of-the-nation address: 'Fans insist that it never went away. Critics wish it would. But heavy metal, that belligerent bastard son of American blues and macho English rock-star attitudes, is back,' wrote the estimable David Fricke in the magazine's 26 June 1980 issue. 'It's also bigger, louder and – hard as this may be to believe – better than ever, rising to punk-rock's challenge by adding some new risks to the old riffs.'

In a review bracketing Van Halen's third album – already certified platinum in the US, having sold a million copies since its release on 26 March – alongside *On Through the Night*, the promising debut from New Wave of British Heavy Metal upstarts Def Leppard, and *Animal Magnetism*, the seventh studio set from German hard-rock veterans Scorpions, Fricke singled out the California quartet for their ability to deliver riff-heavy, high-octane thrills without ever becoming beholden to heavy-metal orthodoxy.

'Van Halen toss melody – along with subtlety and good manners – straight out the barroom door,' Fricke wrote. 'Specializing in decibels and cock-strutting bravado, they put forth the proposition that Might Is Always Right, and the proof on their third LP, *Women and Children First*, is pretty convincing. "Romeo Delight," "Everybody Wants Some!!" and the mad, triple-time dash, "Loss of Control," are works of high-volume art. Each features banshee guitars, hellish drumming, lead vocalist David Lee Roth's cries of hedonistic ecstasy, and ensemble harmonies that sound like the Byrds singing through a sewer pipe – all violently competing for attention in an explosive sound mix.

'But underneath the noisy chutzpah, Roth and his mob are exceptionally good players,' Fricke continued. 'This is especially true of guitarist Eddie Van Halen, who harnesses feedback almost as well as Jimi Hendrix did and displays smarts plus speed in his solos. As for David Lee Roth and his big mouth, he puts up a lot better than he shuts up, baying at the moon with far more spirit and comic panache than most of his competition. Megalomania of this kind is an acquired taste, yet the haste with which *Women and Children First* bullied its way into the Top Ten suggests that there's a little Van Halen in everybody.'

No one in Van Halen, of course, considered *Women and Children First* a heavy-metal album. Speaking in *Rock Stars* magazine, David Lee Roth offered his by-now-familiar description of the band's sound as 'folk music delivered with high impact', but added, 'as far as resemblance to the first two Van Halen records goes...I think *Women and Children First* makes them look little.

'On the first album, we went to the edge and we looked down. On the second album, we didn't discuss the matter, and on the third album Van Halen has jumped over.'

'I think it's our best one yet because it's got more variety,' Eddie said. 'It's not *too* guitar dominated . . . It's got acoustic, it's got piano, it's got the ball bustin' rock. It's got it all.'

Work began on *Women and Children First* in December 1979. Comfortable with familiar routines, the band elected to record at Sunset Sound once again, and once again Ted Templeman and Donn Landee were entrusted with the task of capturing magic in a bottle. In Eddie's recollection, the production wrapped in just ten days. 'It took four days for the music and six days for the singing,' he estimated. 'A bunch of songs were first takes. We don't go for perfection, we just go for spirit.'

Though the guitarist implied to Jas Obrecht that all nine tracks on the album were new compositions, this was not the case. 'Take Your Whiskey Home' and 'In a Simple Rhyme' featured on the demo cassette recorded with Mark Stone at Cherokee Studios in 1974 and given to Michael Anthony ahead of his live debut with the band, while a version of 'Fools' featured on set lists from 1977, titled 'I Live with Fools' at the time. But there were opportunities for the group to stretch in new directions too: album opener 'And the Cradle Will Rock . . .' featured Eddie on keyboards for the first time on record, its insistent riff pounded out on a Wurlitzer electric piano fed through the guitarist's Marshall amp, while the charmingly retro 'Could This Be Magic?' found Eddie using a slide to create bottleneck blues riffs, with Roth playing acoustic guitar.

'That was one of the first songs I wrote on guitar,' the singer told *Classic Rock* writer James McNair. 'I bought my first acoustic guitar at the Crown City pawn shop. Think it cost $130. I moved instantly to open tuning, which was easier to play in, and began to express my Black rage (*laughs*). If you go back to the root and not the fruit, you can find a greater treasure trove of energy. I think what really makes you a complete person is trauma. How much have you gone through? That's what puts the shine on the shoe. That blues guitar will not sound right until it's been in the pawn shop at least once, James – or your heart or your voice has.'

'Our stuff, to me, keeps you on the edge of your seat,' Eddie told *Guitar Player*. 'It builds tension. Whether you like it or not, it slaps you in the face. It's almost like you're just waiting for us to blow it . . . It's like winding something up and just waiting to see when it's gonna break. It's just inner feelings coming out.'

'The Japanese have a great term: *wabi-sabi*,' Roth added. 'It means an appreciation of something completely imperfect. It's easy to take all the cracks out of the woodwork, but that's not my style. With Van Halen you're dragged into it, screaming, because of the imperfection of it all.'

Due to an unforeseen change in Ted Templeman's schedules, which saw the producer unavoidably detained in Paris, the quartet were required to travel to the French capital in January 1980 to finish vocal overdubs on the album. At night, the five men would check out Paris's fabled nightlife, 'partying hard', according to Templeman.

'We hung out in all the biggest and hippest places,' he told his biographer Greg Renoff, 'but unlike in the States, nobody knew who we were; nobody recognised the guys. Those nights were surreal, and a ton of fun.'

As the first pressings of *Women and Children First* flew out of record shops worldwide in late March, a surprise awaited early adopters: tucked alongside the twelve-inch vinyl disc was a tastefully erotic/artistic two-foot-by-three-foot poster of a bare-chested Roth chained to a wire fence, shot in Los Angeles by acclaimed German fashion photographer Helmut Newton at the singer's request.

'We put the poster in because it upsets people,' the singer told *Creem*. 'It's disturbing. It's one of those beautiful things where there's actually nothing going on in the picture, and you're forced to use your filthy little imagination, which is always gonna be better than any picture. Helmut Newton is into creating *tension*, really, creating tension wherever he can. And that's what rock 'n' roll is all about. A lot of tension.'

Privately, Eddie and Alex Van Halen wondered whether there was more to Roth's sudden interest in erotic European art, but for now, the brothers kept their counsel.

Van Halen's World Invasion tour promoting *Women and Children First* launched on 22 March, four days ahead of the album's scheduled release, at Lane County Fairgrounds, in Eugene, Oregon. Unofficially, it was dubbed the Party 'Til You Die tour by the band members, and their appetites for self-destruction made for some wildly uneven, if thoroughly entertaining, performances. *Sounds* writer, and early supporter, Geoff Barton caught the quartet's 17 June show at Newcastle City Hall and pronounced it 'a complete shambles'.

'While most bands start off stubbly and eventually become clean-shaven, with Van Halen it seems to have worked the other way round,' he noted. 'Tonight's gig is often in danger of falling apart at the seams. More ragged than the knees of Joey Ramone's jeans, Van Halen steam through "Runnin' with the Devil", "And the Cradle Will Rock . . .", "Dance the Night Away" *et al* with an almost Faces-style devil-may-care drunkenness.'

For Barton, the sloppiness of the performance made the gig 'a spontaneous delight'.

'It wasn't like staying at home listening to the albums,' he concluded, 'it was a *live performance*. It was a jumble. A hotchpotch. Often untidy. Muddled. Dishevelled. Disorganised. A chaotic classic of its kind.'

Van Halen's audience the following evening, at the Apollo in Glasgow, Scotland, would be less forgiving.

'Roth was so drunk all he could do was swig from endless bottles of wine,' recalled audience member Duncan Nicol. 'He didn't sing many songs, but did tell us constantly how many "chicks" he had fucked since becoming a star. It's the only concert I've ever been at where everyone sat down all through the concert then booed the band off at the end.'

'I could honestly say that no band had more fun than Van Halen,' says Noel Monk. 'It was, by then, a party that had turned spectacularly messy. The sex never stopped, and the groupies never went away.'

'Everyone likes to think that they're the bad boys of rock 'n' roll,' says Neil Zlozower, 'but honestly, the things that I witnessed with Van Halen were the most debauched. We had the hottest chicks you could imagine. Led Zeppelin was gone, and Van Halen cleared up.

'There would be, like, seventy-five girls in the hotel room. It was a fuck-fest. Back then, it was pre-AIDS, no one wore condoms, and it was just one big bone-fest, day after day. Even just being the photographer, I got two or three chicks every night.

'I also knew when to put the camera down, and they trusted

me in that. Plus, I didn't want to be just documenting the parties, I wanted to be part of them. Who wants to be photographing naked girls when you could be with them instead?

'Everybody liked to partake – whether with blow or alcohol or chicks – and they all had their own demons. But I never really saw Eddie go overboard. In fact, I never saw any of the band so fucked up that they couldn't play.'

One notable indicator that the band members were more switched on and focused than their indulgent offstage antics might have suggested was introduced for the first time on the World Invasion tour. In the 'Munchies' section of the band's backstage rider, amid stipulations that their dressing-room food tray must contain potato chips, nuts, pretzels, twelve Reese's Peanut Butter Cups and twelve assorted Dannon yoghurts (on ice), Van Halen now additionally requested M&M's candies, stating, in capital letters: '(WARNING: ABSOLUTELY NO BROWN ONES)'. Initially, the clause was interpreted as either a mischievous band in-joke or a calculatedly ludicrous request inserted purely to stress out promoters pre-show for the group's own amusement. In fact, the demand was made in order to gauge whether or not show promoters had actually read, understood and fully implemented the complicated paperwork drawn up ahead of each gig.

'Van Halen was the first to take 850 par lamp lights – huge lights – around the country,' Roth explained. 'At the time, it was the biggest production ever. If I came backstage, having been one of the architects of this lighting and staging design, and I saw brown M&M's on the catering table, then I guarantee the promoter had not read the contract rider, and we would have to do a serious line check.'

The efficiency of this sugar-coated early-warning system was illustrated within weeks of the group launching the first leg of their North American tour.

'I did several shows with Van Halen over the years and in 1980, I had three shows in Colorado,' recalled legendary Denver concert promoter Barry Fey in his 2011 memoir *Backstage Past*. 'The first one was at the University of Southern Colorado in Pueblo on March 30 which was a warm-up for the summer World Invasion Tour of Europe and North America.

'The Pueblo show was the first time I'd heard about the brown M&M's,' Fey admitted. 'If there were brown M&M's, then whoever was supposed to read the rider didn't, and other important details . . . might have been overlooked. In their Pueblo dressing room, the band found brown M&M's, and the boys, who had proven that they didn't need much of an excuse to damage hotel rooms and the like, tore up the college's dressing room. Tore it up so badly that the University banned not only Van Halen, but all rock concerts at the school.'

'I came backstage,' Roth remembered. 'I found some brown M&M's, I went into full Shakespearean, What is this before me? . . . you know, with the skull in one hand . . . and promptly trashed the dressing room. Dumped the buffet, kicked a hole in the door, twelve thousand dollars' worth of fun.

'The staging sank through their floor. They didn't bother to look at the weight requirements or anything, and this sank through their new flooring and did eighty thousand dollars' worth of damage to the arena floor. The whole thing had to be replaced. It came out in the press that I discovered brown M&M's and did eighty-five thousand dollars' worth of damage to the backstage area.

'Well, who am I to get in the way of a good rumour?'

The legend of Van Halen's M&M's grew in the wake of national press coverage of the trashing of the University of Southern Colorado's dressing room. So much so that ahead of the tour rolling into Shreveport, Louisiana, on 29 August, a local radio DJ offered Van Halen fans David and Patrick Bertinelli tickets and backstage passes for the gig at the Hirsch Memorial Coliseum if they could sweet-talk their celebrity sister into presenting each of the four band members with a bag of M&M's backstage. A TV star since her mid-teens thanks to her portrayal of the adolescent Barbara Cooper in popular CBS sitcom *One Day at a Time*, Valerie Bertinelli knew damn well that her brothers were exploiting her here. But with industrial action halting the filming of her show, the twenty-year-old actress had free time on her hands and figured she could easily give a little back to her supportive siblings. For research purposes ahead of the gig, Bertinelli bought a copy of *Women and Children First* and realised that she already knew the effervescent hornball anthem 'Everybody Wants Some!!' from its radio airplay.

'I'll tell you what I really liked,' she told her brother Patrick, as he sought to mansplain the quartet's importance within contemporary culture. 'The guitar guy – Eddie. Oh my God, what a cutie!'

Having upheld her part of the deal to secure access to the gig for her brothers, Bertinelli watched from the side of the stage as the headliners rocked her home town.

'It was adjacent to the space where Ed's guitars were set up,' the actress recalled in her best-selling 2008 memoir *Losing It*. 'Each time he came over to change guitars, he flashed me a smile. He didn't seem inhibited or distracted by the 15,000 people watching him flirt with me. He was having a good time . . . I understood why girls fell so easily for rock stars. With a whole arena chanting "Ed-dee! Ed-dee!" he kept smiling at me. It was an intoxicating experience that left me giddy and wanting more.'

In a particularly mean-spirited and bitchy anecdote from *Crazy from the Heat* that revealed much more about his own fragile ego than the subject of his catty comments, David Lee Roth recalled meeting Bertinelli backstage at the same show.

'I had no idea who she was,' Roth wrote dismissively. 'Had

no interest at all, so she fixed her eye very seriously on the door to Ed's dressing room. Disappeared backstage with Ed, and they were an item from then on.'

'After Edward dried off and changed his clothes, I introduced him to Valerie,' remembers Noel Monk. 'It was kind of cute to see them together – they were both clearly nervous and somewhat reticent. This struck me as a sign of genuine chemistry. Here was a guy who went out onstage every night and performed, wizard-like, in front of thousands of adoring fans. In the presence of this young woman, however, the rock star facade melted away. He was clearly drawn to her, yet too shy and intimidated to take control of the situation.'

Though he insisted that he was never a 'smooth operator', with his boyish good looks and perfect smile Eddie Van Halen was very rarely starved of female attention. But interested parties always faced a challenge in holding his attention for long as, from his teenage years onwards, Eddie seemed utterly fixated on pouring his heart into playing guitar.

'It's definitely my first love,' he admitted. 'Got in a fight with my girlfriend before. I used to go over to her house and play my guitar in her bedroom, and she'd go, "You love your guitar more than you do me!" And I'd go, "You're right! Hey, I'm sorry – it's part of me."'

Eddie was still in his mid-teens when his first steady girlfriend became pregnant. After speaking to Planned Parenthood, she made the decision to undergo an abortion. 'We were worried about her parents and my parents finding out,' Eddie admitted to *TeenAge* magazine. 'Eventually her parents did find out, and their reaction surprised me. It was, "Why didn't you come to us and let us help?" I thought they'd call us scum.'

One can imagine why self-isolating in his bedroom with just a guitar for company might have seemed like a less complicated option for the shy and sensitive schoolboy.

'Everything was music for Edward,' says Pete Angelus. 'Edward wasn't as social a person as anyone [else] in the band, because he was dealing with his thoughts, his ideas all the time. And usually locked in a hotel room playing the guitar, or locked in the bus playing the guitar, or sitting in his bunk playing that guitar. That guitar never left his hands.'

'I got into the groupie thing in the beginning, but I was kind of shy,' Eddie claimed. 'Dave would have these girls come backstage, and half the time Alex would end up with them. We were bunking together, Alex and I, so I'd hear everything. Once Alex was banging this girl all night, and I was sleeping, and then he had her wake me up by sitting on my face . . .'

In *Kicking & Dreaming: A Story of Heart, Soul and Rock & Roll*, the 2013 memoir she co-authored with her sister Ann, Heart guitarist Nancy Wilson recalls the Van Halen brothers clumsily propositioning her and her sister in a hotel bar in 1979. 'Eddie and Alex let it be known that if Ann and I wanted to sleep with them, they would be amenable to that,' she wrote. 'The concept was two brothers with two sisters . . . except they wanted us in one bed. It wasn't the only time we had that offer, and as with every other request, we turned it down.'

A year on, Eddie's courtship of Valerie Bertinelli progressed with rather more class and chivalry, and it would be just north of two weeks before the young couple slept together for the first time, on 15 September. Not that they actually slept much at all during this all-consuming honeymoon period.

'We were punch-drunk in love,' Bertinelli wrote. 'And just plain punch-drunk. We drank Southern Comfort and vodka tonics. He also drank his Schlitz malt liquor . . . He was almost nocturnal, and if I hadn't stayed up drinking and doing coke with him, we would have been on completely different schedules. I would destroy my body trying to stay up with him.'

On 8 December, the same day on which John Lennon was

murdered in New York, Eddie asked Bertinelli if she would marry him, and the young actress agreed. The couple had been dating for just fifteen weeks, much of that time shared in hotel rooms and tour-bus bunks. The speed at which their relationship was moving alarmed many in the Van Halen camp, and Roth, in particular, repeatedly urged Eddie to reconsider his decision. On one occasion, Bertinelli recalled, Eddie overheard the singer say, 'That fucking little prick, not only is he winning all the guitar awards, he's also the first to marry a movie star.'

'The guys didn't want him to get married,' admits Ted Templeman. 'He said, "Ted, I don't know, what should I do?" I said, "Fuck those guys! They can't tell you your life. You want to walk out right now? I'll walk out with you." That night, I saw Valerie [Bertinelli], and she said, "Oh, Ted. Thank you so much." It was like the band was deciding whether he was getting married or not. And I was like, "It's your life. Screw the band."'

'To an extent, Valerie was treated like Van Halen's Yoko Ono,' recalls Neil Zlozower. 'She was this hot, young, sexy chick, and suddenly she hooked up with Ed, and Ed was all ga-ga goo-goo, totally in love. Eddie liked to have fun before Valerie – there was never, ever any shortage of girls backstage at Van Halen shows – but obviously things changed.'

The couple set 11 April 1981 as the prospective date of their wedding, booking St Paul the Apostle Catholic Church in Westwood, California, for the ceremony. Invitations were sent out to over four hundred guests, with Neil Zlozower offering his services as the wedding photographer, and the lovebirds set aside $35,000 for a lavish reception at the grand Beverly Hills mansion featured in the Barbra Streisand/Kris Kristofferson remake of *A Star Is Born*. As with all weddings, there were teething problems in the run-up to the big day – David Lee Roth snubbed Eddie's invitation to be a groomsman but generously paid for a stylish white tuxedo for the groom, while

Valerie agonised over who to select as her maid of honour, before ultimately plumping for singer Nicolette Larson, on whose 1978 Ted Templeman-produced debut album Eddie had played uncredited – and consideration was given more than once to the idea of simply eloping and telling no one of their plans. There was some minor unpleasantness, too, involving one of Eddie's casual hook-ups, who claimed that he was the father of her child. 'I swear to God, I never fucked her!' the guitarist protested indignantly to Noel Monk. 'Is there any way she could have gotten pregnant from giving me a blowjob?'

'I cringe at how we prepared,' Valerie admitted in *Losing It*. 'The priest we tapped to perform the ceremony gave us questionnaires so he could get to know us better and offer more personal words. As we filled out the forms at home, we each held a little vial of coke. If you ask me, these aren't two people who should be making decisions about the rest of their lives.'

In the end, the ceremony passed without drama – 'Ed looked dashing in his tux,' Valerie recalled – and the happy couple, and their respective families and friends, proceeded to the reception. Which very quickly, as Neil Zlozower remembers, turned into 'a pretty rock 'n' roll party'. Roth recalls doing fat bumps of krell with the groom in a restroom, 'taking turns holding each other around the waist so we don't plunge head first into the toilet from dry heaving'.

Ahead of the meal, Noel Monk realised that the newlyweds were AWOL and set off around the building to locate them, eventually finding them sharing a bathroom.

'There I found Valerie in her beautiful white lace wedding gown, looking every inch the angel – except for the tears streaming down her cheeks,' he recalled. 'Valerie was holding her husband's head over a toilet bowl, pulling his hair back to make sure it didn't become encrusted with puke.'

'I'm sorry,' Eddie mumbled, repeatedly. 'I'm so sorry.'

5
LOSS OF CONTROL

As they listened to Noel Monk break down exactly how, where and why their money was going to be spent, no one in Van Halen could have been oblivious to the cold, hard, undeniable fact that the proposition they were being invited to consider was, by the letter of the law, illegal. The practice of 'payola' – the offering of cash, gifts, holidays, drugs or sexual favours to influential individuals at radio stations in exchange for airplay – may have been as well established as the music industry itself, but just because everyone else did it, or turned a blind eye when it was sanctioned on their behalf, this didn't make the act any less palatable. When the entertainment trade magazine *Variety* first used the term in 1916 in a front-page editorial condemning the practice, its use of the phrase 'direct payment evil' was fairly unambiguous.

And yet, as Van Halen's manager patiently explained that in the considered and trusted opinion of Warner Bros. Records, offering financial inducements to selected radio stations for guaranteed airtime was the only realistic option now available to them in order to boost sales of their new album from gold to platinum status, the decision to be taken seemed like a no-brainer to the attentive band members. As Monk recalls, it was David Lee Roth who authorised the action plan on the group's behalf. More than anyone, Roth understood that perception is everything in the music business. The industry placed a huge premium on forward momentum – rising chart positions, swelling box-office receipts, deeper penetration on the radio, promotion to magazine front covers – and the notion that Van Halen might be perceived as being on the slide after just three years in the limelight was inconceivable, unthinkable.

'Bottom line is, we can't afford to be just a gold band anymore,' Roth bluntly stated. 'So, do what you have to do. We trust you, Noel. Make it happen.'

The emergency band meeting had been convened in the wake of a difficult conversation between Noel Monk and Warners' head of artist development Carl Scott. While *Women and Children First* and its predecessor, *Van Halen II*, had racked up a million domestic sales within three months of being filed in record shops, by mid-summer 1981 *Fair Warning*, the group's fourth album, released on 29 April that year, had barely broken the 500,000 mark. Accustomed, since day one, to being regarded, and treated, as a priority act by Warners due to Ted Templeman's endorsement, Van Halen faced the prospect of slipping to second-tier status if they were deemed incapable of keeping pace with the label's big hitters. Revisiting the conversation with Scott in his memoir *Runnin' with the Devil*, Monk recalls asking, 'Isn't there something we can do?' and receiving the reply, 'Yeah, there is. But it's not cheap.'

No innocent with regard to the shadier side of the record business, by his own admission, Monk had naively assumed that payola had gone the way of piano rolls and 78 rpm discs by the dawn of the 1980s. That same afternoon, he would receive a crash course in the dark arts from the label's head of publicity. Guaranteed airplay at a market-leading station in New York, Los Angeles, Boston or Chicago, he was told, had been costed at $5,000. Acquiring the same preferential treatment in a secondary, but significant, music market would merit a $3,000 pay-off. Greasing the right palms at the smaller stations would require $1,000 to be slipped across a table.

'I wrote a check for more than two hundred grand and gave it to our promotion guy,' Monk admitted, 'who in turn handed it over to the payola brokers, who in turn wrote smaller checks – or handed over wads of cash – to scores of individual radio stations. And lo and behold, *Fair Warning* began to get significant airplay. Tracks that were not even intended as singles started showing up in regular rotation. Go figure.

'The album reached platinum status on November 18,' he recalled, 'and we all breathed a sigh of relief.'

The irony here was that pound-for-pound, *Fair Warning* was a better album than the two collections which preceded it. It was, however, darker and denser, devoid of a hit single and, at points, a demanding listen. It was also, unequivocally, Eddie Van Halen's album, from the jaw-dropping tapped intro of opener 'Mean Street' to the dirty synth rumbles underpinning set closer 'One Foot Out the Door', which was written in the fraught, stressful winter months before the guitarist and his fiancée were due to marry, a time Eddie later remembered as 'a dark period'.

'I was angry, frustrated and loose,' he admitted. 'We started doing things my way, and we all kind of butted heads – me versus them.'

'*Women and Children First* was real spontaneous,' recalled engineer Gene Meros. 'We went in and did it in about four days. It was like total energy and real quick. *Fair Warning* was more of a painful process. There was much more experimentation going on. There was more time spent on arranging things in the studio, getting sounds, and laying down the various tracks. Edward was getting more and more into studio techniques at that time, whereas before, they would just come in and bang 'em out without even thinking about how they were recorded.'

'I worked my ass off,' Eddie told Steven Rosen. 'Everything on it I came up with within two weeks. I also weighed 125 pounds; I lost a lot of weight and a lot of sleep because I knew it had to be done.'

'Ed typically worked all night in the back bedroom, where he'd set up his equipment, or at a studio in Hollywood,' recalled Valerie Bertinelli, already concerned about how little time she was getting to spend with a fiancée she barely knew. 'He sat there with his engineer and tinkered with ideas until he either got them the way he wanted, or ran out of booze, coke, energy, inspiration, or all of the above.'

'I'm pretty much a loner,' Eddie told Jas Obrecht. 'I just can't get along with people. They don't understand me . . . I have nothing to say. I spend a lot of time alone, playing my guitar. It's just more satisfying.

'In order for me to come up with anything different . . . I gotta sit totally in silence by myself, playing my guitar for about two or three hours. It's almost like meditating. I get in the state of mind where I'm not consciously thinking of writing.'

'He put tremendous pressure on himself to create, and the band added even more stress,' Valerie insisted. 'Even though he wrote like a machine, he always said that he had to come up with another song; something better, something catchier, something Dave approved of, something the record company liked, something that everyone – from the band to the execs in the record company boardroom – thought was a hit.'

Determined to push the group forward and challenge himself as a writer and musician, the guitarist largely chose not to exhume material from earlier demos, except on 'Mean Street', which borrowed from the unreleased 'Voodoo Queen' and 'She's the Woman'. As a result, much of *Fair Warning* sounds thrillingly unfamiliar. 'Push Comes to Shove' mixes dub reggae, bubbling funk and one of the most outrageous solos of Eddie's career, a jazz-fusion improvisation reminiscent of Allan Holdsworth. Superficially jaunty and upbeat, 'So This Is Love?' shows its dark underbelly in Roth's bitter lyric ('The grass is never greener, and there's plenty around'), the prom-queen-turned-porn-queen-themed 'Dirty Movies' ladles a futuristic new-wave synth sheen atop a filthy boogie, and the swampy, oppressively heavy instrumental 'Sunday Afternoon in the Park', written on an Electro-Harmonix Mini-Synthesizer, sounds like a 1970s Italian horror theme. Eddie told his fiancée that she had inspired it: 'It's us fighting all the time,' he said.

The experimentation and diversity of the album makes the more 'traditional' tracks all the more potent. With its killer riff, stacked vocal harmonies and a lyric celebrating liberation and life's endless possibilities, 'Unchained' might be *the* definitive Van Halen rocker, 'a blazer' in Eddie's eyes. 'I love that song,' he admitted. 'It's rare that I can listen back to my own playing and get goosebumps, but that's one of them.' Famously, the track sees David Lee Roth break the fourth wall, responding to an exhausted-sounding Ted Templeman pleading, 'Come on, Dave, gimme a break . . .' with a filthy cackle and a hollered, 'One break, coming up!'

'One of my biggest obligations as director was to make sure that all the best mistakes stayed in the movie,' Roth later explained. '"Don't sew that up! Leave it bleeding! Leave it lying there and we'll act around it!" So that moment in "Unchained" when Ted's talking to me from the control room was part and parcel of that approach. Let's leave in all the things that will keep you in the moment with us.'

Roth's lyrics throughout the album were a revelation, often downbeat, cynical, jaded and laced with anger. If the underlying theme of the band's joyous debut album was 'Life's a beach!', here the tone switched to 'Life's a bitch!', nowhere more so than on the album opener, the film noir-inspired 'Mean Street', with its wired protagonist walking a 'stinkin' street', avoiding the neighbourhood 'crazies'. The only issue here is one of credibility: while Roth's earlier fables of living life large on Sunset Boulevard fitted his persona like a diamante-studded codpiece, it was harder to believe lyrics laced with ennui and frustration. At points, however, there was a sense of real life and fantasy converging. On the surface, 'One Foot Out the Door' is a snapshot of the bitter end of an affair, filled with recrimination and regret. With the benefit of hindsight, the lyric carries a weight and significance that may not have been immediately apparent at the time. Roth would later deny, however, that the bleak lyrics were a reflection of growing tensions in the band, offering up a bizarre alternative explanation that may or may not be tongue-in-cheek.

'I had bought a parrot,' he explained to James McNair, 'a big, red Amazonian parrot named Ricky. Man, that bird was bad! You couldn't go anywhere near that bird, much less its cage, without it shrieking. It made more fucking noise than a preacher in a strip club on a Sunday morning. At the time I was living in a small apartment in North Hollywood, and I would walk past the bird's cage at two metres' distance, and the thing would start up a holy shriek to raise the devil and his henchman. Talk about anxiety overload! So, when I sat down to write the lyrics for that album, that was what I was dealing with. Everything was clenched fist and stiff upper lip.'

'The truth is, I don't think he sang as good as I played,' Eddie told Steven Rosen bluntly in an interview for *Guitar World*, before following up with an out-of-character broadside that poured cold water all over the usual portrayal of Van Halen as a unified gang.

'At least Dave pulls his weight,' the guitarist conceded. 'Mike [Anthony] doesn't. He doesn't do anything; he has no input whatsoever. Period. But he has remodelled his whole house and bought himself a [Porsche] Turbo Carrera off the money he's made off of us. Whatever.'

Pulling the curtain back further, Eddie added: 'I wasn't very happy with the way things were going or the way people were approaching the whole recording process. I would sneak back into the studio at 4 a.m. with Donn Landee, the engineer, and completely re-record all the solos and overdubs the way I wanted them. The fucked-up thing was, no one even noticed. That's how uninvolved they were on a musical level.'

The guitarist's assertiveness and control over the work did not go unnoticed. The most perceptive and insightful review of the album, written by J. D. Considine, appeared in the October issue of *Musician* magazine.

'From the opening flash of distortion-charged harmonics, guitarist Eddie Van Halen clearly dominates the album,' noted Considine. 'The structure of most heavy metal songs is predictably rigid. Riffs are deployed in maddening symmetry, verse chorus form is adhered to as if sacramental, and once tonic has been established it is stuck to like glue (unless the last verse is modulated up a key for flash). Much of *Fair Warning*, however, boasts a surprising fluidity in its structural ideas. Once Van Halen (the group) has established a riff, Van Halen (the guitarist) often as not will move on to another idea. More significantly, the instrumental tracks generally seem to lead, with David Lee Roth's vocals added on almost as commentary. Where the song structure is most conservative, on "So This Is Love?" and "Push Comes to Shove", the results are fairly predictable; but where guitar and vocals take almost independent directions, as on

"Mean Street", "Unchained", and the remarkable "Dirty Movies", the effect is devastating.

'Where previous albums offered brawn at the expense of brain, *Fair Warning* turns in an impressive combination of melodic savvy and sonic excess. If what you want is progressive gentility, pour yourself a cup of tea and listen to Genesis. If, on the other hand, you want to listen to some hard rock that assumes the listener is smarter than the average lap dog, this is the album for you.'

'You cannot label us,' the band's newly emboldened guitarist insisted to Steven Rosen. 'You cannot call us heavy metal; you cannot call us progressive; you cannot call us mellow . . . We do whatever we want to do, and that's it. Take it or leave it.

'If you don't like it, you don't like it; if you do, you do. But we do what we want to do. Period.'

For all the tension, anguish and uncertainty that fed into the campaign, the promotional cycle for *Fair Warning* climaxed in spectacular fashion. The tour wound up, on 24/25 October 1981, with the quartet playing two enormous shows in front of 60,500 music fans at the Tangerine Bowl in Orlando, Florida, as support to the Rolling Stones, still the biggest rock band in the world as they approached their thirtieth anniversary. Van Halen may have grown up fast over the course of the previous twelve months, their innocence long since shattered, but they weren't yet so jaded as to write this off as just another weekend. When Mick Jagger approached as they gazed out over the empty stadium post-soundcheck, America's loudest and brashest band fell into awed silence and respectfully bowed their heads. 'It was like God himself had entered our midst,' recalled Noel Monk.

When Eddie looked up, Jagger was looking straight at him.

'You know, Edward,' he said, 'you are a fucking *brilliant* guitar player.'

• • • •

It was when the dwarves started dishing out magic mushrooms to the cast and crew that Pete Angelus began to suspect he'd lost control on the set of the video shoot for Van Halen's cover of Roy Orbison's '(Oh) Pretty Woman'. The band's lighting director and creative consultant, Angelus had pitched Warners a conceptual fantasy piece revolving around the quartet rescuing a damsel in distress from the clutches of evil villains. The goofy, light-hearted, knowingly cheesy promo, Angelus argued convincingly, would cement the band's public image as everyone's favourite naughty-but-nice all-American rock gods.

Like many of their hard-rock peers, Van Halen were initially dismissive of the value of music videos. Before MTV's launch on 1 August 1981, most rock bands tended to view making promotional films as a waste of time, money and energy, even if the notion hadn't been beneath the consideration of their heroes, the Beatles, the Rolling Stones, the Who or Queen. Though Warners had commissioned videos for 'Runnin' with the Devil', 'Jamie's Cryin'' and 'You Really Got Me' as part of the marketing for Van Halen's debut album, the three clips were secured in a single day's filming at the Whisky a Go Go, and their impact was regarded as negligible in the album's subsequent success, particularly when weighed against the inarguable value of radio airplay and the word-of-mouth buzz generated by the quartet's kinetic, feel-good live performances. But as the cover of '(Oh) Pretty Woman' was envisaged as a stand-alone single, a stopgap release to buy the band some downtime following their six months on the road promoting *Fair Warning*, it seemed prudent to devote a little more time, creativity and imagination to the video, not least because MTV's influence on the record-buying public was evidently becoming increasingly significant. And so Pete Angelus's storyboard got thoroughly Van Halen-ised, fleshed out with irreverent, tongue-in-cheek details.

For reasons best known to themselves, the band decided to dress as different characters: Roth was to be Napoleon Bonaparte, Eddie would play a cowboy, Alex would adopt a Tarzan look and Michael Anthony would appear as a samurai warrior. A decision was then taken to cast two dwarves, a hunchback and transgender entertainer International Chrysis in the key supporting roles. To loosen nerves and inhibitions, the on-set catering was to consist largely of beer, weed, Jack Daniel's and cocaine; hallucinogenic fungi were a bonus. Notwithstanding two cameramen quitting the set because they were tripping hard, it was all fun and games, until Angelus lost his dwarves.

'I stood on the set, going, "Seriously, can anybody find the little people?"' Angelus recalled in *I Want My MTV*, Rob Tannenbaum and Craig Marks's illuminating oral history of the music channel. 'After 20 minutes of searching for them I thought, I'll walk around and see if I can turn up anything. I got to the transvestite's dressing room and opened the door . . . The little guy was wearing a black cape. He was holding the transvestite's penis, which seemed kind of erect, and he was pretending it was a microphone. And he was singing "Satisfaction" by the Rolling Stones while doing a Mick Jagger impersonation. I thought, This is not going well.'

Blame Roth. It was Roth, twitching with nervous energy as the post-tour withdrawal symptoms kicked in at the end of 1981, who pushed for the band to record a cover version in order to maintain a presence in the market during what was supposed to be an extended hiatus. The singer had actually suggested taping a remake of Martha and the Vandellas' 1964 hit 'Dancing in the Street', but Eddie nominated Roy Orbison's seven-million-selling single from the same year instead. The quartet returned to Sunset Sound Studio with Ted Templeman

and tracked three pieces of music – the single A-side, perenni-
al live favourite 'Happy Trails', written by Roy Rogers and his
wife Dale Evans, and instantly recognisable as the theme song
for their long-running radio/TV show, and the dense instrumental 'Intruder', required to fill out the space in the video
soundtrack – in a single day. With the accompanying video in
the can, the plan was to launch the song into the marketplace
and then have the band ease back into the shadows for a well-
earned break.

But God laughs when men make plans. Though MTV bri-
dled at the video's gleeful political incorrectness and pulled it
from daily rotation within weeks after receiving thousands of
complaints, radio leaped on the effervescent, energised cover.
As the song hurtled up the *Billboard* Hot 100 chart, where it
would peak at number 12 in mid-April 1982, Mo Ostin and
Lenny Waronker at Warner Bros. contacted Ted Templeman
to demand the delivery of a new full-length Van Halen album
within weeks, exactly what the band *didn't* want.

With considerable reluctance, the quartet acquiesced to the
pressure, brokering a compromise with their paymasters: they
would deliver a new record, but having no time to work up new
material – and once again curiously unwilling to dig too deep
into their vault of unreleased material – it would lean heavily on
cover versions, in keeping with the raw energy of their unanticipated hit single. With Sunset Sound booked out, the band were
shunted into Amigo Studios, owned by Warners, where Templeman and Landee would cut the album in just twelve days.

Diver Down was released on 14 April 1982, the same week
in which '(Oh) Pretty Woman' peaked on the *Billboard* chart.
Of its twelve tracks, three songs – 'Cathedral', 'Intruder' and
'Little Guitars (Intro)' – are sub-two-minute instrumentals
and no fewer than five are covers, with the Roy Orbison remake joined by versions of the Kinks' 'Where Have All the

Good Times Gone!', the previously spurned 'Dancing in the Street', 'Big Bad Bill (Is Sweet William Now'), a 1924 composition from Milton Ager and Jack Yellen, and the aforementioned 'Happy Trails'. Of the original material, 'Secrets' was a leftover from the *Fair Warning* sessions, 'Hang 'Em High' was a reworked version of 1977 demo track 'Last Night', 'Little Guitars' was 'a song for señoritas', according to Roth, and album highlight 'The Full Bug' featured Roth in lairy 'cocksman' mode, bragging about giving some young lady 'the best part of a man'.

Testing the definition of 'long-player', the whole album clocked in at just over thirty-one minutes in length, a fact that did not go unnoticed by reviewers.

'Not only is this album an insult to the average consumer who will have to pay upwards of ten dollars for it,' wrote Jeffrey Morgan in *Creem*, 'it is an exceptionally vicious kick in the teeth to Van Halen fans everywhere; fans who – by buying their albums, attending their concerts, and wearing their merchandise – have made David Lee Roth, Alex Van Halen, Eddie Van Halen and Michael Anthony millionaires.'

Writing in *Rolling Stone*, Parke Puterbaugh labelled the release 'a cogent case for consumer fraud'. Choosing to interpret the scarcity of original material as an indication that the band were 'running out of ideas', Puterbaugh's pithy two-star review neatly concluded, 'There's a little Van Halen in everybody, these guys are fond of saying, but there's too little on *Diver Down*.' Not that hardcore fans cared too much, at least initially: *Diver Down* passed the one-million sales mark in just ten weeks, peaking at number 3 on the *Billboard* 200, two places higher than its 1981 predecessor.

Ever ready to uncork a fresh bottle of snake oil, David Lee Roth was able to put a positive spin on the hastily compiled set. Referencing the album's minimalist artwork – a 'diver down' flag intended to mark the presence of a scuba diver beneath the waves – the singer told *Sounds'* Sylvie Simmons that it signified that 'there was something going on that's not apparent to your eyes . . .'

'A lot of people approach Van Halen as sort of the abyss,' he said. 'It means, it's not immediately apparent to your eyes what is going on underneath the surface.'

Given Roth's astute understanding of the machinations of the Fourth Estate, this hint at the internecine tensions within the band was surely no careless, unguarded slip of the tongue. While a fan listening to the quartet giggling through the four-part-harmony a cappella vocals on 'Happy Trails' or hearing Eddie and Alex's clarinet-playing father Jan trilling throughout 'Big Bad Bill . . .', at Roth's invitation, might have imagined that the unit was closer than ever, this was an illusion. And an exasperated Eddie would quickly tire of manicuring the truth.

Discussing his newest solo turn, 'Cathedral', in an interview later in 1982, he informed regular confidante Jas Obrecht that he'd wanted to include the piece on a previous record but had been overruled by Roth, who bluntly told the guitarist, as Eddie remembered it, 'Fuck this, man. No more fucking guitar solos.'

'He's on an ego trip,' Eddie stated. 'He has always been. Ted didn't know that that's the way Dave felt. One day when Dave wasn't there [in the studio], I said, "Ted, what do you think of this? And what do you think of that?" I played him "Little Guitars", the intro, the little flamenco-sounding thing, and "Cathedral", and he's going, like, "God! Why the fuck didn't you show me this earlier?" And I explained to him, "Dave just said, 'Fuck the guitar hero shit, you know, we're a *band*.'" So Ted just said, "Fuck Dave." So we put it on anyway.'

Though he didn't call him out with the same ferocity, Eddie was quietly seething at Templeman also, as he felt that the producer had 'wasted' a keyboard riff he had envisaged turning into a Peter Gabriel-style track by plonking it on top of the 'Dancing in the Street' riff. Never the confrontational type, Eddie sulked rather than vetoing the idea, but the incident gnawed at him.

'I hated every minute of making *Diver Down*,' the guitarist would later state boldly. 'David had the idea that if you covered a successful song, you were halfway home. C'mon . . . Van Halen doing "Dancing in the Street"? It was stupid. I started feeling like I would rather bomb playing my own songs than be successful playing someone else's music.

'*Fair Warning*'s lack of commercial success prompted *Diver Down*,' he admitted. 'To me, *Fair Warning* is more true to what I am and what I believe Van Halen is. We're a hard rock band, and we were an album band. We were lucky to enter the charts anywhere.'

Soon enough, Roth, too, made his true feelings known, offering telling insights into the working dynamic between himself and the guitarist.

'What Eddie and I do is argue,' he told *Creem*. 'We come from different backgrounds, musically, philosophically, socially, our hobbies. I have trouble understanding, more times than not, why he does what he does. There are meeting grounds, of course. But in the musical end, there is no meeting ground. We're arguing. Sometimes we reach a compromise. No one is ever happy except the public.'

Originally scheduled to run for eighty shows across North America, beginning on 14 July in Augusta, Georgia, the amusingly titled Hide Your Sheep tour (also known as the Kicking Ass and Taking Names tour) was intended to paper over the fractures beginning to undermine the group's foundations. In reality, it only exacerbated the simmering tensions between the band's frontman and its musical mastermind. When the caravan reached California in September, Eddie took some time away from the hothouse atmosphere to visit his friends in Kiss, who were recording what would become their *Creatures of the Night* album at the Record Plant Studio, this time as a trio following troubled guitarist Ace Frehley's departure. Exactly what transpired on that autumn afternoon remains a subject of debate, but Gene Simmons swears to this day that Eddie was so over working with David Lee Roth that he offered to quit his own band in order to fill the vacant guitarist slot in Kiss.

'He was so unhappy about how he and Roth were – or weren't – getting along,' says Simmons. 'He couldn't stand him. And drugs were rampant. And so he took me to lunch, to a diner right across the street from the Record Plant. And Eddie said, "I want to join Kiss. I don't want to fight any more with Roth. I'm sick and tired of it." But I told him, "Eddie, there's not enough room. You need to be in a band where you can direct the music. You're not going to be happy in Kiss." I talked him out of it. It didn't fit.'

When this writer spoke with Paul Stanley about this rumour, he confirmed that Eddie did indeed visit Kiss in the studio – 'I remember him listening to the solo for "Creatures of the Night", which he thought was amazing,' he remembered – but had no recollection whatsoever of any conversation with either the guitarist or indeed his louder-than-life bassist about Eddie joining the New York band. When it was suggested to Stanley that had Van Halen really offered to team up with the band during his powwow with Simmons, one might have imagined the bassist mentioning it upon returning to the studio, Stanley was absolutely adamant that this did not happen.

'You'll have to make of that what you will...' he noted, diplomatically.

'I don't buy that Simmons story for a second,' says Jas Obrecht, who was in regular contact with Eddie at the time. 'And you know why? There's no way on earth Eddie would ever leave Alex. It's impossible, it would never happen. Eddie is intensely loyal to his family, and it just would not happen, under any condition. I'm calling bullshit on that.'

Unbeknown to all but their closest and most trusted friends, Alex had, in fact, talked Eddie out of quitting their band just one year earlier.

'In 1981, when Ed got married to Valerie, things got a little loopy,' the drummer revealed. 'He was getting press that he didn't want, and things became unbearable. Ed wanted to quit. I told him, "Look, we've spent too much time to give this up. The lyrics and the image may not be exactly right, but people are getting to hear your music." I said, "Hey, we're playing! That's what every musician wants to do."'

Whatever the truth of the matter, ultimately the Hide Your Sheep tour was not derailed, save for the cancellation of three October shows in New Jersey, following another contentious incident, in which the guitarist fractured his wrist after punching a wall in anger. Later that month, however, properly healed, Eddie found the time to contribute to Michael Jackson's upcoming *Thriller* album, popping into Westlake Recording Studios in Los Angeles to add a guitar solo to 'Beat It' as a favour to producer Quincy Jones.

Jackson had written 'Beat It' as a rock song, centred around a driving riff from Toto guitarist Steve Lukather, a long-time friend of the Van Halen brothers. When Eddie arrived at Westlake to track his parts, Jones gave him carte blanche to improvise over Lukather's work.

'Michael left to go across the hall to do some children's speaking record,' Eddie recalled. 'I think it was *E.T.* or something. So I asked Quincy, "What do you want me to do?" And he goes, "Whatever you want to do." And I go, "Be careful when you say that! If you know anything about me, be careful when you say, 'Do anything you want!'"'

'I'm not gonna sit here and try to tell you what to play,' Jones insisted. 'The reason you are here is because of what you do play.'

'I listened to the song, and I immediately go, "Can I change some parts?"' Eddie remembered. 'I turned to the engineer and I go, "OK, from the breakdown, chop in this part, go to this piece, pre-chorus, to the chorus, out." Took him maybe ten minutes to put it together. And I proceeded to improvise two solos over it.'

Lost in the music while recording the second of these solos, Van Halen wasn't initially aware that Jackson had walked back into the booth to check out his contribution.

'I said, "Look, I changed the middle section of your song,"' Eddie recalled. 'Now, in my mind, he's either going to have his bodyguards kick me out for butchering his song, or he's going to like it. And so he gave it a listen, and he turned to me and went, "Wow, thank you so much for having the passion to not just come in and blaze a solo, but to actually care about the song, and make it better."'

Eddie walked away from his encounter with the King of Pop without asking for royalty points on the record or even a session fee. More significantly, he didn't bother to inform his bandmates, his manager or his record label of his decision to guest on the album either, or indeed consider for a minute that it might, perhaps, have been good etiquette to do so.

'I said to myself, "Who is going to know that I played on this kid's record, right? Nobody's going to find out." Wrong! Big-time wrong.'

The guitarist was even more secretive about his involvement in another 1982 studio session, which saw him co-producing (alongside Donn Landee, with the pair credited as 'The Vards') a two-track single for Frank Zappa's twelve-year-old son Dweezil. Co-written by Zappa Sr's guitarist Steve Vai and Dweezil's fourteen-year-old sister Moon Unit, A-side 'My Mother Is a Space Cadet' featured an unmistakeable Eddie guitar intro and a chorus reminiscent of the Police. 'It cooks!' Eddie told Jas Obrecht. 'It smokes! The whole band was fucking twelve years old! They couldn't play for shit, but when you hear it, it'll blow you away.'

When Dweezil's band – which included future Adele/Foo Fighters producer Greg Kurstin – entered a high-school talent contest, their rock-star mentor came along to show his support and presented the youngster with a brand-new Kramer Explorer guitar. Post-gig, the guitarist joined his young pals in an alley behind the school building for a debrief and a cigarette.

'I remember that a teacher came up and saw us all in the alley,' the band's bassist Scott Marshall recalled. 'She says, "What are you kids doing back here?" Eddie popped up from his 930 Turbo Porsche, and jokingly said, "Gettin' high!" She freaked out and ran away. I don't think she got the joke.'

6
JUMP

Three thousand feet above the sun-cracked deserts and mountain slopes of San Bernardino County, Valerie Bertinelli looked on with quiet concern as her husband, twitching and squirming in his seat, stared through the helicopter window in silence. It was the afternoon of 29 May 1983, and bound for the 500-acre Glen Helen Regional Park in Devore, where his band were set to headline one of the largest, most ambitious live events ever staged in the US, Eddie Van Halen's nerves were showing.

Bertinelli couldn't help but draw comparisons between the tightly wound, anxious artist by her side and the relaxed, playful lover who'd cradled her hands in his own as they cruised along the waterways of Amsterdam on a gaily painted canal barge just one month earlier. The pair had been in the Dutch capital to celebrate their second wedding anniversary, and Eddie's thoughtfully plotted itinerary for the pair had taken in a visit to the Anne Frank House and a double bill of Bartók symphonies and Chopin, before a meander through the city's lively night markets. If that brief European vacation offered a vision of the man Bertinelli loved at his most unguarded, sweetly laying bare his humble roots, today was all about a flexing of ego and status, a public demonstration of exactly how far the hard-working immigrant musician had come.

The US ('Unite Us in Song') Festival was an ambitious vanity project for Apple Inc. co-founder Steve Wozniak, who nurtured dreams of establishing a 'new festival for a new age', an undertaking he envisaged developing into an annual 'Super Bowl of rock parties'. The event's inaugural staging, held over the weekend of 3–5 September 1982, featured headline sets from the Police, Tom Petty and the Heartbreakers, and Fleetwood Mac; it also ended up with Wozniak out of pocket to the tune of somewhere between $5 million and $12 million, a fact which seemingly didn't faze the tech entrepreneur at all. No sooner had the 1982 festival stage been broken down by local crew members than 'Woz' was pledging that his baby would return bigger and bolder in 1983. This second coming, he promised, would be convened over Memorial Day weekend, 28–30 May, and themed around 'New Wave', 'Heavy Metal' and 'Rock' bills. The San Jose-born businessman had earmarked west London punks the Clash, riding high on the US success of their 1982 album *Combat Rock*, to headline the event's opening night, was chasing the mercurial David Bowie to close the festival and aimed to cajole Van Halen out of the studio to provide a beefy, all-American filling between the two English acts.

'You are going to be part of something so big, so different, it will begin a whole new chapter in the history of live music,' Wozniak boldly predicted in the advance promotion for the weekend, which subsequently added a Willie Nelson-headlined 'Country Day', to be held on 4 June. 'We will be joining together in a celebration that will mark the end of the "me" decade and the beginning of the "us" decade.'

These noble, high-minded intentions were rather undermined in the pre-production stage by increasingly bitter arguments about the festival finances. Having initially accepted a $500,000 appearance fee for their Saturday-night headline slot, the Clash were outraged to discover that Van Halen were set to bank twice as much for their bill-topping set the following evening, a disparity which would become even more pronounced.

With the European leg of his Serious Moonlight Tour, promoting the hugely successful *Let's Dance* album, scheduled to run from mid-May through to early July, Wozniak favourite David Bowie was initially, and understandably, loath to commit to a one-off show on the other side of the Atlantic in mid-tour, given the considerable logistics involved in re-routing the whole caravan to California between scheduled gigs in France and England. But with just forty-eight hours remaining before Wozniak was due to unveil the festival line-up in a blaze of publicity, Bowie finally accepted the booking, in exchange for the promise of a chartered 747 plane for the Atlantic crossing and a guaranteed fee in excess of $1 million. This, however, created a fresh problem for promoter Barry Fey, as a 'Most Favoured Nation' clause in Van Halen's contract stipulated that no other act on the three-day bill could be paid a fee larger than they were due. Fully aware that the festival organisers had the narrowest of windows in which to negotiate, Primary Talent, Van Halen's live-booking agency, boldly requested, and swiftly received, an extra $500,000 for their clients' scheduled performance. Already aggrieved, the Clash were incandescent with anger when they learned of this new arrangement, and on the eve of the festival Joe Strummer threatened to take his band back to the UK, before bruised egos were soothed and the quartet talked down off the ledge.

'The people out there want us to play,' the Clash's manager Bernie Rhodes told the media, attempting to put a positive spin on the Londoners' unseemly hissy fit. 'Besides, if we didn't play, Van Halen would call us communists.'

David Lee Roth was never going to let the English punks have the final word.

'The thing the Clash don't understand is that you can't take life so goddam seriously,' he mocked. 'No one gets out alive. The difference between us and the Clash is just a matter of haircut and shoes...We're just here doing our usual: confusing business with pleasure.

'When you play the game of life,' Roth concluded, 'you play it with all your guts. It's not a question of whether you win or lose, it's how good you looked.'

Ultimately, it would be the fans who would decide who would emerge on top in this phoney war, and the final ticket receipts left no doubt as to which act Californian music fans saw as the People's Champions: out of the 670,000 $20 tickets sold for the event, approximately 375,000 were purchased for the Van Halen-topped 'Heavy Metal Day', which also featured LA newcomers Quiet Riot and trainee Sunset Strip hellraisers Mötley Crüe, Van Halen's old friend and former touring partner Ozzy Osbourne, Birmingham's studs-and-leather-plated metal gods Judas Priest, Canadian progressive-rock trio Triumph, and Teutonic hard-rockers Scorpions playing ahead of the headlining home-state heroes. Vince Neil, Mötley Crüe's David Lee Roth-aping bottle-blond frontman, would later declare, with admirable gravitas, and no little truth, 'It was the day new wave died and rock 'n' roll took over.'

Everything was set, then, for Van Halen to own the weekend. As a playful pre-show joke, Barry Fey placed a bowl of brown M&M's in the group's dressing room, secure in the knowledge that he'd done everything in his power to lay the groundwork for a night to remember. The gesture tickled the Van Halen brothers greatly, though their smiles would fade as the day wore on.

'This was not a good night for me or my band,' Noel Monk later acknowledged. 'In front of a couple hundred thousand people, and the largest collection of media ever assembled for a concert, Van Halen went out, and nearly shit the bed.'

The problem, bluntly stated, was David Lee Roth. In the run-up to his band's headline set, the crowds out front at Glen Helen Regional Park were shown riotous party scenes on jumbo TV screens, purportedly being filmed live in the star-studded backstage compound. Body-painted models strutted around wearing just stiletto heels and a smile, as dwarves dressed in cowboy suits and riding saddled-up sheep gatecrashed a lavish buffet. One cheesy segment depicted a rogue cameraman straying into a restricted area behind thick black curtains to find Roth, in leopard-print briefs, on the verge of 'schtupping', to borrow a verb from the singer's vocabulary, a bikini-clad friend sprawled over a piano. This seemingly spontaneous bacchanalian excess had been scripted, filmed and edited weeks in advance, but on the day, holding court in a huge guest hospitality area accessible via a pathway signposted 'Van Halen Trail: No virgins, Journey fans or sheep allowed', Roth seemed hell-bent on staging a one-man encore performance of its grossest excesses. By mid-afternoon, the singer, fucked off his head, could barely stand upright. Interviewed pre-show by MTV's Mark Goodman, a visibly krelled-up Roth, swaying and barely coherent, mugged furiously for the camera and laughed maniacally at slurred half-jokes that landed only in his own head. Amid this vulgar vaudeville act, one nugget of news was disclosed when, asked about the status of the band's next album, Roth revealed that the quartet had already tracked songs earmarked as future singles.

'Edward has a studio, you know, and we've been in and out,' he said. 'We've been working our tails off.'

Onstage several hours later, stumbling around with a bottle of Jack Daniel's whiskey in his hand and tripping over lyrics, Roth was a hot mess. The tone was set from the opening track of the set, *Women and Children First* deep cut 'Romeo Delight', when, coming out of the first chorus, Roth bellowed, 'I forgot the fucking words!' The vast majority of the audience, determined to throw down hard with California's party kings, were too drunk or high to care. Three songs in, Roth improvised an entirely random set of lyrics for the second half of 'The Full Bug' and threw in a harmonica solo so out of time and out of tune that it could have been performance art. Halfway through the set, during 'Somebody Get Me a Doctor', Eddie incorporated a snippet of Cream's 'I'm So Glad' and a teasing hint of unreleased new song 'Girl Gone Bad' into an extended solo, presumably just to amuse himself. Michael Anthony accidentally tugged the cable from his bass during his solo spot and received one of the biggest cheers of the night for hurling his instrument into the air and letting it drop on the stage – it was one of those nights. Granted an encore their ramshackle two-hour performance scarcely merited, Roth strutted onstage in 'ass-less' chaps to lead the band into 'You Really Got Me', seemingly oblivious to the dark scowls on the faces of the seething Van Halen brothers.

'This was Van Halen's audience,' wrote Sylvie Simmons, reviewing the event (using the witty pseudonym 'Laura Canyon') for *Kerrang!*. 'David Lee Roth had the crowd in the palm of his hand, and kept turning them over between his fingers . . . Van Halen were as over-the-top as ever, probably more so, knowing they could have gotten away with murder up there – almost did, what with Roth inciting the crowds to riot! Predictably, Eddie and Alex Van Halen played like maestros – half a dozen solos each, and we're only up to the second song – and David strutted and posed and stood with his hands on his hips and his mouth open, gaping at the cheering crowd, in-between classics like "Dancing In The Street", "Jamie's Cryin'" and "Runnin' With The Devil".'

'More people have been arrested tonight than in the entire fucking weekend last year,' screamed Roth at one juncture, as the crowd roared its approval. 'You are one bunch of rowdy motherfuckers.'

Wired to the tits as he was, this particular Roth spiel was rooted in fact. There were reportedly 130 arrests over the course of the weekend, one man was beaten to death with a tyre iron in a parking lot, another died following a drug overdose, and any number of bloodied and beaten bodies lay prone in the dust as 'Happy Trails' brought the festival's Sunday night to a conclusion. Exiting the arena, some overexcited fans rammed police vehicles with their cars. 'They even hit a horse,' one bemused deputy reported. As his men scraped human detritus from the park grounds, San Bernardino County sheriff Floyd Tidwell told the assembled media, 'There are some people I'd be happy never to see back in this county again – Van Halen, for example.'

When Steve Wozniak's accountants produced their calculators in the aftermath of the festival, it emerged that the weekend had cost the tech guru $13 million. He would never attempt to stage another music event. Still, Wozniak did get a photograph with Valerie Bertinelli, which he kept on display in his office for years afterwards, so it wasn't *all* bad news.

As shambolic as the whole affair was, radio and television coverage of Van Halen's sloppy performance, broadcast on the Westwood One network and cable channel Showtime, made their pouting, smirking master of ceremonies David Lee Roth a national star, America's latest poster boy for unbridled rock 'n' roll excess. For the ensuing six months, Roth's chiselled face and artfully tousled blond mane were almost permanent fixtures in American music magazines, as media coverage of hard rock and heavy metal expanded in tandem with MTV. If Eddie Van Halen was embarrassed and irritated by his singer's increasingly self-obsessed showboating, and he assuredly was, the guitarist consoled himself with the hope that he would soon wrestle back control of his band.

• • • • •

To inspectors from the Los Angeles zoning commission, the plans submitted by Mr Edward Van Halen for the construction of a racquetball court on the grounds of his Coldwater Canyon estate appeared somewhat extravagant. No one was disputing the popular musician's right to squander his money in whatever legal manner he deemed appropriate, but were two-foot-thick, concrete-filled cinder blocks strictly necessary for this particular project, they questioned, as the guitarist guided them around the proposed site.

'When we play, we play *hard*,' the unassuming, low-key rock star patiently explained with a smile. 'We want to keep it quiet and not piss off the neighbours.'

Application approved.

Donn Landee can take the credit for the naming of Eddie's covert recording facility. While eavesdropping on LAPD bulletins on an illegal scanner, the engineer learned that the reference '5150', derived from the California Welfare and Institutions Code, warned of the escape from custody of a mentally unstable individual diagnosed as a potential danger to themselves and/or others. Aware that many in the Van Halen camp considered Eddie crazy for seeking to build his own studio, Landee shared his discovery with the guitarist, and the pair gleefully appropriated the code as a shared badge of honour. In truth, Eddie's motivation for embarking upon the project was logical and pragmatic: with his own bespoke studio available 24/7, the obsessive, workaholic guitarist reasoned, he would no longer be forced to sync his productivity to anyone else's work schedule, would no longer need to place dead-of-the-night phone calls to Ted Templeman, Landee or his bandmates when inspiration struck. The construction of 5150 was his own declaration of independence.

Donn Landee proved an eager and enthusiastic lieutenant in facilitating Eddie's grand designs, with the pair sharing 'a common vision', the guitarist recalled. It was Landee who located a dilapidated Universal Audio console for sale, which Eddie hastily snapped up for $6,000, and Landee who personally dusted down, rewired and breathed new life into the vintage board. In a subsequent *Guitar World* interview, Eddie would approvingly label his new best friend 'a man-child genius on the borderline of insanity'. To some in Van Halen's inner sanctum, the description might have been equally applicable to the twenty-nine-year-old guitarist.

In April 1983, Eddie informed Ted Templeman that he wanted to record the next Van Halen album at his still-unfinished studio. Templeman was far from enthusiastic, but reluctantly acquiesced when he saw how much the prospect excited the guitarist, figuring that he could patch things up at Sunset Sound or Amigo during post-production or mixing if needs must.

The first new song Eddie previewed for the producer was a synth-driven, hook-laden instrumental he'd been toying with for over a year, written in his bedroom on a Sequential Circuits Prophet-10 and finessed on an Oberheim OB-Xa. Templeman was nonplussed.

'Wait a minute,' he recalls saying. 'I signed a heavy-metal band.'

If this seemed like a curiously out-of-character comment from a commercially minded producer and record executive who had encouraged the band to record 'You Really Got Me', taken a proactive role in writing melodies for 'Dance the Night Away', and produced and signed off on '(Oh) Pretty Woman', 'Dancing in the Street' and 'Where Have All the Good Times Gone!' just twelve months earlier, Templeman was quick to emphasise that he had nothing against Van Halen using keyboards, but that he considered Eddie's work on 'And the Cradle Will Rock . . .' and 'Sunday Afternoon in the Park' bolder, more exciting and more 'on brand'. This new idea, he ventured, sounded like the kind of plinky-plonky vamp one might hear at a baseball game or travelling funfair. Eddie told Templeman that he was wrong, and that he would prove him wrong, and the pair parted company for the day agreeing to disagree.

Long after midnight, the guitarist phoned his mentor from 5150 once more. 'Ted, you've got to hear this,' he enthused. 'I'm gonna come and get you.'

'He drove down in his Porsche to Century City and picked me up at three in the morning and drove me up there,' Templeman recalled. '"Listen to this." And they had "Jump" down. Donn had worked on it. And it did work; it sounded great. And I said, "Yeah, OK." The next morning, I said, "Dave, write some lyrics."'

Roth was even less impressed with the initial demo of the song than Templeman, and was equally direct in voicing his opinion to Eddie. 'Dave said that I was a guitar hero and I shouldn't be playing keyboards,' Eddie recalled. 'My response was if I want to play a tuba or Bavarian cheese whistle, I will do it.' Nevertheless, the vocalist trusted Templeman's commercial instincts. After an hour spent jotting down ideas on a notepad in the back of his 1951 Mercury Lowrider, Roth returned to the studio and presented his lyrics, pivoting around a phrase he'd written down while watching a dramatic television news report one evening. Ironically, one of the most life-affirming songs of the decade would have its origins in a news segment covering a potential suicide bid.

'It was the five o'clock news, and there was a fellow standing on top of the Arco Towers in Los Angeles, and he was about to check out early, he was going to do the 33 stories drop, and there was a whole crowd of people in the parking lot downstairs yelling, "Don't jump, don't jump!" and I thought to myself, "Jump,"' Roth explained to writer Lisa Robinson in an interview for *Rock Video* magazine. 'It's easy to translate it the way you hear it on the record as a "Go for it" attitude, positive sort of affair.'

From this encouraging start, the making of Van Halen's sixth studio album rapidly descended into chaos. Fuelled by a seemingly never-ending supply of cocaine and alcohol, Eddie and Donn Landee would retreat into their private clubhouse for days on end, shunning sleep and often literally locking Templeman and Roth out of the sessions. Valerie Bertinelli would ring Noel Monk in tears, begging him to drag her husband out of the studio. During Monk's frequent concerned phone calls to the complex, he could hear the guitarist snarling and screaming as he smashed up expensive audio equipment, while an audibly wired Landee assured him that all was going just fine. 'After a while', Templeman noted, 'that kind of zombie existence is going to hollow you out.'

'We were always disagreeing,' said Roth. 'We were always at each other's throats about what was the appropriate thing to do. But it was that belligerent, argumentative, confrontational chemistry that created the music. The best medical accomplishments are not achieved when everybody is sitting around going, "You're great! Do you think I'm great, too? You do? Great." There's no spark. No challenge.'

'Everybody was afraid that Donn and I were taking control,' said Eddie. 'Well . . . yes! I just didn't want to do things the way Ted wanted us to do them. I'm not knocking *Diver Down*. It's a good record, but it wasn't the record I wanted to do at the time. *1984* was me showing Ted how you really make a Van Halen record.'

Long before work at 5150 was complete, the marketing team at Warners decided that releasing the new Van Halen album on the stroke of midnight on New Year's Eve, as 1984 came blinking into view, would be an easy way to generate publicity. With that in mind, they set Templeman a late-October deadline to deliver the fully mixed and mastered album. Given the chaotic scenes at Coldwater Canyon, Templeman was anxious about hitting this mark, not least because no one else involved in making the record seemed at all concerned, least of all Eddie, who would, at whim, sporadically switch his attention to recording music for side projects, without a word of warning to his increasingly exasperated bandmates. The producer's anxiety was compounded, during the mixing process, when he was continually outvoted by Eddie, Alex and Donn Landee during disagreements over sound balances, but in order to maintain harmony, he accepted the majority verdicts. By late October, the mixes were complete, and Templeman left Landee to oversee the mastering of the tapes. Eddie, however, still wasn't entirely satisfied and continued to covertly tweak the 'finished' mix. It was only when Templeman heard from the staff at Amigo that Landee had yet to show with the multitrack tapes that he realised the guitarist and engineer were still at work on the album . . . and, even more alarmingly, were point blank refusing to release it to the label until they were fully satisfied.

'Nobody was happy with Donn and me,' Eddie admitted to *Guitar World*'s Chris Gill. 'They thought we were crazy and out of our minds. Ted thought that Donn had lost it and was going to threaten to burn the tapes. That was all BS. We just wanted an extra week to make sure that we were happy with everything.

'Ted just didn't see eye to eye with the way I looked at things. That was my whole premise for building the studio. I wanted to make a complete record from end to end, not just one hit. As soon as "Jump" was done, he looked at the rest of the album as filler. It wasn't that to me.'

As Templeman applied what he imagined were the final touches to the album, on Halloween Queen guitarist Brian May released a mini-LP, *Star Fleet Project*, which he had recorded in collaboration with Eddie Van Halen, bassist Phil Chen, Queen keyboard player Fred Mandel and drummer Alan Gratzer at the Record Plant in Los Angeles on 21 and 22 April. Credited to Brian May + Friends, the twelve-inch vinyl record featured just three tracks: 'Star Fleet', May's hard-rock reimagining of English musician Paul Bliss's theme to Japanese sci-fi anime series *Star Fleet* (originally composed, like 'Jump', on an Oberheim OB-Xa synth); May original 'Let Me Out'; and 'Blues Breaker (Dedicated to E.C.)' a thrillingly freewheeling twelve-minute blues jam inspired by May's and Eddie's mutual love of 'The Beano Album', 1966's *Blues Breakers with Eric Clapton*, recorded by John Mayall and the Bluesbreakers.

'*Star Fleet* was a Japanese animated series for children which used to be on Saturday-morning TV,' May explained to this writer in 2013. 'I used to watch it with my little boy Jimmy. We'd get up early on Saturday mornings to watch it, and the recording was originally Jimmy's idea, because he said, "You should play that, Dad." I was living in Los Angeles at the time, Jimmy was attending nursery school there, and one day I found myself with some time off, which was rare, and I thought, "What an interesting idea it would be to do this." And so I made some phone calls to friends in LA: Ed, whom I'd met through my friend Tony Iommi; Alan Gratzer, who was a neighbour; and Phil Chen, a great bass player from Rod Stewart's outfit at the time. We had a little bit of discussion in advance, but basically we just bowled into the studio and laid into it.'

'I'd made a little acoustic demo of the track "Star Fleet", which I sent to everyone, and then Ed and Phil came to my house to work on it,' May told *Total Guitar*. 'I'd done this whole arrangement that was a bit complex . . . The idea was to go through a lot of changes and then arrive at a big all-out soloing section, and obviously I wanted Ed to solo. So we ran through it a couple of times and Eddie said, "Yeah, we can do that."

'We'd never played together before, and yet the chemistry is there. In "Blues Breaker" . . . we're not just noodling, we are listening to each other and playing off each other, as is the whole band. Alan was really in tune with it, Phil was like a rock, and Fred Mandel was doing lovely sympathetic things on the keys. [Eddie] said to me, "I'm glad we're doing this, because you're making me go back to my roots. I love playing blues, and I love not doing the Eddie Van Halen stuff, I love not tapping and doing all the fireworks. It's great to get back to just playing from the soul."'

'It was exhilarating, I must say, like flying by the seat of your pants,' May told me. 'They were all excellent musicians, so everyone could keep up, and it just evolved as we were going. I love being challenged in different scenarios, and I think Ed relished that too. That record is a document of one afternoon of pure, spontaneous, empathetic musicianship.'

● ● ● ● ●

Van Halen's sixth album did not emerge on 31 December 1983.

A nicely worded Warners advert on the front cover of the 7 January 1984 issue of *Billboard* magazine, however, alerted both fans and industry figures that new music was imminent from the label's most high-profile rock band. 'Van Halen *1984* is here,' it read. 'We're talking big, brother.'

The following week's issue recorded that the album's lead-off single, 'Jump', had debuted on the Hot 100 at number 47, sandwiched between the Kenny Rogers/Dolly Parton duet 'Islands in the Stream' and Bonnie Tyler's 'Take Me Back'. The 21 January issue of the trade mag carried one of the first press reviews of the set:

'Pasadena's platinum quartet strikes again in a market riper than ever for their raucous hard rock. Funnier and more versatile than most of their metal brethren, they add traces of modern rock – notably Eddie Van Halen's prominent use of synthesizers for the title overture and chordal dressing elsewhere – without diluting the classic guitar focus of the band. David Lee Roth's vocal mien remains as salacious as ever, even without the usual off-the-wall cover tune, and production is typically strong. "Jump" is already off to a strong start, and this set will follow suit.'

1984 was finally released on 9 January, debuting on the *Billboard* 200 at number 18. Given the circumstances in which it was made, it's astonishing just how cohesive, coherent and confident it sounds across its nine tracks, even as it shifts from synth pop ('Jump' and 'I'll Wait', co-written with Michael McDonald from the Doobie Brothers) to hard rock (the lairy, lascivious turbo-shuffle 'Hot for Teacher' and the AC/DC-inspired 'Panama', featuring the growl of Eddie's Lamborghini revved to 8,000 rpm, wherein Roth trolls critics who claimed he wrote only about women, partying and cars by delivering a lyric that could be about all three subjects, or one of the above) to space-age blues ('Top Jimmy', written about Los Angeles club legend James Paul Koncek, leader of Top Jimmy and the Rhythm Pigs) and stadium-friendly jazz fusion ('Drop Dead Legs', likened by Eddie to 'a jazz AC/DC' and boasting arguably the most outrageous solo of his career). While Eddie deserves the lion's share of the credit for facing down Templeman and refusing to allow anyone to subvert his

singular vision, the whole band stepped up magnificently under considerable pressure, and *1984* sounds (ironically) like
the work of a fully unified, integrated collective driving forward with a shared belief and unstoppable momentum. 'This
is no mere arena-rock band,' noted *Rolling Stone* in a four-star
review of the album. 'And *1984* is the album that brings all of
Van Halen's talent into focus.'

On 25 February, the anthemic 'Jump' knocked Culture
Club's 'Karma Chameleon' off the peak of the *Billboard* Hot
100 and would remain the country's best-selling single for a
total of five weeks. Its parent album, meanwhile, took up a five-
week residency at number 2 on the *Billboard* 200, kept from
the summit, perhaps inevitably, by Michael Jackson's *Thriller*,
which, between 26 February 1983 and 14 April 1984, racked
up no fewer than thirty-seven weeks at number 1, with the Police, Lionel Richie, the *Flashdance* O.S.T. and, for a solitary
chart-topping week, LA hard-rockers Quiet Riot offering the
only challenges to its hegemony.

'Of course, everyone blamed me,' Eddie told CNN. 'They
said, "If you hadn't played on 'Beat It' that album wouldn't be
Number One." We'll never really know who helped who more. I
do know that when I played on his record, it helped expose Van
Halen to a different audience.'

Roth claimed that he only learned about his bandmate's
cameo on *Thriller*'s third single when he heard 'Beat It' blasting
from a Mexican girl's pick-up truck in a parking lot outside
a 7-Eleven supermarket on Santa Monica Boulevard. 'I heard
the guitar solo, and thought, now that sounds familiar,' he recounted in *Crazy from the Heat*. 'Somebody's ripping off Ed Van
Halen's licks. It was Ed, turns out.'

In public, Roth laughed off the guitarist's moonlighting –
'What did Edward do with Michael Jackson? He went in and
played the same fucking solo he's been playing in this band for

ten years. Big deal!' – but, in private, he was seething, furious
at what he perceived, not for the first time, as Eddie's disloyalty
and disrespect.

Revisiting his feelings in his autobiography, he wrote, 'I said
to myself, hey, how many solo projects will he do while I stand
guard at the gate of dreams worth dying for here?' His resent-
ment festered even as the band took to the road once more.

The schedule for the quartet's North American tour was
daunting, with multiple nights booked at some of the country's
biggest sports halls and most storied music rooms: two nights at
New York's iconic 19,500-capacity Madison Square Garden on
30/31 March, three nights at the 19,000-capacity Meadowlands
Arena in New Jersey at the beginning of April, followed by two
nights at Detroit's 12,000-seater Cobo Hall. After seven shows
in Canada, the caravan was scheduled to hit America's west coast:
three nights at the 16,500-capacity Cow Palace in Daly City, two
nights at the Forum in Inglewood, then on to the Midwest and
southern states, wrapping with six nights in Texas, split evenly
between the Summit (16,000 capacity) in Houston and Dallas's
Reunion Arena (17,000 capacity). On a business level, capitalis-
ing on the band's assimilation into the mainstream made perfect
sense, but with fault lines already cracking the veneer of band
unity, Noel Monk, for one, must have looked at the lengthy, gru-
elling itinerary and wondered whether the four men he would
count off their (separate) tour buses as they arrived in Jackson-
ville, Florida, on 18 January would be the same four men he'd
welcome back on board in the early hours of 17 July, following
their final Dallas performance.

Valerie Bertinelli, too, was concerned: 'The fun and camaraderie was gone,' she noted. 'The party-time spirit was over.'

Monk can't recall exactly how far into the tour his band
were before he realised that Eddie had his own personal drug
dealer on the road. Van Halen's accountant had flagged up the

fact that the guitarist was drawing out large cash advances, which Monk knew from experience was indicative of either serious financial issues or a costly drug habit. Soon after, Monk identified the recurring appearance backstage of a man not on his crew payroll, and he quickly realised what the individual's purpose was. He chose to turn a blind eye, figuring that with high-grade cocaine on tap from a trusted source, the guitarist was less likely to spend the pre-show hours trawling unfamiliar neighbourhoods in unfamiliar cities in search of a connection serving up a 'product' whose purity could not be taken as read. Still, as he observed trusted crew members racking out thick slugs of cocaine on top of Eddie's amps before showtime night after night, Monk couldn't help but wonder where this might end. Touring with Van Halen had always been a blast, a non-stop party, but the atmosphere was now strained and combustible, with the band members, excluding the ever-stoic and dependable Michael Anthony, constantly bitching and whining about one another, and the tension spilling over onto the stage.

'It was obvious to anyone in their orbit that there were real problems between the band members,' says music writer Malcolm Dome. 'In May '84, I was in Vancouver doing a feature on [Swiss hard-rock act] Krokus, and they said, "Van Halen are playing tonight, shall we go?" We went backstage [at the Pacific Coliseum], and Roth had a huge set-up, almost a PA set-up, to play his music, while Eddie and Alex were almost cowering in the corner, not enjoying themselves one little bit and looking like they didn't want to be there. There was no connection at all between the musicians and Dave, the party animal. It was like they were completely divorced. There were four different limos sitting outside, and onstage it felt like David Lee Roth and his backing band. You could sense that there was genuine friction. They weren't hiding it at all.'

'I shot the band in Detroit and Houston, and I saw the two nights at the Forum in Los Angeles, and it was all about Edward,' recalls photographer Ross Halfin. 'In the early days, the gigs were all about Roth, because he was such a commanding frontman, but by then the centrepiece of the show was Edward's fifteen-minute guitar solo. By then, it was very much the Roth camp on one side and the Van Halen brothers on the other.'

Rolling Stone joined the tour in Cincinnati, from where writer Debby Miller filed an insightful, perceptive story for the magazine's 21 June issue, under the headline 'Van Halen's Split Personality: How a Geek and a Physique Created Thud Rock's Most Successful Oddsemble'.

'Most heavy-metal bands', she observed, 'have so little personality they have to come up with a gimmick to sell the act, but Van Halen has two larger-than-life characters. Dave is the guy MTV zeroes in on because he's charming, a joke machine, a man Eddie thinks ought to replace Johnny Carson someday . . . He's moody and indulges his temperament; one person in their entourage says, "We're *all* childish, but Dave hasn't been born yet."

'Eddie, on the other hand, is so shy he can't even dance,' Miller wrote. 'He just plays music; many consider him the most innovative guitar player since Jimi Hendrix.

'Eddie has a smile so sweet it ought to be on a rubber doll. You get the feeling that the smile and the guitar are the two things he's developed to fight off the world. But it still heaves in at him.'

During her interview with the guitarist, Eddie apologises for 'not being a good talker'. Miller tells him that he expresses himself just fine and asks why he has the impression he's not articulate enough.

'I guess it's been too many goddamn years I've been told that I'm stupid,' Eddie replied.

. . . . .

After the fourth leg of the band's North American tour wrapped
in Dallas, Van Halen had a month to recuperate ahead of flying to Europe to play five festival shows as support to AC/
DC, under the Monsters of Rock banner. Given the palpable
tension clouding their relationship, Eddie was surprised when
Roth chose to sit alongside him in the Concorde Lounge at
New York's John F. Kennedy airport ahead of their superson-
ic flight to London, and more surprised still when the singer
pulled a small cassette recorder out of his bag and passed him
a set of headphones, asking him to have a listen to the tape
within. As Roth pressed the device's 'play' button, he watched
the guitarist's expression switch quickly from curiosity to
confusion as he recognised the familiar sun-kissed melody of
'California Girls'. Eddie's initial thought was that the singer
wanted Van Halen to record a Beach Boys cover, but Roth
excitedly explained that he was going to release the song on a
solo EP, with Warners' blessing. He'd had the idea on a beach
holiday in Mexico, he revealed, and having run it past Lenny
Waronker, he'd tapped up Ted Templeman to record the song
and three additional covers – the Edgar Winter Group's 'Easy
Street', Louis Prima's 'Just a Gigolo'/'I Ain't Got Nobody' and
the Lovin' Spoonful's 'Coconut Grove' – during a two-day studio session at the Power Station in New York, alongside Edgar Winter and some jazz-fusion cats. With Van Halen due a
proper break, Warners were going to release the *Crazy from the
Heat* EP in January 1985 as a way of maintaining the band's
profile, Roth explained, and it would serve as a light-hearted
palate cleanser for the quartet's next studio album. He assured
the bemused guitarist that there'd be no overlap with Van Halen business, that his EP was designed purely to scratch an itch
and allow him to reconnect with some of the music he'd loved

before joining the band: Motown, Stax, James Brown, Ohio Players, Marvin Gaye, etc. He hoped Eddie would dig it. The guitarist handed back the cassette recorder in silence.

The Monsters of Rock festival, held annually at Donington Park in the East Midlands, had already acquired mythical status among British rock and metal fans by the mid-1980s. First head-lined by Rainbow in 1980, successive stagings of the single-day event had been graced by performances from AC/DC, ZZ Top, Whitesnake, Slade, Judas Priest and more. The 1984 event could lay claim to hosting the strongest bill to date, as it featured AC/DC, returning for a second headline bow, Ozzy Osbourne, back on home turf and riding high thanks to the success of *Bark at the Moon*, Belfast-born guitarist Gary Moore (now a solo artist following his on/off stints in Thin Lizzy), the Sunset Strip's lat-est feral hellraisers Mötley Crüe and Van Halen's old club-days pals, San Francisco's Y&T (formerly Yesterday & Today). Mak-ing their first appearance in the UK since 1980, Van Halen were tipped to steal the show; once more, with glory within their grasp, the quartet failed to rise to the occasion.

'Donington was a massive let-down,' says Malcolm Dome. 'It was supposed to be their day, playing the UK for the first time in four years, off the back of the biggest rock album of the year. But they just didn't deliver.

'Before they played, Dave tried to upstage an AC/DC photo call for the media backstage. He came out of his dressing room, put his big boombox on and began doing his warm-up exercises, expecting that everyone would go, "Oh, it's David Lee Roth!" and ignore AC/DC. In reality, it was the other way around: ev-eryone ignored Dave, and it was a bit embarrassing to see.

'It didn't get much better when they went onstage. Dave's quips didn't work, and the band seemed pretty listless. It wasn't like the crowd had an attitude because they were flashy Ameri-cans – Mötley Crüe were on the same bill, and they went down really well – but Van Halen just didn't live up to expectations.

In fairness, those expectations were probably so high that they couldn't possibly have lived up to what we all hoped for.'

Backstage, post-show, coked-up and drunk, Eddie was furious, raging about technical difficulties that had ruined the gig for him. Noel Monk recalls Valerie Bertinelli being so alarmed by her husband's outbursts that she fled the dressing-room area, fearful for her own safety. It wasn't an ideal time for a well-known photographer to stroll over to grab a few candid shots.

'It was a strange day for Van Halen,' says Ross Halfin. 'I remember shooting them onstage, and Edward was smiling at me, so I was smiling back. I went backstage to see them afterwards, and Eddie was hanging out with Neal Schon from Journey and John Entwistle from the Who, so I took a few photos. Then Eddie said, "Hey, fag, what's your fucking problem?" I said, "What?" And their tour manager said, "Oh, look, just ignore him." But he kept going, "What's your fucking problem, fag? Smiling at me like a fucking fag." He just turned completely nasty. I realised he was drunk, and when he was drunk, he could turn from the nicest, most charming guy to the most horrible person in the world. But I noticed, too, that he only acted like this when he had a security guard around, so that no one would thump him.'

The 1984 tour concluded not with a bang, but with a whimper, the quartet performing on autopilot as the Monsters of Rock caravan docked in Stockholm, Winterthur, Karlsruhe and, on 2 September, the huge Zeppelinfeld complex at Nuremberg. There were no end-of-tour celebrations, no champagne bottles uncorked, no group hugs exchanged ahead of the journey back to Paris to catch homeward-bound flights.

'We were all tired,' said Noel Monk. 'Tired of the travel, tired of the tour, tired of each other.

'The trip home at the end of a tour usually feels celebratory; this time I was filled with resignation.'

7
LOVE WALKS IN

It's 31 December 1984, and MTV is hosting its 4th Annual New Year's Eve Rock 'N Roll Ball live from New York City. Former Runaways guitarist Joan Jett is set to make her live TV debut with the Blackhearts during the four-hour broadcast, Duran Duran, Frankie Goes to Hollywood, UB40 and Whoopi Goldberg are among the invited studio guests and, co-hosting alongside MTV's petite, perky, star VJ Martha Quinn, 'Diamond' David Lee Roth is ready to share a world-premiere screening of the video for his debut solo single, 'California Girls', with an estimated worldwide audience of 42 million 'screaming, beady-eyed, slack-jawed, drooling party monsters'.

'I bring a message to all of you from Edward and Alex and Michael and all the rest of the Van Halen travelling circus and animal act tonight,' Roth, resplendent in a black tuxedo, white bow tie, red and white gloves and white-rimmed shades, tells the pumped-up studio audience. 'Tonight is an excellent time for everybody to make your new year's resolutions . . . and the midnight hour is soon upon us . . . You know it's a dog-eat-

dog world out there, rock fans, and now's a good time to de-
cide whether you're going to be a hot dog . . . or a little wiener.
'I have chosen to remain a little wiener for one more year,'
Roth declares. 'Have a good time, baby!'

Evidently pleased with this bon mot, Roth would repeat the
line on network television on 2 January, as *Late Night with...*
talk-show host David Letterman's first studio guest of 1985.
Having aired a segment of the 'California Girls' video and asked
Roth to confirm or deny some tall tales from a recently published unauthorised Van Halen biography, Letterman casually
asked, 'You're doing solo work . . . does this mean that the band
will soon be breaking up?'

'No, no, no . . .' Roth protested.

'That happens, you know . . .' said Letterman.

'That does happen,' Roth conceded. 'That's the *Spinal Tap*
story. No, I still have very strong tribal instincts, and we'll be
going into the studio, like, the middle of this month to start arguing again, and we'll come back out with an album sometime
this year. Hopefully . . .'

The *Billboard* 200 chart for the week ending 5 January 1985
saw Van Halen's *1984* at number 39, on its fiftieth week on the
chart; with over five million copies sold, it was America's sixth-
best-selling album of 1984. Two weeks later, in the week ending
19 January, Roth's cover of 'California Girls' debuted on the
Billboard Hot 100 at number 43; on 2 March, it would peak on
the chart at number 3, behind REO Speedwagon's 'Can't Fight
This Feeling' and Wham!'s number 1 single 'Careless Whisper'
(credited to 'Wham! featuring George Michael').

Thrilled as he was, Roth dismissed any suggestion that this
success might precipitate his exit from Van Halen, pronouncing
himself 'perfectly content' within the band. 'It's just that there
ain't enough time in Van Halen's day for me to sing and dance
as much as I want,' he explained. 'I saw it as an opportunity to

kinda spread my wings in directions the Van Halen band will not go.

'I'm not going solo. I'm ready to go back in the studio with those guys and argue my way into the Top 10 again.'

Though the quote was delivered with a wink and smile, Roth admitted that relationships within Van Halen had changed over time.

'Right now, in real life, I never see Edward,' he told *San Francisco Chronicle* journalist Ben Fong-Torres. 'I never call him; he doesn't call me. On the road, we get along great. We have a mutual thing going then. In the studio, fine. In the office?' Roth shrugged indifferently. 'Eh.

'It's business conflicts. The wealth and power we have has different effects on different people. We get a big swell when we're not doing anything; when everybody has a chance to sit around and dwell on things for a while, then they start complaining.'

It was, perhaps, no coincidence that in a contemporaneous conversation with writer David Gans for *Record* magazine, Roth bluntly hinted that the continuation of Van Halen was no longer about four music-obsessed kids getting together to make noise and party hard; more than just a band, Van Halen was now a brand, a business.

'We have a commitment to making rock music with our rock band, for years and years and years,' he stated. 'The way to make that happen is to make new music at frequent and regular intervals. We *have* to make a new record – it's that simple.'

Writing sessions for the seventh Van Halen album were volatile from day one. 'The chemistry had turned rotten,' said Roth. 'There were constant delays and screaming. It sounded like a sack of sick cats.

'The arguments became more and more vehement, loud and venomous, with threats, hands balling into fists.'

Exactly what happened next remains a matter of debate. Roth claimed the new music Eddie was writing was melancholy and morose; Eddie said Roth had no interest in hearing it anyway. Roth said the Van Halen brothers wanted to scale back the group's touring plans and promote their next album with just a handful of stadium shows. 'He was the one who suggested not doing a record and just cashing in on the summer circuit,' Eddie shot back. Roth claimed that Eddie told him the album would take a year to make; the guitarist didn't deny this, but said he was taking a helicopter view of the whole process, estimating that between writing, recording and mixing, plus conversations about artwork, merchandise and tour scheduling, a year would fly by. '[He] put it in the press like I just wanted to rot in the studio for a year,' the guitarist fumed. In April, against Roth's wishes, Eddie and Alex fired Noel Monk from his role as Van Halen's manager. Eddie would later claim that Monk was Roth's 'goddamn puppet'.

The fast-deteriorating situation was further complicated when Roth, buoyed by positive feedback for his directorial work on the 'California Girls' video, wrote a film script, titled *Crazy from the Heat* and centred around a rock star named Dave, and began to actively seek financial backing to fund shooting. The singer detailed the proposed storyline of *Crazy from the Heat* – 'a musical with a very left-of-centre plot' – in his autobiography of the same name with a gravitas worthy of Francis Ford Coppola. However it may have sounded in his head, on paper the synopsis makes for a truly excruciating read. Roughly summarised, the story would revolve around a nefarious scheme by Dave's crooked managers to swindle the rock star out of his earnings, a plan they could only launch once Dave had been shipped off on a post-tour vacation to the fictional 'Dongo Islands' – 'your worst Third World' – where the hapless innocent and his pals would stumble into 'cannibal country' and face a fate worse than death. Somehow, Dave's original managers, honourable men who'd been shafted by the aforementioned evil, unscrupulous 'suits', would get wind of his new handlers' wicked plot and seek to warn him of their villainy, only to happen upon a Japanese criminal cartel that is financing unethical and highly illegal experiments aimed at isolating brain serum which, when synthesised, would give geeky white people the gift of rhythm. Dave would become embroiled in this twisted stratagem when the conspirators identified 'some problem with crossing the races' and determined that the only suitable guinea pig to experiment upon would be a white guy with rhythm . . . 'and they can't think of anyone but Dave'.

Astonishingly, someone at CBS Pictures loved the idea and pledged $10 million to green-light the project, a testament to the strength of both Roth's public profile in 1985 and the cocaine the Medellín Cartel were flying into Los Angeles in the mid-1980s. Feeling vindicated by the studio's support, Roth duly announced to the Van Halen brothers that he was taking a sabbatical from the band.

'I can't work with you guys anymore,' Eddie recalled Roth telling him in a showdown at his Pasadena mansion. 'Maybe when I'm done with my movie, we can get back together.'

'I ain't waiting on your ass!' the guitarist snapped back. 'So long, and good luck!'

· · · · ·

On 3 July 1985, some Van Halen fans thought they were getting a preview of the band's seventh album from an unorthodox source, when a blast of the guitarist's trademark 'shredding' featured in a pivotal scene in time-travelling sci-fi feature film *Back to the Future*, wherein Marty McFly, played by Michael J. Fox, slips a cassette marked 'Edward Van Halen' into a Walkman and wakens his sleeping father with a high-decibel alarm call. Geeky debates over whether or not this 'bunch of noise', as Eddie described it, was or wasn't a new Van Halen song were, however, almost instantly overshadowed when, on 4 July, American Independence Day, *Rolling Stone* reported that 'Van Halen is on permanent hold'.

'Eddie, who's rumored to be scouting around for a new lead singer, is writing songs with Patty Smyth and planning to collaborate with Pete Townsend [*sic*],' the shock story revealed. 'As for David Lee Roth, he intends to pursue an acting career full time and is developing his own movie.'

Official confirmation of the news was slow in coming. But, in August, Eddie broke ranks and admitted to *Rolling Stone*, 'The band as you know it is over.

'Dave left to be a movie star,' the guitarist explained. 'He even had the balls to ask if I'd write the score for him. I'm looking for a new lead singer.

'It's weird that it's over,' Eddie said. 'Twelve years of my life putting up with his bullshit.'

Ted Templeman was working on Aerosmith's 'comeback' album *Done with Mirrors* when news of the split broke. The producer assumed the argument would quickly blow over . . . until word reached him as to the identity of the singer Van Halen were lining up to replace Roth.

As concerned musician friends rallied around him in the wake of the news of Roth's exit, Eddie's first instinct was to re-emerge into the spotlight with an all-star 'various artists' compilation album, featuring the likes of Joe Cocker, Phil Collins and Journey's Steve Perry voicing his songs. Alex Van Halen talked his younger brother out of the idea, encouraging Eddie to seek out a gifted vocalist who could restore balance and harmony to their musical family. The notion of a possible

collaboration with Pete Townshend was also abandoned, partly because the Who's guitarist wanted to work in London and
Eddie was loath to exclude Alex and Michael Anthony from
the project, but more prosaically, because Eddie lost Townshend's home phone number. Instead, Eddie began focusing
his energies on trying to charm a family friend into the fold.

It was Valerie Bertinelli who initially brought Patty Smyth to
her husband's attention. The actress had become mildly obsessed
with New York rock band Scandal's 1984 hit 'The Warrior', and
when she saw that the quartet were co-headlining the Hollywood
Palladium with John Waite later that year, on 7 November, she
asked Eddie to take her. The guitarist went one better, joining
Scandal onstage for their cover of Ike and Tina Turner's 'River
Deep, Mountain High' and Scandal's own 'Maybe We Went Too
Far', then taking Valerie backstage to meet vocalist Patty Smyth.
The trio got on so well that Eddie and Valerie flew out to see
Scandal at two Texan shows the following week, with the guitarist again joining the New Yorkers onstage for their encores.
Smyth would later visit the couple in Los Angeles on several occasions, staying over in the family home even when Valerie was
filming out of town. When Roth departed, Eddie asked Smyth
if she might consider trying out for his band, but with the singer, then married to New York punk pioneer Richard Hell, pregnant, the timing was hardly ideal. Rejecting advice from Warners to park his band and work on a solo album – 'If they think
I'm going to experiment and futz around, doing a solo project
as opposed to what I really want – just to wait and see if Roth
comes back – they're off their nut,' he vented – Eddie's entreaties to Smyth continued as late as 27 July 1985, when he invited
the singer, then eight months pregnant, to join him and Valerie,
Late Night with David Letterman band leader Paul Shaffer and

musician friends for dinner in New York, following the couple's appearance on the chat show.

'He said, "Look, I gotta know. You gotta tell me now,"' Smyth recalled. 'And I said, "I can't." He definitely wanted me to do it. He asked me over the course of a year, several times. But when he really needed the answer, I just was not ready to move my whole world to California . . . I didn't see that as my immediate future. I wish he had just said, "Hey, let's just do a record, we can call it whatever." But the way that he asked me made it seem like I had to move to California, and I just wasn't hormonally in the right mindset for that.

'Eddie was ballsy and smart, and that was a pretty ballsy idea, especially for rock 'n' roll, which is so sexist. He was just like, "You're a badass. You can do it." And I'm like, "I *know* I can do it, but I'm eight months pregnant!"

'I think we would have completely crushed it. I think that the fans and everybody would have responded well, because they trusted Eddie and they loved him – like, he knew what he was doing. There may have been some scepticism in the press or whatever, sure, but I think that we would have crushed all of that.'

· · · · ·

Ultimately, and somewhat appropriately, Van Halen's second act would begin at a repair shop for high-end vehicles. Based in Van Nuys, former Ferrari test driver Claudio Zampolli had built up an enviable reputation, and clientele, as a seller of imported luxury automobiles and the go-to mechanic for the clueless Valley millionaires who collected them like baseball cards. While having Zampolli look over his Lamborghini Countach, Eddie's eye was drawn to a Ferrari 512 in the shop.

'Nice car,' he said. 'Whose car is that?'

'Sammy Hagar's,' Zampolli replied. 'You should call him and get him in the band.'

'You got his number?' Eddie asked.

Resting up at home having cancelled a scheduled summer tour of Japan in support of his Ted Templeman-produced album *VOA*, Hagar was expecting the call.

'I'd been working with Ted Templeman, conjuring up another record, and he was telling me about all the bad blood in Van Halen,' he recalls. 'He'd be saying, "Oh, boy, those guys, man, they've got a lot of problems." And when Ted said, "I think Roth is gonna leave the band," I thought, "They're going to call me."

'I mean, look, this is one of the biggest rock bands in the world, who can they get? They can't just get some kid off the street, because Roth was too big of a character. I thought, "Well, there's Ronnie James Dio, there's Ozzy Osbourne and there's Sammy Hagar, and that's about it." I couldn't have imagined Dio in Van Halen, Ozzy was a mess back then, and I was playing two nights in almost every arena in America. So I just thought, "They gotta call me." I'm not saying I'm psychic, but I get feelings about things, have done my whole life, and I just knew.'

As with David Lee Roth, Hagar was not a man overburdened with self-doubt or lacking in self-confidence. Born on 13 October 1947 in Salinas, California, Hagar was just fourteen years old when he first stepped onstage with a band, fronting the Fabulous Castilles, and just twenty-five when he knocked on Ronnie Montrose's front door in Sausalito, wearing a silver suit and glam-rock boots, to ask the former Van Morrison/Herbie Hancock guitarist if he'd like to start a band.

'I never lacked confidence,' says Hagar. 'Once I had a band and started performing in front of people, I thought, "This is what I'm here to do, and I'm good at it." I wasn't arrogant, but I never lacked self-belief. I was a kid who wanted fame and fortune so bad that he would have done *anything* to get it. I'd seen

Ronnie the night before playing at a sold-out Winterland with the Edgar Winter Group, who had one of the biggest albums in the country at the time [1972's *They Only Come Out at Night*], and so to me Ronnie was a big rock star and my ticket to the big time. I had real belief that I could make it.'

Impressed by Hagar's confidence and chutzpah, Montrose decided to hear the kid out. Within days, the pair had amassed an album's worth of songs and committed to forming a new band.

'The chemistry between Ronnie and I was fantastic at first,' says Hagar. 'We could write a song in twenty minutes. He wasn't a songwriter – he basically had one riff, for "Rock the Nation" – but I had a bunch of songs – "Make It Last", "I Don't Want It", "One Thing on My Mind", "Bad Motor Scooter" . . . – and I showed him the lyrics to "Space Station #5", and we wrote that together instantly.'

Soon after, Ronnie Montrose called Ted Templeman and asked if he could arrange a meeting to talk about a new band he was putting together. Templeman had worked with Montrose on Van Morrison's *Tupelo Honey* album, liked the San Franciscan guitarist, and was reminded of Cream when he listened to Montrose's demo. By the summer of 1973, he'd installed the band at the Sunset Sound and Amigo studios to record their debut album for Warners. By his own admission, Templeman was 'flabbergasted' when *Montrose* failed to connect with US rock fans, peaking at number 133 on the *Billboard* 200. On the road, supporting acts such as Black Oak Arkansas, Foghat and Humble Pie, Hagar remained buoyant, however – 'I would have loved to have had overnight success, but the prospect of hard work didn't bother me, because with my poor, blue-collar working-class background, I only knew how to do things the hard way,' he says – and was encouraged by reports that the album was selling steadily in Europe. Touring the continent for the first time in support of the group's second album, 1974's *Paper*

Money, the singer was convinced that the quartet's big break lay just beyond the horizon.

'I remember we played in Belgium, and we were reviewed in a national newspaper and they printed my photo,' he says. 'I wanted to feel special, and getting that attention makes you feel like a somebody, so I was really happy. But it flipped Ronnie out that I was the focus of the review. His ego couldn't take it.'

Days later, ahead of a brace of sold-out shows at the Olympia in Paris, Montrose informed his singer that he was breaking up the band.

'It felt like I'd been punched in the gut,' says Hagar. 'Ronnie was getting more and more distant, so I knew something was coming, but it was devastating. I was so disappointed. It was so unexpected, and so wrong, that I really couldn't figure it out. I resented it terribly. I didn't have a penny in the bank, and I'd a wife and a baby at home, so it was a pretty insecure time. Ronnie could be a piece of work.

'That band never got past the sophomore stage, never graduated; what you heard from us was infantile, barely hatched out of the egg. If we'd held it together and grown up together, we could have made some great music and become a great, great band. But Ronnie decided otherwise.'

Equally dismayed by the band's implosion, Templeman advanced Hagar the money to make a demo tape for Warners but opted to pass on signing the singer as a solo artist.

'It was disheartening initially,' says Hagar, 'because Ted was very powerful at Warners, and all his projects got attention. But with hindsight, it was a blessing in disguise, because I had to go back to square one and do it all over again by myself. I was naive and innocent and made mistakes, but it set me off on my own path.

'I think I do my hardest work, and get the best results, when I've got a little bit of "I'll show you sons of bitches!" in my head.

I think that's good for any artist or any elite athlete. It's healthy to be a little pissed off. You need some kind of fire.'

By the time Templeman reunited with Hagar to work on 1984's *VOA*, the 'Red Rocker' was on a roll. Signed to Geffen Records by A&R hotshot John Kalodner, Hagar scored a platinum album with 1982's *Standing Hampton*, his first release for the label, and landed a first Top 20 hit with the first single from 1983's *Three Lock Box* album, 'Your Love Is Driving Me Crazy'. With an iconic video featuring the singer's Ferrari 512 being pursued by the California Highway Patrol, 'I Can't Drive 55', the first single from *VOA*, reached number 26 on the charts and pushed its parent album past the one-million sales mark within the year. Which was right around the time Eddie Van Halen got in touch via the phone at Claudio Zampolli's repair shop. Out of curiosity as much as anything, Hagar agreed to a meeting.

'He said, "Wow, this could be something,"' Eddie recalled to Steven Rosen. 'He wanted to come down to meet us first and see what kind of condition we were in. Because he'd heard some horror stories about my being . . . way out there, a space case. He came down with Ed Lefler, his manager. We said, "We don't just want to do a project with you. We want you as a permanent member of the band."'

'At the time I was thinking, "What am I going to do now?"' Hagar recalls. 'At that point in my life I was looking for a reason to go on. I'd come from such a poor background and worked so hard my whole life, and I was always fame- and fortune-driven, but I had plenty of fame and fortune at that stage, with four platinum albums in a row and selling out double arenas in almost every city in America. I was thinking, "I don't need any more money, and I don't need any more fame." I was wealthy, I was eating in the finest restaurants and wearing the finest fucking clothes, I was driving Ferraris. I was becoming a little too sophisticated, and it was killing my music.'

Hagar turned up to Van Halen's 5150 studio in a pressed Armani suit, wholly unprepared to discover that the biggest hard-rock album of the past twelve months had been conceived and recorded in a facility that looked and smelled like 'the worst bar on the planet'.

'These guys had cigarette butts and empty beer cans and whisky bottles everywhere, multi-thousand-dollar guitars lying upside down on the ground,' he recalls with a laugh. 'It stunk like shit because of the smoke. Eddie comes walking out with a pair of sunglasses, jeans with holes in them, just outta bed, cracking a beer and smoking a cigarette. Alex was still drunk. Mike hadn't even been home. They'd been up all night waiting for me. I'm looking at these guys, then I'm looking at myself in a suit, and I go, "I look like a fucking idiot." This is a real rock 'n' roll band.'

Hagar had first met the members of Van Halen in 1978, when the two bands shared afternoon stage times at the Black Sabbath-headlined Summerfest at Anaheim Stadium on 23 September, the gig notable for Roth, Anthony and the Van Halen brothers pretending to parachute into the stadium. Backstage, Eddie told Hagar that the band used to perform Montrose songs during their club days. Hagar, for his part, recalls thinking that the guitarist was 'one of the nicest, sweetest, humblest rock stars on the planet'.

'From the outside, I was impressed by Van Halen,' he says. 'What I liked about them was that they wrote hard-rock pop tunes. Eddie's guitar-playing was so musical, and because he used major chords, it was very unique, very cool, edgy but sweet. It was almost wimpy and heavy at the same time. It was Ted Templeman and Donn Landee's production that made the band sound heavy, and in the same way that [Led Zeppelin drummer] John Bonham always made Jimmy Page sound heavy, so Alex always made Eddie's playing heavy, even when he was playing cutie-pie riffs. I didn't like Roth's antics. I didn't see how any guys could like him, but I guess they did. It's like [radio host] Howard Stern once said: "If David's biggest fans ran into him in a bar, they'd kick his ass!"'

There was no love lost between the two singers. At the dawn of the decade, when Roth wondered aloud to a journalist 'quite what manner of a man was Sam, writing songs only about cars and not women', Hagar responded by calling Roth a 'faggot' and suggested that Van Halen's frontman wanted a 'relationship' with him. ('Sammy definitely has a social problem,' Roth fired back in 1982. 'I think it's based on lack of education.')

'Dave always hated Sammy,' Eddie later revealed to Steven Rosen. 'I never understood why. Dave would always talk shit about him: "Ahhh, that little mother, he ain't got nothin' on me." I'd wonder, "Where's that even coming from? Why the animosity?"

'But I'll never forget the first song we jammed on with Sammy. It was "Summer Nights". Donn Landee had the tape rollin'. When we listened back, it was like, "Holy shit. Where have you been all our lives?"'

'We just cranked up,' recalls Hagar. 'They had written some ideas for the music to "Summer Nights" and "Good Enough", and I just start scatting and singing. Alex is making fun of my haircut 'cause I'd just had most of it shaved off, apart from a little poodle poof on top. And I'm going [jokingly], "Fuck you guys, let's step outside . . ." We ran cassettes all day, recording what we did. I got home at two in the morning and played one of these cassettes, and it was so rock 'n' roll. I went, "Fucking wow!" When I heard how musical Ed and Alex were, and how Michael could sing above me, it just sounded really fresh. I thought, "Wow, this is like Cream." It was really tasteful and melodic, and I thought, "This is wonderful, this is fucking good, this is better than what I can do on my own." I was looking for inspiration, and Eddie Van Halen brought me inspiration.'

'I'm doing it,' Hagar told Ed Leffler.

Regardless of the good vibes between the two parties and their shared desire to see where pooling their talents might lead, there was the small, but not insignificant, matter of Hagar being contracted to Geffen Records. An astute, savvy businessman, David Geffen knew that he held the whip hand when Mo Ostin came calling to discuss the idea of Hagar transitioning to Van Halen and the Warners stable, and conducted their negotiations accordingly. As Hagar recalls, Geffen were prepared to loan their biggest asset to Warners for one album, after which they wanted the rights to a new Hagar solo album. David Geffen asked for 100 per cent of the label profits on that solo album and 50 per cent of the cut on Hagar's first recording with Van Halen. 'Sammy, you have no fucking idea what you cost me,' Ostin would tell Hagar, when the horse trading was finally settled to the satisfaction of all parties.

In the autumn of 1985, Ostin accepted an invitation to see the newly formed quartet perform some new material at 5150. Having bet the farm on hard rock's newest supergroup, one can only imagine the grimace on the veteran music mogul's face when he stepped into the grimy studio to find the greatest guitar player of his generation standing behind a keyboard. The first song the quartet chose to air was the infectious, keyboard-driven 'Why Can't This Be Love'. When the song ended, the four musicians looked to Ostin for a reaction.

Smiling, Ostin licked his finger, held it in the air and declared, 'I smell money!'

The creative union between Van Halen and their new frontman was made public on 22 September, during Hagar's set at the inaugural Farm Aid concert, a huge fundraising event organised by Willie Nelson, John Mellencamp and Neil Young to help American farmers facing financial ruin, staged at the Memorial Stadium in Champaign, Illinois. On an incredible bill featuring Bob Dylan, Tom Petty and the Heartbreakers, Johnny Cash, John Fogerty, Roy Orbison, Joni Mitchell, Billy Joel and more, Hagar, Foreigner and Bon Jovi were the only hard-rock acts scheduled, and Hagar had an ace up his sleeve, with Eddie waiting in the wings to join his band for a set-closing cover of Led Zeppelin's 'Rock and Roll'. The impact of this big reveal was slightly dampened when, after Hagar introduced 'I Can't Drive 55' as 'a song for all you tractor-pulling motherfuckers', the live feed of the band's set was unceremoniously yanked from the TV and radio coverage, meaning only the more attentive members of the 80,000-strong crowd in the stadium would hear his good news. But 'Van Hagar' were now unchained.

With Ted Templeman booked to work on David Lee Roth's solo album, the new-look group required a new producer. Enter, at Hagar's suggestion, Foreigner guitarist Mick Jones, cautioned to expect the unexpected.

'Sammy said, "Mick, you and I have been around awhile,"' recalled Jones, '"but let me tell you, this is something else. Hold tight and enjoy the ride!"'

By way of an introduction, Van Halen opted to play the well-spoken, well-mannered English guitarist one of their heavier collaborations, the full-tilt, metallic 'Get Up'.

'I've never heard anything like that in my life,' Jones told them. 'It sounds like four guys fighting inside the speaker cabinets, beating the shit out of each other. I'm in.'

As the quartet set to work with Jones at 5150, Van Halen fans worldwide wondered what kind of future the band might have without their talismanic former lead singer. So, too, unable to keep himself from weighing in, did David Lee Roth.

'I don't know if there's a Van Halen without David Lee Roth,' he mused. 'But I know that nobody cares about Van Halen without David Lee Roth.'

Labelling Roth a 'clown', Eddie Van Halen responded in the most cutting terms. 'The problem with Roth was that he forgot who wrote the songs,' he noted. 'I wrote them. And the songs are the heart of our music. I never listened to his words. I couldn't have cared less what he was singing about.'

'I'm sure that Edward will play every bit as well as he ever has,' Roth conceded. 'I never said he was anything but a wonderful guitar player. He's just a shitty human being.'

8
FEELS SO GOOD

Ed Lefler fought hard to keep a smile from his face as Sammy Hagar, Michael Anthony and Eddie and Alex Van Halen trooped into his suite in Atlanta's Ritz-Carlton hotel and slumped, one by one, into their seats. Three weeks into a run of live shows projected to stretch from late March into early November, the four musicians were still finding their tour legs, still refining the daily routines and rituals that would serve to minimise anxiety, or at least blur reality, in the dead hours between hotel check-ins and gig stage times, before the familiar surges of adrenaline kicked in and all sense of decorum was abandoned once again. Hastily arranged early-afternoon band meetings with management were part of no one's plans.

Lefler stared in silence at his sullen charges for just a little too long, until an exasperated Hagar finally snapped.

'What the fuck, Ed?'

Lefler reached behind his chair and pulled a bottle of vintage champagne from one of the silver ice buckets he'd ordered up to his suite.

'*Billboard*. Number. One.'

• • • • •

Van Halen's *5150* album was released on 24 March 1986, pre-viewed, four weeks earlier, by the release of 'Why Can't This Be Love', the first song the quartet performed for Mo Ostin at Eddie's studio. 'Only time will tell if we stand the test of time,' mused Hagar in the song's most memorable, and tautological, lyric. The single's first-week sales, ensuring debuts in the Top 10 in the US, UK, Germany and Australia, were a solid start.

The quartet worked on *5150* from November 1985 through to February '86. For Eddie, the making of the album was 'a breeze'. The guitarist was particularly fulsome in his praise for his band's new frontman. 'I don't know if I could have gotten out of Dave what I can get out of Sammy,' he told Steven Rosen. 'I don't know if this is slandering Dave, but Sammy is just a better singer; he can do anything I ask him to do.

'He's changed my life. Seriously.'

'I think Roth's limitations as a singer had held Eddie back,' says Hagar. 'I mean, songs like "Dreams" had been sitting on tape for a year or two, and I can imagine that Ted Templeman said, "No, Dave can't sing that." So when I walked in, Eddie was digging through his cassettes and putting them on, and I'd go, "Wow, fuck, yeah, let's go!" Van Halen was able to go to another level. I think Eddie was frustrated with the former band, and probably it would have broken up. The feeling I got from him was that I was the saviour. We had amazing chemistry.

'Ed was freaking out when he heard me sing, Al and Michael Anthony too. They were going, "Holy shit, this guy has rhythm in his voice, he has pitch and a range from hell." I could pick up a guitar and say, "Hey, Eddie, how about a groove like this?" and play some rhythm, and he'd go, "Holy shit, let me play organ." We were all over the place. It was such an inspiration back and forth that it started elevating both of our musical abilities. Everyone around us got goosebumps. It was magical.'

Organised, calm, patient and encouraging, Mick Jones, too, played his part in the studio, trimming the fat from the original demo of 'Why Can't This Be Love' to accentuate its melodic hooks and co-writing and rearranging 'Dreams', drawing out a lifetime-best vocal performance from Hagar in the process.

'I was able to push Sammy to new heights,' Jones said. 'Literally. He was singing so high that he was hyperventilating. He almost passed out.'

As he revealed to *Classic Rock* writer Paul Elliott, Foreigner's leader took a different approach with Eddie, wisely letting the guitarist do his thing, aware of how he bristled when confronted by authority figures.

'There's not much I could have done to improve Eddie's performances,' Jones said. 'He was completely out there – not drug-wise, he just went into this trance state as he played.'

In such moments, Jones was reminded of the times he spent in the company of Jimi Hendrix in the late 1960s, when Jones was the guitarist for French rock 'n' roll superstar Johnny Hallyday and the American guitarist was the opening act on a European tour.

'When I worked with Eddie, it was the first time I'd met a guitar player who had a similar gift,' Jones noted, 'who had that thing running through him from up above.

'He was just a great guy, very humble. No pretence or airs or attitude. I was mesmerised working with him.'

'We had a good time together,' Jones told *Rolling Stone*. 'We used to race cars after the sessions . . . a selection of high-end sports, racing cars and zoom along Mulholland. He had a Lamborghini. I think Sammy had a red Ferrari. And I had a good old American car. I whipped him several times!'

There was only one real wobble during the process, an echo of the darker days in the creation of *1984*, when Donn Landee had what Jones diplomatically referred to as 'a bad moment'.

'He locked himself in the studio and threatened to burn the tapes,' Jones revealed. 'It was a stand-off for almost a day – like one of those situations where somebody's going to commit suicide. He was very highly strung. But in the end, we talked him down.'

With the album out of Landee's clutches and safely in the can, the quartet began pre-release promotional duties at 5150 with national and international media outlets. English music writer Sylvie Simmons, a long-time supporter who'd first interviewed the band when they supported Black Sabbath in 1978, was one of those summoned to Eddie's studio complex for an audience with the new-look quartet. Talk inevitably turned to the group's former frontman. Initially, Eddie and Alex were tactful, gently batting away the journalist's enquiries and constantly steering the conversation back to express the positivity shared here and now by the band. Eventually, though, Alex tired of pussyfooting around the subject.

'I guess you're going to print this anyway,' he said, 'so I'm going to say it: basically, when Roth was around it was his world. Everybody was afraid to breathe the wrong way with that character around.'

'Not afraid . . .' Eddie interjected.

'Horseshit!' Alex said brusquely. 'That was the truth, man. He told everybody how to dress, he told us how to walk and how to talk. He wouldn't let anyone get a word in edgeways.'

'The guy is an asshole,' Eddie eventually conceded.

· · · · ·

The polished, glossy professionalism of *5150* was never going to appeal to everyone. Some long-time fans lamented its lack of spontaneity, the dearth of humour, the absence of any sense of genuine danger, folly or adventure. For better or worse, the grown-ups had taken over. Hagar wasn't blind to the criticisms – 'I know there are people who're like, "Oh, I liked early Van Halen better, Sammy ruined it," but this was the music that Eddie presented to me,' he stated, on the defensive for once. 'I wrote the lyrics and melodies, but this was the music Eddie wanted to make' – but took vindication from the album's sales figures. Without a single promotional video, *5150* sold a million copies in just two weeks, knocking Whitney Houston's self-titled debut album off the top of the *Billboard* 200 in its third week on sale. Hagar summed up the band's feelings with just three words: 'We felt invincible,' he said.

Behind the public triumph, however, lay a private tragedy. In January 1986, much to Eddie's delight, Valerie learned that she was pregnant. In March, after experiencing severe discomfort, she visited a doctor, who informed her she had lost the baby. Adding to her pain, Valerie convinced herself that the miscarriage was a punishment from God for a brief fling she'd had the previous year, when at a low ebb after being starved of attention from her husband.

Further anguish was to follow. On 24 May, ahead of a second sold-out Van Halen show at the Alpine Valley Music Theatre in East Troy, Wisconsin, Eddie and Alex received phone calls from home informing them that their father Jan had suffered a severe heart attack. A private jet was chartered to fly Valerie and the brothers back to California, and the trio went straight to the hospital where Jan was recuperating. Typically upbeat, Jan tried to make light of his condition, assuring his boys that he'd be discharged and back on his feet in no time. With Van Halen committed to arena shows through to 3 November, maintaining a constant presence by Jan's bedside was not an option for his sons, but over the course of the next five months, the brothers racked up tens of thousands of air miles as they used every available gap in the tour schedule to return home to monitor their old man's recovery. But on 9 December, with his wife Eugenia and his two sons by his side, Jan passed away, aged sixty-six.

Jan's death hit his youngest son particularly hard, and Eddie's alcohol and cocaine usage escalated dramatically, the guitarist locking himself away in his studio to self-medicate for days at a time.

'Every day', Valerie Bertinelli wrote in her memoir, 'seemed to become more and more of a battle, whether we were fighting each other, or just battling the sadness of life.'

In an open-hearted interview with women's magazine *Redbook*, Bertinelli spoke candidly and courageously about the issues the couple were facing, her concern for her spouse evident in every line. 'He doesn't abuse me, but he hurts himself,' she stated.

In June, Roth had broken his silence on his exit from Van Halen in a no-holds-barred interview with *Creem*'s Dave DiMartino, as he and his new band – guitarist Steve Vai, bassist Billy Sheehan and drummer Gregg Bissonette – were completing work on his debut solo album with Ted Templeman. With his former band first out of the blocks in terms of releasing new music, Roth clearly felt the need to grab a few headlines ahead of his album's scheduled July release.

'The guys go on about how they were so miserable for these past 10, 12 years, the music was substandard, now they're gonna go on, and everything is just wonderful . . . Poor Edward Van Halen— forced to live a lie! Struggling to survive the onslaught of Maseratis! Forced to survive Lamborghini after Lamborghini! Can you *imagine* the mental stress the poor kid must be feeling? Except he's *not* a kid anymore, he's 30 years old.

'You don't go bullshitting the public like that,' Roth spat. 'You don't treat your fans like that. A great part of Van Halen was – it *still is* a big part of me, you know? My heart was completely and totally into that band, my whole life dedicated to that band. You just don't go on and treat the public as dummies – you know, mindless word drool poured all over pages about how it "stunk." "Yeah, we hated it," "Dave forced us to do it" . . . Big bad Dave.'

'I said a few things in anger, you know, that I should apologise for,' Eddie admitted to *Rolling Stone*'s David Fricke that same summer, while insisting that he was genuinely saddened by the demise of the original line-up.

'I cried, I was bummed. I slagged him in the press because I was pissed, and I was hurt.'

Roth was unmoved.

'Now that they realise how ugly their little hatchet job on me is reading, now Edward turns that impish little, "Ohhh, I'm so sorry,"' Roth mocked. 'I don't buy it. I don't think the public does, either.'

Introduced by the fabulous swagger of 'Yankee Rose', with former Frank Zappa sideman Steve Vai in dazzling form, Roth's *Eat 'Em and Smile* was a fine hard-rock debut, the album peaking at number 4 on the *Billboard* 200 in late August. But if he imagined that his solo career would eclipse that of his former band – and he surely did not doubt this for one hot minute – he was mistaken: when the time came to take *Eat 'Em and Smile* on the road, he faced half-full arenas that his former comrades had filled twice over earlier in the year. There was more than a hint of desperation in the singer's decision to stage a press conference in Toronto in October 1986, raging against his perceived belief that Van Halen were demanding rigid 'love us and hate him' loyalty from fans torn in their affections.

'I'll rise to the challenge,' Roth insisted, directing his next comment towards Eddie. 'If we have to have a comparison, fine – I'll eat you for breakfast, pal . . . eat you and smile.'

Back in California, terrified that her grieving husband's self-destructive impulses would see him follow his father into an early grave, Valerie issued Eddie with a stark ultimatum: either he dismiss his drug dealer and promise to quit drinking or she would walk away from their marriage. Still numb and immersed in self-pity, Eddie simply watched her go.

As the new year dawned, unwilling to give up on the man she loved, Valerie decided to stage an intervention for her estranged husband. It was an emotional and painful encounter, with an outraged Eddie feeling betrayed, victimised and bullied as his bandmates, family and closest friends took it in turns to implore him to seek help for his alcohol and substance abuse issues. But when passions cooled, the guitarist accepted that his behaviour was threatening to derail all he had lived and worked for, and he agreed to check himself into the Betty Ford Clinic in Rancho Mirage, California, for treatment.

'It's hard to confront someone,' says Sammy Hagar. 'Unless someone is ready to change their lifestyle, you're not going to change it for them, you're not going to convince them, especially a rich and famous rock star. They're going to be like, "Fuck you, you're fired!" if you try to interfere with their lifestyle or habits. When you're rich and famous, most people don't tell you shit, anything you do or say is OK, so you can get away with murder. No one can make those drastic changes until they're ready. I remember talking to Ted Templeman, and he said, "Until you hit bottom, no rock star who's having their ass kissed is going to change anything; it's only when they lose everything that they wake up." And he's damn right.

'At that time both Eddie and Al had a real drinking problem. I saw it, but the reason it didn't alarm me initially was because when we stepped up to the instruments, they could play. These guys could get drunk and play well, so I'd be like, "Wow, there is no problem here." And if we said, "Be at the studio tomorrow at noon," they were there, even if they'd stayed up all night to do it. With alcoholism or drug addiction, you can totally get away with being a rock star. I'm sorry to say it, but you can. You can't if you're a construction worker and you're up every day at five o'clock in the morning to drive a truck, but rock stars are spoiled rotten.'

'At first, Sammy thought Alex and I were drinking because we were so excited to have a singer, that we were celebrating,' Eddie told the *Seattle Post-Intelligencer*. 'Then he realised that that's the way we were every day. I think he was a little scared.'

'I didn't drink to party,' he insisted to *Billboard*. 'Alcohol and cocaine were private things to me. I would use them for work. The blow keeps you awake, and the alcohol lowers your inhibitions. I'm sure there were musical things I would not have attempted were I not in that mental state.

'I was an alcoholic, and I needed alcohol to function.'

In April 1987, after a 'lost' period in the wake of his father's passing, Alex too sought help for his alcohol dependency.

'I over-partied,' he confessed. 'I got home [from the *5150* tour], and we had three months to kill. I just went out and tied a big one on. The guys in the band had the guts to say, "We don't want to see you dead, trust us. You should do something." I was out there.

'Alcohol is funny. It's socially acceptable and part of partying, but it can turn on a dime and get its hooks into you.'

That same spring, Sammy Hagar set to work on the solo album he owed Geffen, roping in Eddie as co-producer. Completed in ten days, with Eddie playing bass and contributing just one guitar solo (on 'Eagles Fly'), *I Never Said Goodbye* would become Hagar's highest-charting solo album, peaking at

number 14 in mid-August. The following month, Van Halen returned to 5150 to begin work on their eighth studio collection.
Self-producing alongside Donn Landee, the quartet approached
the recording with a new-found maturity and a sense of brim-
ming confidence instilled by the six million domestic sales of
5150. This, arguably, was their downfall. Having seen off Roth,
silenced the doubting voices at Warners and demonstrated that
they didn't need their mentor Ted Templeman's guiding hands
or golden ears to deliver commercial success, it's entirely understandable that there was little hunger or urgency firing the
group's songwriting during the leisurely seven months they
spent on *OU812*. By his own admission, Hagar worked best
with a vengeful 'I'll show you sons of bitches!' fire inside, and as
he flitted between his property in Malibu and his holiday home
in beautiful Cabo San Lucas, on Mexico's Baja California Pen-
insula, there was little to rile the self-possessed musician. Eddie
wanted to title the album 'Rock 'n' Roll' – 'That's what it is,'
he said. 'It ain't heavy metal, it's not hard rock, it's rock 'n' roll'
– and he had a point, for across its nine tracks the set dabbles
with raunchy blues ('Black and Blue'), Zeppelin-esque grooving
('Cabo Wabo'), classic VH power-boogie ('Source of Infection',
part of the same lineage as 'I'm the One' and 'Hot for Teacher')
and synth pop ('When It's Love'), without ever getting wild or
threatening to upset the neighbours. On an album designed to
consolidate the group's broad appeal, the only genuinely interesting curveball is the finger-picked acoustic country blues of
'Finish What Ya Started', a song written after Eddie coaxed his
Malibu neighbour Hagar out of bed at 2 a.m., with a bottle of
Jack Daniel's whiskey in one hand and an acoustic guitar in the
other. As with a number of other songs on *OU812* – 'Source of
Infection', 'Black and Blue', 'Sucker in a 3 Piece' – 'Finish What
Ya Started' is blighted by Hagar's creepy, middle-aged sex-pest
lyrics – 'not my best stuff ', he acknowledged – but it's arguably

the only moment on a solid if unspectacular set when Van Halen aren't on cruise control. While Guns N' Roses were setting Los Angeles ablaze with the incendiary *Appetite for Destruction*, Van Halen appeared to be settling comfortably into producing the sort of tastefully manicured arena rock one might expect to hear soundtracking Don Simpson/Jerry Bruckheimer Hollywood blockbusters. As a mark of respect and gratitude to the man who'd shared their every musical dream, Eddie and Alex included the touching dedication 'This one's for you, Pa' on the album's inner sleeve, but, truthfully, there was little of Jan Van Halen's mischievous, maverick spirit present in its grooves.

Confident that the band had another multi-platinum hit album under their belt, it was Sammy Hagar who suggested to Ed Lefler that now was the time for Van Halen to make the leap to headlining stadiums. If Van Halen fanboys Mötley Crüe were deemed capable of drawing 60,000 rock fans to Oakland Coliseum as headliners of Bill Graham's (almost) annual Day on the Green festival in 1987, then surely Van Halen – 'the biggest band in the world', in Hagar's mind – could pull in similar-sized crowds all across the nation with their own bespoke festival package. That no one had ever attempted such a grand-scale undertaking before, Hagar reasoned, would only add to the sense of spectacle and enshrine Van Halen for ever as true legends of rock.

'Van Halen wanted to make rock 'n' roll history, basically,' said Louis Messina, the main man at Texan promoters PACE Concerts. As the promoter of Dallas's long-running and hugely successful Texxas Jam festival, Messina was a highly respected and well-connected player in the live-music industry, and it was to him that Lefler turned first when sounding out the feasibility of Hagar's ambitious idea. The promoter's initial response was encouraging: 'It's such a natural idea', he said, 'that I'm surprised no one's tried it before now.' Within weeks, he put some numbers before Lefler, proposing a twenty-eight-date, twenty-three-city tour to run from the end of May through to the end of July, for a potential audience of 1.7 million. With a suggested ticket price of $25, if *every* ticket sold, the gross box-office receipts would total $42 million. In conclusion, Messina said, packaged correctly, it could work. The next challenge was to secure a supporting bill that would make the event the hottest ticket of the summer.

The first name on the list was a no-brainer, as Van Halen and Scorpions had a history dating back over a decade. As a club band, Van Halen had performed covers of Uli Jon Roth-era songs such as 'Speedy's Coming' and 'Catch Your Train', and Scorpions duo Rudolf Schenker and Klaus Meine had partied with the young Californians when David Lee Roth celebrated his twenty-fourth birthday in Hamburg during Black Sabbath's 1978 *Never Say Die!* tour. Scorpions' 1985 *World Wide Live* double album had sold over a million copies in the US, and with the German quintet set to release their tenth studio album, *Savage Amusement*, in April '88, the timing was perfect. For the bill's middle slot, LA hard-rockers Dokken, featuring another familiar face, former Boyz guitarist George Lynch, seemed a safe bet: the group's fourth album, *Back for the Attack*, was certified platinum in January '88, while its singles – 'Dream Warriors', 'Burning Like a Flame' and 'Prisoner' – had been playlisted on rock radio nationwide. To open the show, Messina nominated Hamburg hard-rock quintet Kingdom Come, newly signed to Polydor, and already attracting attention for the blatant Led Zeppelin steals on their Bob Rock-produced debut album. To fill the show's vacant early-afternoon slot, Dokken's management, Q Prime, suggested Metallica, an uncompromising quartet from San Francisco who were fast outgrowing their 'thrash metal' roots: the group's third album, *Master of Puppets*, had sold a million copies worldwide without a single or video to promote it, and having proved their mettle on arena stages as the support act on Ozzy Osbourne's *Ultimate Sin* tour, James Hetfield and Lars Ulrich's band were seeking to strengthen their national profile ahead of the autumn '88 release of their much-anticipated fourth album, . . . *And Justice for All*. Messina was confident that the mix of acts would appeal to a broad cross-section of hard-rock/heavy-metal fans and proposed licensing UK promoter Maurice Jones's well-established Monsters of Rock brand name to knit the bill together. Lefler bit. Launching the history-making tour with a multi-band press conference at the King Kong Encounter attraction at Universal Studios in Los Angeles, the members of Van Halen talked up the tour as *the* live event of the year.

'When I was younger, I would have *killed* to go to something like this,' said Eddie, while Sammy Hagar expressed his hope that every ticket-holder would walk away from the nine-hour gig saying, 'That was the greatest show I've ever seen in my life.'

'The way I look at it,' said Alex Van Halen, weighing up the package, 'this tour is kinda like one big sandwich, you know? Which is the best, the first bite or the last? Who really cares, as long as you eat the whole thing?'

On every level, the Monsters of Rock tour promised to be an epic undertaking. To facilitate the three-shows-per-week schedule, Van Halen would have three complete stage sets, which would leapfrog one another across the country. The production would require 971 tonnes of equipment, including a 250,000-watt sound system and an 850,000-watt lighting system to illuminate the seven-storey stage – all this transported by fifty-six 48ft-long trucks. Heavy metal indeed.

For Eddie Van Halen, the trek would be significant for one simple reason: it would be his very first sober tour.

'I just asked the guys the other day if we could not have any alcohol backstage,' he told *Rolling Stone* in April 1988, as his group began rehearsals for the biggest tour of their career. 'The last ten years of my life I don't think I've been truly sober. I'd wake up, crack open a beer before I'd eat anything. I've been trying to clean up my act . . . I went to Betty Ford and the whole bullshit, because it worked for my brother. He's been sober a year in April. I've been sober for 20 days. And I'm starting to feel the light at the end of the tunnel, starting to feel good.

'The thing is, you can't do it for other people,' he added. 'You know, my dad died a year ago December, from drinking, and he asked if we'd stop drinking and shit, and partying, and I tried to do it for him. I tried to do it for my wife. I tried to do it for my brother. And I didn't do any good for me. After I got out of Betty Ford, I went on a drinking binge, and I got a fucking drunk-driving ticket on my motorcycle.'

In the same week that *OU812* debuted at number 1 on the *Billboard* chart, the Monsters of Rock tour launched with a three-night (27–29 May) stand at the Alpine Valley Music Theatre, Wisconsin, in front of an aggregated audience of 96,768. Not every show would be so successful: in Oxford, Maine, a day of torrential rain ensured that only around a thousand hardy souls stuck around to watch the headliners at the Oxford Plains Speedway, while a proposed second show at Giants Stadium in New Jersey was shelved due to poor ticket sales, which Louis Messina called 'the biggest mystery in the world'. Los Angeles was more welcoming, with a tour-high attendance of 80,144 filling the Memorial Coliseum on 24 July. But here, on home turf, the California quartet were unceremoniously upstaged, with Metallica stealing the show.

When the band's founding members, James Hetfield and Lars Ulrich, initially moved from Los Angeles in February 1983 to take up residency in San Francisco, they left behind a city almost wholly indifferent to their musical charms. Five years on, LA's metal community welcomed back their prodigal sons with a reception bordering on frenzy. Their first stadium show in the city dissolved into chaos while their intro music, Ennio Morricone's 'The Ecstasy of Gold', was still playing. Initially, it was just those closest to the stage who left their allocated seats to rush to the front, but soon thousands more fans began streaming from the stands to join them, trampling down fences and knocking over security personnel. Five songs in, the band were forced to quit the stage for their own safety as yellow-shirted security staff struggled to contain an audience that was now hurling safety barriers, seats, bottles, plastic glasses and anything else it could lay its hands upon.

'Nothing Van Halen did [on] Sunday altered the earlier impression that Metallica is making the metal of the moment,' *LA Times* reviewer Steve Hochman noted, 'and likely the future.'

The band made a similar impression on Sammy Hagar.

'Metallica will be the new kings of rock,' he predicted, 'just you wait and see.'

As touring in support of *OU812* wrapped, Van Halen's frontman was undergoing something of a crisis of confidence. Noting that his second album with the band had sold roughly half as many as *5150*, a still impressive four million copies, Hagar admitted to thinking, 'Maybe the honeymoon's over.'

Drinking heavily again, Eddie, too, was feeling listless and uninspired. The final night of the 1980s would end in ignominious circumstances for the guitarist who'd done so much to shape its sound. Spending New Year's Eve in Malibu with his wife's family, Eddie's mood darkened with every shot of Jägermeister he downed, and he decided to bail on the celebrations before midnight. Aware that her husband was in no fit state to drive, Valerie attempted to hide his car keys, and a tussle broke out between the pair. When Valerie's father tried to intervene,

Eddie got increasingly aggressive, and backed off only when his father-in-law landed a sweet right hand on the side of his face, cracking a cheekbone.

Valerie took her dazed husband to the nearest hospital, where the circumstances leading to his injury were explained. The doctor examining Eddie's face told him the injury would heal, but cautioned, 'You might want to check yourself in someplace and get help.'

Prepared to listen to an authority figure for once, the guitarist would spend the first twenty-eight days of the dawning decade back in rehab.

9
FIRE IN THE HOLE

The smart money was on Nirvana.

The anarchic 'high-school pep rally from hell'-themed video for 'Smells Like Teen Spirit' didn't merely introduce Kurt Cobain's band to the mainstream and serve as a launch pad for the 30 million global sales of the Aberdeen, Washington, trio's major-label debut album *Nevermind*; it also became a canvas on which faux-concerned cultural commentators could project their ideas and opinions, however half-formed, about the escalating sense of alienation, frustration and joyless ennui gripping Generation X. Beyond being credited for ushering in a new Year Zero for rock music – a questionable and, at best, short-sighted assertion in itself – Samuel Bayer's riotous promo clip was also believed to say Important Things About Who We Are, in a profound manner that Mötley Crüe's video for 'Girls, Girls, Girls', for example, could not match (albeit both videos featured extras sourced from the same Sunset Boulevard strip clubs). 'This was the sound of psychic damage,' *Newsweek* noted, 'and an entire generation recognised it.'

When the video received four nominations at the 1992 MTV Video Music Awards, including, most significantly, a place on the shortlist for the night's top honour, Video of the Year, hopes of Cobain's band collecting at least one coveted 'Moonman' trophy ran high in the offices of their record label, Geffen Records, and their management team at Gold Mountain. Not least because, nominated alongside Nirvana and LA funk-rock knuckleheads Red Hot Chili Peppers, the two remaining acts on the shortlist – Def Leppard (nominated for the Bart Simpson-inspired animated video for 'Let's Get Rocked', from 1992's *Adrenalize*, their second US number 1 album) and Van Halen (nominated for the rather more arty promo clip for 'Right Now', from their third consecutive number 1 album, *For Unlawful Carnal Knowledge*) – were members of the generation of 'old-school' hard-rock bands who, the media maintained, would be vanquished for ever by the Nirvana-helmed grunge/'alternative' rock revolution.

The youngest and oldest bands on the Video of the Year shortlist were, perhaps, not as far removed from one another as they might have appeared on a surface reading. Though Kurt Cobain would frequently tell music writers that the first band he ever saw in concert was LA hardcore godfathers Black Flag, in reality it was Sammy Hagar, touring his *Standing Hampton* album, who first rocked Cobain's world as a seventh-grader, at Seattle's Center Coliseum on 18 March 1982. Cobain's (almost certainly embellished) memories of the night include pissing himself en route to the gig, getting high and setting himself on fire with a Bic lighter when he attempted to hold a flame aloft during one of the set's emotive power ballads. Cobain and Hagar shared another bond: each hated every minute they spent making the videos for which they were being feted by MTV. Famously, Cobain was furious with director Samuel Bayer for the entirety of the 'Smells Like Teen Spirit' shoot, believing, not incorrectly, that the director had diluted a storyline which he had envisaged as a cross between the Ramones' 'Rock 'n' Roll High School' and the 1979 teen movie *Over the Edge*, a film Van Halen had actually been asked to write music for, back in the day. For his part, Hagar believed the treatment conceived for 'Right Now', with director Mark Fenske's thought-provoking text overlaying the visuals, was 'bullshit', and he maintained a policy of sullen resistance throughout the shoot in Chicago.

'I thought: *how dare they?*' he seethed.

'I had pneumonia and a 104-degree temperature,' he recalled. 'When you see me in the video folding my arms, refusing to lip-sync, it's because I was pissed off. The director's going, "Oh, that's great!" When I slammed the door into the dressing room at the end of the video, that was for real. I was pissed off.

'Mo Ostin, the chairman of Warner Bros. Records, called me personally when he heard I hated it. He goes, "Sammy, this is going to be the biggest video you've ever had." I go, "You're crazy. This stinks." I didn't want to talk about it.'

In total, the video for 'Right Now' received seven nominations, making it the most nominated video of the night. Mark Fenske and Mitchell Sinoway had already picked up their trophies for Best Direction in a Video and Best Editing in a Video for their work on 'Right Now', when Van Halen were announced as the Video of the Year winners.

Eddie was only half joking when he told *Guitar World*'s Steven Rosen that it 'took 13 years' to write 'Right Now'. The guitarist had composed the song's basic structure on piano in 1983, envisaging it coming together in a manner similar to Joe Cocker's version of Traffic's 'Feelin' Alright', as heard on the Yorkshire-born singer's 1969 debut album *With a Little Help from My Friends*. He recalled that 'nobody wanted anything to do with it' at the time, and Sammy Hagar wasn't feeling it either when Eddie put forward the idea during writing sessions for his band's ninth studio album, which began in March 1990, a full thirteen months after the *OU812* world tour concluded in Hawaii.

'I just couldn't hear Joe Cocker singing over what he was playing,' Hagar admits. 'We weren't fighting or anything, we just couldn't hear what the other guy was hearing, so it'd be like, "OK, no problem, next . . ." and we'd work on something else.

'I had the lyrics to "Right Now" from the beginning, and I kept singing them to Eddie, saying, "Think of it as a stadium song, imagine a whole stadium of people singing it with their hands in the air." But nobody was really buying it. So then one day Eddie is in one room playing the piano, and I'm next door playing pinball, and I'm singing, "Right now . . ." and I realised I was singing to what he was playing. I went running in to him, singing it, and we both went, "Yeah!" And Andy Johns, the producer, was like, "Fuck, yeah! That's great!" I've goosebumps on my arm remembering this, because it was such a crazy miracle that it took more than six months for those two ideas to come together; usually when Eddie played me a piece of music, I had a melody and lyrics for him the next day. So that was really unique, a special moment for a special song. It's like there were angels flying over our heads that day, saying, "What have we got to do to make these two hear this? Hit them over the head with a baseball bat?"

'"Right Now" is one of those songs that elevated Van Halen to a new level, which they'd never have got to with Dave,' Hagar adds. 'From four little punks coming out of Pasadena, yelling and screaming and playing loud, to writing a sophisticated song like "Right Now" is quite a path.'

Eddie had recruited English studio technician Andy Johns, best known for his engineering work with Led Zeppelin, the Rolling Stones and Free in the 1970s, to produce the album following a conversation with his brother.

'I can always make my guitar sound the way I like,' he explained to Jas Obrecht. 'To me, the main problem is always [the] drums. So, we sat down and said, "Who the fuck makes drums sound the way you like, Al?" He goes, "Well, Led Zeppelin." And who did all the happenin' Zeppelin? Andy Johns. So I called him up, he came over, and we just hit it off right off the bat. That guy is so rock and roll it's ridiculous.'

As Johns remembered, he had to call in sick on his first scheduled day at 5150, on 21 May 1990, as he'd been celebrating his fortieth birthday the previous night and was in no fit state to work. Initially, he recalled, the quartet were 'a bit paranoid' as to how the sessions might unfold, 'a bit suspicious', but after the powerful, propulsive 'Judgement Day' emerged from an early studio jam, the group let down their guard, with Eddie later hailing Johns as an 'inspirational' collaborator.

'He gets sounds that make you want to play,' he recalled. 'It's really that simple.'

'I had a house on Mulholland [Drive] and he lived on Coldwater, which was only two traffic lights [away],' said Johns. 'I'd get these phone calls at one in the morning... "Hey, Andy, you gotta get over here, I got an idea." "Ed, I'm in bed!" "Yeah, yeah, yeah, screw that, come over here." He was a spontaneous cat.'

For his part, however, Hagar recalls the making of the album as 'like pulling teeth'. The singer's wife, Betsy, was seriously ill, requiring twenty-four-hour medical care, and understandably, he was loath to leave her side and couldn't commit to a set schedule in the studio. 'It's really hard to concentrate when your wife is curled up in a ball on the floor, crying,' he noted. The singer was also much less enamoured of Johns' work ethic. 'He was bombed a lot of the time,' he recalled. 'He crashed his car into the studio wall. There started to be a little tension.'

When Johns accidentally erased a Hagar vocal track, the singer decided he'd had enough. At his insistence, Ted Templeman returned to the fold. 'Ted helped pull it all together,' Eddie admitted. 'It was great working with him again.'

Introduced, memorably, by Eddie 'playing' a Makita 6012HD power drill on opening track (and lead-off single) 'Poundcake', *For Unlawful Carnal Knowledge* was released on 17 June 1991 and debuted at number 1 on the *Billboard* 200, selling 243,000 copies in week one. It was also an international success, reaching number 12 in the UK and number 6 in Germany. A back-to-basics set, characterised by Eddie as sounding 'big and bad', the eleven-track album featured the dirty funk grind of 'Spanked' (surely the only major-league rock song ever written about phone-sex chat lines), the infectious pop rock of 'Runaround', which was given extra bite by Eddie's growling solo, and in 'Top of the World', a sunny delight to rival 'Dance the Night Away'.

It also saw the return of an Eddie Van Halen solo showcase, in the form of the sweet acoustic lullaby '316'. The track took its title from a calendar date: 16 March, the day in 1991 when Valerie Bertinelli gave birth to the couple's son, Wolfgang William Van Halen.

'Having a son is probably the most beautiful thing that's ever happened to me,' Eddie told *Guitar Player*. 'Obviously, I'm a little bit more responsible. Now I've got to wake up three or four times a night, and I'm legitimately burnt instead of just fucked-up burnt! He's just starting to smile and really being able to see things – it's such a trip! It's life!'

'Sometimes I caught Ed staring at Wolfie with a look of disbelief, as if he couldn't have helped create something that miraculous,' Valerie recalled. Less happily, she knew her husband had started drinking excessively again and braced herself for trouble ahead.

From its opening night in Atlanta, Georgia, on 16 August 1991, at least two members of Van Halen took the title of the F.U.C.K. tour rather too literally. Having spent months watching over his stricken wife, Sammy Hagar shamelessly 'took full advantage' of the debauched, hedonistic opportunities offered up as the nation's biggest hard-rock act rolled from city to city. In his 2011 memoir, *Red*, the singer admitted: 'I fucked everything that walked.

'I sent roadies into the crowd to bring back girls I pointed out. During Eddie's guitar solo, which was always about 20 minutes, I'd have five or six girls in my tent [under the stage], naked, all of us, having brutal sex while Eddie was out there doing his thing. When I went back out, I had to stuff my hard-on back in those tight pants.'

Eddie, too, was promiscuous and reckless, behaving, in the words of Hagar, like a 'dirty dog', flying female 'friends' across state lines when craving companionship. 'Everyone knew but me,' his long-suffering wife later confessed, embarrassed at her own naivety. On occasion, Eddie found his demons harder to hide. During one gap in the band's schedule, while on holiday with his wife, his son and mother-in-law in North Carolina the guitarist flew into a violent drunken rage, smashing up a rental car and leaving Valerie sobbing on the floor of the couple's beach house. In a bid to bring some stability to their increasingly joyless marriage, the couple agreed to undertake extensive therapy, individually and together. Encouraged to unburden themselves of shame and deceit, both admitted to incidents of infidelity and pledged to try to work out their issues.

The release, in February 1993, of a first Van Halen live album, *Live: Right Here, Right Now*, recorded over the course of 14 and 15 May 1992 at the Selland Arena in Fresno, California, bought some breathing space for a relationship, and a band, that was fast spiralling out of control.

Fortunately for Van Halen's leader and frontman, the eyes of the music industry were trained elsewhere. On 11 January 1992, Nirvana succeeded in accomplishing a feat beyond Van Halen's powers eight years earlier, when they knocked Michael Jackson from the top of the *Billboard* 200. Though no one paid too much attention at the time, on the day *Nevermind* replaced *Dangerous* as the best-selling album in America, another Seattle rock band chalked up a minor, yet significant, chart success. For Pearl Jam, news that their debut single, 'Alive', had broken into *Billboard*'s Hot Mainstream Rock Tracks chart at number 32 was never going to warrant the popping of champagne corks, but it served as a welcome indication that they had their own momentum. One week earlier, their debut album, *Ten*, had landed on the *Billboard* 200 album chart at number 155. It was clear that Nirvana's milestone achievement had set down a marker. 'It changed something,' said guitarist Mike McCready, a huge Van Halen fan from the moment, in 1979, when his guitar teacher played him 'Eruption'. 'We had something to prove, that our band was as good as I thought it was.'

Four months later, *Ten* was certified platinum by the Recording Industry Association of America, in acknowledgement of a million domestic sales. One year on, its sales figures eclipsed even those of *Nevermind*.

In the summer of 1993, mindful that Pearl Jam and Nirvana had new albums on the music industry's Q3 (third quarter, i.e. autumn) schedule, *Time* magazine approached their respective management teams with a proposal to put both Seattle-area artists on the cover of an autumn issue. Though often cast as bitter rivals in the media – a situation exacerbated by Kurt Cobain's tendency to rail against what he perceived as Pearl Jam's lack of punk-rock credibility – the camps had recently been reconciled, with Cobain and Pearl Jam frontman Eddie Vedder offering a tongue-in-cheek public display of their rapprochement by slow-dancing together backstage at the 1992 MTV Awards. Acutely aware of the additional hype that a *Time* front cover would generate, at a time when they were still tentatively adjusting to the pressures of unanticipated stardom, the groups took a bilateral decision not to participate in the magazine article. Despite this, to their intense displeasure, when the 25 October 1993 issue of *Time* was published, it featured Vedder on its cover, with a cover line hailing 'angry young rockers like Pearl Jam' for giving voice to 'the passions and fears of a generation'. One week later, Pearl Jam's second album, *Vs.*, entered the *Billboard* 200 at number 1, selling 950,378 copies in its first five days in the record shops, a sales record that would not be topped for five years.

Though music magazines continually tried to accentuate the differences between rock's new superstars and its old guard, Eddie Van Halen was a confirmed fan of Kurt Cobain. 'It was just his feel that moved me,' he said. 'There's no particular technical proficiency, but it didn't matter. I loved his voice and his songs. It came from his heart. It was real.' Eddie's admiration for Cobain's craft and spirit, however, would lead to one of the most embarrassing, and problematic, incidents of his career.

For Nirvana's Los Angeles-born touring guitarist Pat Smear, the opportunity to play Inglewood's storied 'Fabulous Forum' on 30 December 1993, as the final date on Nirvana's US tour promoting their album *In Utero*, was a dream come true, just as it had been for Eddie and Alex Van Halen in 1979. Formerly the guitarist with cult Los Angeles punks Germs, Smear was a huge Queen fan, so the idea of standing on the same stage where his hero Brian May had previously performed was almost beyond his comprehension. 'I was *dying*,' he recalled. Had he been warned in advance that he would find another iconic guitar hero, Eddie Van Halen, in Nirvana's dressing room preshow, Smear would have been awestruck.

'When I walked up to Eddie, he was talking to [Nirvana bassist] Krist [Novoselic],' the guitarist recalled. 'I just saw the back of his head, so I didn't know who he was. And Krist goes, "Oh, Eddie, you haven't met Pat? He's our new guitar player." Eddie turns around and sees me, but he doesn't say hello or anything. He just says, "Oh no, not a dark one." At first I thought he was kidding.'

To Smear, Eddie appeared 'drunk out of his fucking mind'.

'He kept asking me, "What are you? Are you like a Raji or something? Are you Mexican?"

'He started begging Kurt to let him play with us. It was so disgusting. He was like, "I'm all washed up; you are what's happening now." It was horrible. He kept saying to Kurt, "C'mon, let me play the Mexican's guitar!"'

Los Angeles film-maker Dave Markey, who'd become friends with Nirvana after meeting them while he was filming a documentary on Sonic Youth's 1991 European tour, released in 1992 as *1991: The Year Punk Broke*, was in the band's dressing room to witness Eddie's outburst. Aware that the guitarist was in bad shape, Markey tactfully turned off his camera, but later spoke about the incident to Kurt Cobain biographer Charles Cross, recalling how 'Eddie went into this racist, homophobic banter, typical redneck. It was surreal.'

A furious Cobain eventually brought the ugly encounter to an end.

'Actually you can jam,' he promised Eddie. 'You can go onstage after our encore. Just go up there and solo by yourself!'

'I was just shocked,' Smear recalled. 'I was thinking, "God, Eddie Van Halen hates me."

'Eddie Van Halen is the perfect example for me of not wanting to meet your heroes 'cause you'll be disappointed,' the guitarist concluded. 'I blame that incident totally on the alcohol. I've done a lot of bad things when I was drunk, too.'

Though he would never address, much less apologise for, this deeply unfortunate and unpleasant encounter, made all the more disappointing when one considers the racist abuse which he and his family had encountered in both Holland and America, Eddie's life was undeniably in free fall in the closing months of 1993, particularly after the passing, on 16 October, of the band's manager, Ed Lefler, aged fifty-seven, from thyroid cancer.

'He was like a father to us, a fifth member,' said Sammy Hagar. 'When he died, the thing that went through my mind was how vulnerable we really were because we trusted this man so much. And he made it so we didn't have to think about certain things. He kept the vultures, the wolves and the thieves away so we were free to just have fun, fun, fun. The only responsibility we had was to make a good record.'

Eddie took over the band's business affairs while they sounded out candidates to take the reins on a full-time basis. This was a level of responsibility for which the guitarist, at this moment, was both utterly unqualified and wholly unsuitable. As he and Alex met with, and summarily rejected, some of the most high-profile managers in the industry – Alice Cooper's manager Shep Gordon, Neil Young's Elliot Roberts, future Elton John manager Johnny Barbis – the pressure piled up, and cocaine and vodka could offer only temporary respite. It wasn't hard for family and friends to figure out the exact moment in the spring of 1994 when Eddie snapped.

'I was sitting around here with Tim Collins, who manages Aerosmith,' Eddie told *Rolling Stone* writer David Wild, 'guzzling a bottle of wine down. Finally, I said to Tim, "I'll be right back." I walked down to the house, grabbed my Norelco shaver and just shaved my head. Cut it completely off. I looked like an Auschwitz victim. I guess everything in my life all came to a head, literally. I was losing it. I was so frustrated and pissed off that I just didn't know what else to do.'

Desperate to alleviate his brother's anxiety before his mental health unravelled further, Alex Van Halen approached his brother-in-law, Rush's manager Ray Danniels, to manage the band, against Hagar's wishes. 'Sam was distant,' Danniels observed. 'He felt a loss of control.'

'We started arguing amongst ourselves, about everything, and pretty soon we just weren't getting along,' Hagar recalls. 'Everything started to fall apart.'

As tensions simmered, Eddie pushed for a return to the studio, hoping that, once again, music might provide sanctuary and solace in a time of trouble.

'The studio can be a place to go to get away from shit,' he said. 'It's very therapeutic.

'It blows my mind, each time. Even after eleven albums [*sic* – at this point VH had released nine studio albums], it's like we learn how to do it all over again. At first you don't really have much written, so you start focussing on jamming, and all of a sudden, things just start to happen. You never know exactly where it will come from... you just go into that zone, and let it flow.'

The problem was that this time, the music wasn't flowing. Conscious that the group might benefit from bringing in a producer capable of unlocking their creativity, Eddie spoke to Andy Johns, Mike Clink (producer of Guns N' Roses' *Appetite for Destruction*) and Bob Rock, before electing to work for the first time with Bruce Fairbairn, the Vancouver-born producer who had scored multi-platinum successes with Bon Jovi (*Slippery When Wet*, *New Jersey*), AC/DC (*The Razor's Edge*) and Aerosmith (*Permanent Vacation*, *Pump*, *Get a Grip*).

'We tried to find someone who we could get along with, mentally and musically,' said Alex, 'and just in terms of the general vibe. You're going to be in the studio with someone for eight hours at a stretch, and it can really be a chore if the personalities aren't right. There was something about Bruce . . . he commanded respect, but he also respected the band.'

'Being a producer is a very elusive job title,' Eddie remarked, 'part baby-sitter, part amateur psychologist. Bruce was different. He made us listen to our music from another perspective and with our added input, we ended up with more real musical insight than with most other producers we've worked with.'

The album sessions started in earnest at 5150 in June and wrapped at Vancouver's Little Mountain Sound Studios in October. Fairbairn sought to impose a strict schedule upon the band – 'Bruce just said, "Work, motherfuckers!" He's a serious guy,' said Eddie – but wasn't prepared for quite how fractious relationships within the band had become. Sammy Hagar maintained that Eddie, officially sober since October 1994, stashed bags of cocaine and bottles of vodka in the studio bathroom during the sessions, an accusation the guitarist furiously denied, though he did admit to drinking on occasion in order to facilitate re-recording certain guitar parts he deemed 'stiff' with a looser feel.

'I didn't drink too much,' he insisted. 'When we made the last record, I had at least 12 to 15 beers in me each day. If I got a little overboard, I'd say, "I'm outta here, I'm too far gone," and call it a day.

'I drink more when I'm playing and writing and working than when I'm not,' he admitted. 'For me, leisure time is not the problem area. My problem is that I go to the office to drink. It's completely ass-backward. And the only reason that I keep doing it, is because it still works, believe it or not. It just breaks down the inhibitions.

'It's easier for me to just let go and not judge what I'm doing. It's all about just opening up and being free.'

Against the odds, *Balance* measured up remarkably well against the other Hagar-era albums. Introduced by a record-

ing of chanting Buddhist monks, a left-field opening a lifetime removed from the screeching car horns prefacing 'Runnin' with the Devil' in 1978, the album mixed traditional VH
rockers ('Aftershock', 'The Seventh Seal'), another full-tilt
boogie-shuffle ('Big Fat Money'), a heartfelt Hagar elegy for
Nirvana's Kurt Cobain, who'd taken his own life in April '94
('Don't Tell Me (What Love Can Do)'), straight-up pop rock
('Can't Stop Loving You') and experimental instrumentals (the
John Cage-style prepared piano piece 'Strung Out', excavat-
ed from hours of tape Eddie had recorded in summer 1983
during a stay at film composer Marvin Hamlisch's Malibu
beach house, after he'd 'tricked out' the composer's Yamaha
grand piano with batteries, cutlery and ping-pong balls; and
Alex's rhythmic sound collage 'Doin' Time'). It also featured
a stirring full-band instrumental, 'Baluchitherium', titled by
Valerie Bertinelli in tribute to the largest land mammal of the
prehistoric age, and a neat, knowing wink to those who now
considered Van Halen rock dinosaurs.

'Dinosaurs are great,' Eddie said. 'Dinosaurs are huge, right?'

Released on 24 January 1995, *Balance* became the band's
fourth number 1 album in America, shifting an impressive
295,000 copies during its first seven days on sale. Two days
later, Eddie celebrated his fortieth birthday in Holland, during
a brief European promotional tour. The following day, 27 January, Van Halen premiered four songs from the album at a 'secret' gig for fan-club members at the Luxor Theater in Arnhem,
Holland, that was broadcast live on Dutch TV.

'It's about life being in balance,' said Eddie of the album's
title, 'and about how things have gotten out of balance.'

'It's a musical concept as well as a statement about what's
going on around us,' said Hagar. 'We're all looking for a little
equilibrium.'

On Valentine's Day, Eddie invited *Rolling Stone* writer David Wild to his home to conduct an interview for the 6 April issue of the magazine. When Wild arrived, the guitarist was out, dropping four-year-old Wolfgang off at school, leaving Valerie to entertain the journalist. To break the ice, Wild produced a copy of a just-published issue of *BAM* magazine, which included a high-school yearbook photo of Eddie.

'Isn't he adorable,' Bertinelli said with a smile.

'The thing I love about Ed is his heart,' she added. 'I don't know if you can understand that just by talking to him for a few hours, but the guy has the biggest heart in the world.'

When Wild asked if Valerie was confident that her husband's sobriety would hold up this time, she replied, 'If I wasn't, I wouldn't be here. Fourteen years living with an alcoholic is my limit.'

When the man of the house returned home and the interview began, Wild asked him the same question.

'It's not an alternative anymore,' Eddie insisted. 'Drinking does not work for me.

'During the recording of *Balance*, I'd be drinking these non-alcoholic Sharps and a couple real ones in between. All of a sudden, my mind and body started retaliating. It wasn't fun anymore. I'd wake up in the morning and puke. The next morning I'd wake up and have the dry heaves. And I'm realizing I'm a fucking alcoholic. I'd have to drink a six-pack to feel normal. I'm doing it for myself this time because nobody can tell you to quit.'

'You recently turned 40,' Wild noted. 'Was that traumatic for you?'

'Not at all,' Eddie responded. 'I feel 18. I don't feel any different...Listen, my dad played until he died. I think it's something you're born with. You're either rock and roll or you're not.'

The editors of *Rolling Stone* placed that quote on the cover of the magazine when it was published in April. By then, Van Halen were three weeks into an American tour promoting *Balance*, having launched the new album with an MTV Spring Break show from Pensacola, Florida, on 11 March. Performing in front of 9,000 fresh-faced college kids, the group looked their age. Alex Van Halen had collapsed in a hotel lobby on the day of dress rehearsals for the show, having ruptured three vertebrae while playing with his son, and Eddie was in constant pain too, having been diagnosed with avascular necrosis, a bone disease associated with alcoholism. His doctors recommended immediate surgery, but Eddie insisted that the show must go on. On 7 April, however, the tour ground to an unanticipated halt when Eddie was arrested at Burbank airport, ahead of boarding a United Airlines flight to Oakland, when a loaded gun, a .25-calibre Beretta, was found in his carry-on luggage. 'He was very cooperative,' said airport police chief Tony Lo-Verme. 'He stated he normally travels by charter, where you more or less do what you like. This time, he traveled by commercial aircraft and forgot to take [the gun] out.'

Briefly detained, and later charged with unlawful possession of a firearm, the guitarist pleaded no contest to the charge. On 13 April, he was fined $1,000 and sentenced to one year of probation. His gun, seized at the airport, was destroyed. Eddie later called the incident 'a stupid mistake'.

'We'd been traveling for a month on our own plane, and I carry a gun with me for protection,' he explained. 'I forgot to take it out of my bag on a commercial flight. It wasn't like I was trying to sneak it on the plane. I just totally spaced and forgot to take it out of my bag.'

He made no apology, however, for carrying the gun.

'Just two weeks ago at our house,' he said, 'there's a van out in front of my house for a week, with people stalking us. It happens all the time. The cops come up, they chase 'em away, they come back in the middle of the night. I don't know if they're just nice fans or if they're freaks. I have no idea, and I have to protect my family. So I carry a gun.'

• • • • •

Summer 1995 found Van Halen touring Europe for the first time since their final shows with David Lee Roth in the summer of 1984. Mindful that the group's profile in Europe had suffered during their long absence, Ray Danniels decided against booking a headline tour for the band and instead secured the group a slot playing as special guests to Bon Jovi in stadiums. If the decision made sense in pure business terms, ensuring that the group would perform nightly for audiences numbering between 40,000 and 80,000, the bill was a mismatch, with only a fraction of the headliners' fans paying Van Halen the slightest bit of attention.

As the opening band on the bill, Californian hard-rockers Ugly Kid Joe could sense Van Halen's mounting irritation and observed Eddie's behaviour becoming more erratic.

'It was getting silly,' recalls frontman Whitfield Crane. 'Bon Jovi made that tour harder than it needed to be. My only request on the rider was clean socks every night, but that was nixed by Bon Jovi's people. One day we were sitting backstage in Germany, and I was talking to Eddie, bitching, like, "Can you believe that motherfucker [Jon Bon Jovi] won't give me socks?" And Eddie just snapped. He said, "He won't give you socks?" And he just jumped up onto the table, pulled his shoes off and said, "I'll give you *my* socks," and pulled them off and handed them to me. When Eddie Van Halen is giving you his socks, you know your life is getting weird.'

On 4 July, Eddie was back at home in California, resting up ahead of the *Balance* tour's resumption in New Jersey in the middle of the month, when US tabloid magazine *The Globe* published a story from one Andi Remington detailing a torrid two-year affair with the guitarist. The article was accompanied by photos of the pair in Valerie and Eddie's bed, with Eddie naked save for a strategically placed MTV 'Moonman' and his guitar.

'What were you thinking?' Valerie's manager asked Eddie when the scandal broke.

'I'd had a couple of beers,' Eddie sheepishly replied.

The *Balance* tour limped on until 5 November, closing with a brace of shows in Hawaii. By now, the relationship between the Van Halen brothers and Sammy Hagar had deteriorated to the point where they were travelling separately to shows and staying in separate hotels. When Hagar expressed a desire to take some proper time off, Eddie told him that he was evaluating various options for his next creative project. 'I'll let you know if it involves you or not,' he said.

'OK,' said Hagar. 'Fuck you.'

The exact reasons why Van Halen parted company with their second vocalist are detailed and disputed. The 'Fall '96' issue of the band's unofficial but well-connected fanzine *The Inside* devoted three whole pages to a timeline of the break-up, citing Eddie's anger at Hagar releasing his *Unboxed* greatest hits album and the singer going 'off doing his solo fucking career when we were supposed to be close', the Van Halen brothers taking issue with Hagar's 'frat boy unleashed in the red light district' lyrics for *Balance* clunker 'Amsterdam', arguments over the band's participation in the soundtrack to disaster film *Twister*, and Hagar's vehement rejection of the idea of Van Halen releasing their own *Best of* collection.

On 16 June 1996, Eddie called Hagar at home and told him that he'd had enough.

'You never do what I ask you to do,' Eddie said. 'You're really stubborn. You're a solo artist in this band, so you might as well really be a solo artist.'

Depending on whose version of history you believe, Hagar responded with either a simple 'Thank you' or the more colourful reply, 'Fuck you, you fucking motherfuckers', and hung up the phone.

'Things had got very dysfunctional by then,' he told this writer in 2019. 'People in the band started changing...and it wasn't me and it wasn't Mike. Drugs and alcohol and insecurity and bad management killed that band.

'When I came in, Eddie and Alex were so happy, and so willing to make things work. Dave had totally led that band, but by the end their relationships were broken, and when I came in we wrote and played and laughed and partied and drank and had a great time. The first record [5150] went straight to number 1 [in the US], we sold out every building we played, and it was just like, "Wow! Wow! Wow!"

'Those early years were idyllic. We were having so much fun, and accomplishing so much – number 1 albums, selling out stadiums across America, picking up loads of awards. It was the never-ending honeymoon. The only negative I'd say was that we got so confident that we could do anything that it spilled into arrogance. And then Ray Danniels came in. I appreciate now what he was trying to do, but at the time I just wanted to break his neck, because he'd side with Eddie and Al on everything. There were so many decisions I didn't agree with. It's like, "We've had four consecutive number 1 records and now you want to make a *Greatest Hits*? You want us to support Bon Jovi?" Fuck that! Once Ray took over, that was kinda the end of Van Halen, certainly in terms of being on top of the world.

'But did I see it coming when Ed kicked me out? No, to be honest. I'd been in bands that got along worse than that, at least we weren't getting into fist fights on stage! I thought it was still good. I mean, we were living the fucking dream. I was driving Ferraris, eating at the best restaurants, drinking fine wines, taking beautiful vacations and really enjoying life to the fullest. But when the smallest amount of bullshit would come, I'd be like, "Fuck you, I ain't doing that!" In my head I'd gotten a little arrogant, like, "Fuck those guys, they can't do anything without me." I didn't want to get thrown out of the band, and I didn't want to quit the band . . . well, I did wanna quit the band, but I knew better. I just thought, "If we can make it through this year, maybe it'll all come back together." But, no, Ray Danniels had poisoned them against me.'

'I understand him being upset and angry,' Danniels told the media. 'This is a guy who somehow managed to blow being a member of the biggest American rock band, period, and he's smarting. But unfortunately, he's created the situation for himself. He's been his own worst enemy and continues to be.'

'And the next thing I know,' Hagar recalled, 'they'd got Roth back...'

• • • • •

'The band that made history in 1978 is making even bigger history in 1996, with possibly the biggest and most important musical reunion in our lifetime. Short of Elvis actually being alive, this rock and roll news is as big as it gets, folks.'

With these words, the editors of *The Inside* broke the news of David Lee Roth's return to Van Halen to its readership. 'Our sources say they are working on a day-by-day basis, focussing their energy on new music,' editor Jeff Hausman wrote. 'Equally exciting is the appearance of a new *rumour* that MTV had asked Van Halen to open the 1996 Video Music Awards with a live performance! If Van Halen has, in fact, decided to debut their new/old line-up live we're really in for a treat. The awards will air on September 4th, with or without Van Halen.'

After eleven years of bad-mouthing his former bandmates, on 14 June 1996, David Lee Roth phoned Eddie at home after being tipped off by Carl Scott at Warners that Van Halen were readying a greatest hits collection. From the highpoint of 1988's two-million-selling *Skyscraper* album, the singer's solo career had tailed off to the point where, in 1995, he was performing as a lounge act, David Lee and His Blues Bustin' Mambo Slammers, featuring Nile Rodgers and Edgar Winter, in Las Vegas casinos.

In the course of their initial conversation, Eddie mooted the possibility of Roth recording one new song, maybe two, for their upcoming compilation.

'The idea of the *Best of...*album came from Alex,' Eddie told this writer, 'because he'd read stuff from these thirteen- and fifteen-year-old kids on the internet who thought *Balance* was our first album. Alex said, "It's been twenty years, let's put together a couple of songs from each record in chronological order so that fans can decide what they'd like to buy from our back catalogue." Sammy wasn't into it at all, and he decided to go back to being a solo artist. Then I got a call from Dave. He wanted to know how he was being represented on the *Best of...*in terms of songs and pictures and whatever. After being on the phone for thirty minutes, I sensed a change in the guy, the LSD – that's Lead Singer Disease – had disappeared a bit. After a week or so, I decided to stop by at his house, and he really did seem different from the old Dave: maybe he'd been taking acting lessons.'

On 23 July, Eddie welcomed Roth back to his 5150 studio. 'No matter what happens,' Roth recalls the guitarist telling him, 'we're going to be friends, right?' Working with producer Glen Ballard, by 2 August the reconstituted band had recorded two new songs, 'Me Wise Magic' and 'Can't Get This Stuff No More' (a reworked version of *Balance* reject 'The Backdoor Shuffle'), and their prodigal-son frontman was itching for more activity, to the bemusement of his old friends.

'At the time, we had put out a press release, which said, "Van Halen are in the studio with Roth recording a new song for the *Best of . . .* album and are currently looking for a permanent replacement for Hagar,"' Eddie told this writer, 'but Dave just didn't want to believe what I was telling him. One day he told me he'd pulled a muscle, and when I asked how, he said, "Getting ready for the tour, man." I said, "What tour?" Every other day I had to ring him and say, "Cut the crap, Dave, or we're not doing anything."'

This being the case, the decision to appear with Roth at the MTV Video Music Awards at New York's Radio City Music Hall – not performing, as had been rumoured, but to present the Best Male Video award – was a bold one. Having been introduced by host Dennis Miller as 'three-quarters of one of the greatest rock 'n' roll bands ever', Eddie, Alex and Michael Anthony walked on stage to 'Runnin' with the Devil', before the audience spotted David Lee Roth bringing up the rear and rose to give the quartet a minute-long standing ovation. 'I think we're here to present the Best Male Video of the year award,' Eddie began, before Roth leaned across him and spoke into the microphone.

'No, no, no,' he said. 'Instead of the Best Award thing, we have to make an announcement. We have to address a subject here. This is the first time we've actually stood onstage together in over a decade.'

Eddie had to physically drag Roth away from the podium so that Michael Anthony could introduce the nominees, before Roth took centre-stage once more to announce Beck (for 'Where It's At') as the winner. As Beck made his acceptance speech, Roth continued gyrating and mugging for the cameras, to his bandmates' visible discomfort. The night went downhill from there. As the group quit the stage and entered the backstage media run, Eddie's attempts to stress the 'one day at a time' nature of the group's reunification were continually undercut by

Roth's overenthusiasm. At one point, after Eddie stated that the band would be doing nothing more until he went under the blade for his much-delayed hip surgery, Roth rounded on him and said, 'This night's about me, not your fucking hip!'

'Nobody ever talks to me like that,' Eddie spat back. 'You ever fucking talk to me like that, I'm going to kick you in your fucking balls, you fucking hear me?'

And with that, 'the biggest and most important musical reunion in our lifetime' was over.

• • • • •

If the world's press and the millions watching at home were confused by what exactly they were witnessing in New York, one can only imagine what thoughts were racing through the mind of North Dakota native Mitch Malloy as he watched the awards ceremony that night, having previously understood that he was to be Van Halen's new frontman.

Malloy's roller-coaster ride with Van Halen began when he received a phone call in the summer of 1996 from Steve Hoffman, Ray Danniels's assistant and formerly Malloy's day-to-day manager.

'OK, you can't repeat anything that we're about to tell you,' Hoffman said. 'Please sit down. Sammy has been fired and it's very top-secret.' He then told Malloy that he'd shown the Van Halen guys the video for Malloy's 1992 single 'Anything at All' and that Eddie was interested in meeting him. They had first-class plane tickets and a limo on hold; Malloy just needed to let them know when he was available.

At 5150, the band ran through 'Panama', 'Ain't Talkin' 'Bout Love' and *Balance* single 'Don't Tell Me (What Love Can Do)' with Malloy during a first rehearsal. Eddie then took him into another room, containing a grand piano, and asked him to sing *OU812* ballad 'When It's Love'. He also played Malloy rough sketches of some new songs he'd been writing, revealing that, after seeing a therapist, he'd finally begun to create new music while sober. On his third morning at 5150, the singer was told to be in the studio's control room at 8 a.m. for a band meeting.

'The door opened, and there was a silhouette of Ed, because the sun was shining,' Malloy told *Rolling Stone*. 'The door closes behind him and he doesn't step forward. He stays where he is. So, I'm sitting in the chair behind the console and he's maybe eight feet away, at the front door to the control room which leads outside. He stops and he goes, "Well, we just had a meeting." He goes, "You're the nicest guy I've ever met. Best singer I've ever heard in my life. Congratulations, you're in the band."

'I jumped out of my chair and went around the console, went down to where he was. He put his hands on my shoulders, hugged me, kissed me on both cheeks, said, "Congratulations!" Turns and walks out of the room. I go back up, sit down again at the console and my body's actually giggling. I can't control it. I'm giggling like a 12-year-old girl, and I actually uttered the words, "I'm in Van Halen." And that was that.'

As he watched MTV on the night of 4 September, however, Malloy knew in his heart that things had changed. 'That moment that Roth walked out behind them, I knew it was over. I am not going to be in Van Halen. I just knew.'

The following week, on 11 September, Malloy's manager Wynn Jackson sent a fax to Ray Danniels.

'Mitch has asked me to pass along his regrets that do [*sic*] to his strong commitments and excitement about his solo career in Nashville, he will have to respectfully pass on the opportunity to be considered as the new lead vocalist in Van Halen,' Jackson's fax stated. 'After spending time with Eddie and the guys,

Mitch feels a strong bond that he will carry with him throughout his life. Thanks again for the opportunity. Best of luck with
the endeavour and please pass along our best to the band.'

It's unlikely that Danniels lost too much sleep over Malloy's withdrawal, for by then, unbeknown to David Lee Roth,
he'd already set up one of his former clients, Extreme vocalist
Gary Cherone, with an audition to join Van Halen. When Roth
learned of this, he was outraged. On the morning of 2 October,
the singer sent out a fax, bearing the title 'An Open Letter from
David Lee Roth', to every major media organisation in America.

To Whom This May Concern,

You've probably heard rumours that Van Halen and I will not
be consummating our highly publicised reunion. And since neither
Edward, Alex, nor Michael have corroborated or denied the gossip, I
would like to go on record with the following: Eddie did it.

It's no secret, nor am I ashamed of my unabashed rapture at the
prospect of resurrecting the original Van Halen. A 'couple of songs'
was all I knew for sure when Edward and I got together three months
ago to write them. At that time, the band tip-toed around me sprin-
kling sentiments like, 'This isn't a sure thing, Dave; this doesn't mean
anything long term, Dave; we're still auditioning other singers, Dave.'
I was cool. I was happy. I was in the moment.

The next thing I knew, the four of us are doing a surprise walk-on
at the MTV Awards. I told Edward at that time that I didn't think it
was a good idea for the band to go to New York half-cocked; and that
I didn't want to imply by our presence that we were 'back' if in fact it
was just a quickie for old times' sake.

Well ain't hindsight always 20/20 . . . Had I asked for something
in writing, this wouldn't have happened. Had I acknowledged the
occasional icy grip in my stomach, maybe this wouldn't have happened. But I didn't. Like I said – rapture. And I love these guys. Do
I trust them? That question never entered my mind.

Then, a series of events last week led me to discover at about the same time the press did, that the band, along with their manager, had already hired another lead singer, possibly as long as three months ago. I wonder how he felt the night of the MTV Awards. It certainly explains why on that night Edward looked as uncomfortable as a man who just signed a deal with The Devil. I can't think of a reason Edward would lie to me about being considered for the lead singer when he had already hired someone, and then let me appear on MTV under the impression that there was a great likelihood that Van Halen and I were reuniting. As I said, I told him in no uncertain terms that I didn't want to do the MTV gig as a band unless we were, in fact, a band.

And so I apologize to my fans and my supporters, and to MTV. I was an unwitting participant in this deception. It sickens me that the 'reunion' as seen on MTV was nothing more than a publicity stunt. If I am guilty of anything, I'm guilty of denial. I wanted to believe it just as much as anyone else. Those who know me know that trickery was never my style.

Van Halen's response, delivered to the same media outlets within twenty-four hours, opened with a smackdown so brutal that World Wrestling Federation owner Vince McMahon could have signed it up on a three-year contract. 'We parted company with David Lee Roth 11 years ago for many reasons,' it began. 'In his open letter of October 2nd, we were reminded of some of them.

'The intention all along was to do two new songs with Dave for the *Best of Volume 1* package,' the statement continued. 'He was never led to believe anything but that. When the four of us were asked by MTV and Warner Bros. to present an award at the 1996 MTV Video Music Awards, the four of us agreed. Dave was never an "unwitting participant". We appeared in public just as we do before releasing any other Van Halen record. For the last two weeks we have been working with someone who we hope will be part of the future of Van Halen, although no final decision can be announced until contractual considerations have been resolved. Van Halen will go forward and create the best possible music we can.'

'We are not going to make this a nostalgia band,' Ray Danniels told live-music-industry magazine *Pollstar*. 'This is a band that's selling out arenas and sheds and coming off a record that's sold well over four million copies. They're a current band, whether David's the singer, or somebody else is. We're not going to trade that in.'

On 22 October, Van Halen's seventeen-track *Best of – Volume 1* compilation was released. It would become David Lee Roth's first and only number 1 album with the band. That same week, on 26 October, an interview with Eddie was published in the *LA Times*. Asked to reflect upon the events of a turbulent year, Eddie summarised the period for writer Chuck Crisafulli in just two words: 'Utter lunacy'.

When talk turned to Roth and Hagar, Eddie repeated one of his favourite phrases, diagnosing the pair as suffering from 'LSD – Lead Singer Disease', before stating that he didn't feel good taking cheap shots at their expense. 'They're both talented, we made a lot of good music together, and we had a lot of fun together,' he said. 'I still respect them both, but it's going to be hard to ever be friends again.'

Eddie would make just one appearance on stage in 1996, hosting a benefit gig at the Riviera Theater in Chicago on 17 November for one-time David Lee Roth guitarist Jason Becker, who had been diagnosed with amyotrophic lateral sclerosis (ALS, also known as motor neurone disease). He assembled a one-off supergroup, dubbed the Lou Brutus Experience in tribute to a Chicago radio host and featuring Steve Lukather, Billy Sheehan and Sheehan's Mr Big bandmate Pat Torpey, for the gig and recruited a supporting cast featuring hot young guitarists Marty Friedman, Tony MacAlpine, Richie Kotzen, Vinnie Moore and Zakk Wylde.

The Lou Brutus Experience played a thirty-minute set to close the seven-hour show, starting with a raucous cover of 'Wipeout', which led into covers of Led Zeppelin's 'Good Times, Bad Times' and Jimi Hendrix's 'Little Wing'. Van Halen's 'Ain't Talking 'Bout Love' followed, before versions of the Beatles' 'She's So Heavy' and Hendrix's 'Fire' brought the 2,300-capacity crowd to its feet. Closing out a challenging year for the guitarist, the gig was a welcome reminder that playing music could still be kept separate from the business of music.

Aware that the unseemly debacles with Hagar, Roth and – within industry circles at least – Mitch Malloy had rather damaged the 'good times, all the time' Van Halen brand, as the group began its third act with *Van Halen III* in 1998, they launched a major charm offensive on the media, inviting members of the Fourth Estate, this writer included, to interview the band, now featuring Gary Cherone, at Eddie's home. Their eleventh album was an eclectic affair, and very much Eddie's baby, with the guitarist playing bass and drums on several tracks, and even taking rasping lead vocals on its closing piano ballad, 'How Many Say I', on which he sounded not unlike Pink Floyd's Roger Waters.

When I asked Cherone if he was overawed at the prospect of joining America's biggest rock band, Eddie placed a fatherly hand on his shoulder and said, 'Let me answer that.'

'The first day he pulled up with his bag in his hand, I knew Gary was the right guy for Van Halen,' he said. 'He's very talented, very gifted, and a down-to-earth human being. Gary's very much like me, in that he's quiet and not really out-going, but he's always thinking.

'I believe that the man or woman upstairs put us both here to play music, and it feels like I've been waiting twenty years for this guy to come along.'

Van Halen III, Eddie declared, represented 'a whole new beginning for this band'.

'The Rolling Stones are pushing 60, and they're paving the way for us,' he said with a smile. 'We'll see who drops first. I'm a musician, and I'm going to be making music until I die.'

Talk turned to David Lee Roth's recently published, free-wheeling memoir *Crazy from the Heat*. 'I don't recommend that anybody follow this book as a blueprint for anything,' Roth wrote in its final chapter, titled 'Coda'. 'There's no answers here.'

'I haven't read the book,' Eddie admitted. 'He didn't send me a free copy. Someone from Japan rang me and said, "It's comedy fiction, right?" Maybe Dave thinks what he says is reality, but I know what happened in this room.

'Anyway,' he concluded, 'if I'm supposed to be such an asshole, why does he still want to work with me?'

Before our allotted time with the band expired, I felt obliged to confess that the publication I was filing this story for, UK rock and metal magazine *Kerrang!*, was about to run a pretty damning review of *Van Halen III*. Awarding the album a rating of just 1 out of 5 (or K out of KKKKK, to be true to the magazine's unique rating system), my colleague, and long-time Van Halen fan, Paul Elliott had written, 'The fundamental problem with this album is the songs. They're shit.'

Eddie took the news remarkably well.

'That's life,' he said with a shrug. 'It's a deep record, and I think people will get it if they give it a chance. We never set out to please all the people all the time, and when things are contrived, and you're not making music from the heart, you're double fucked if people don't like it.'

The world got the opportunity to hear *Van Halen III* for the first time on Thursday 12 March 1998, during a special live radio broadcast from the Billboard Live club on Sunset Strip, formerly the site of Gazzarri's. After fielding questions from host Tommy Nast and competition winners, the band left the stage, with Eddie mouthing the words, 'We'll be back.' Shortly afterwards, the curtain in front of the stage was drawn back, and the invited audience got to see the very first live performance by Van Halen Mk III. The set drew upon songs from the David Lee Roth era ('Unchained', 'Mean Street', 'Ain't Talkin' 'Bout Love') and from the quartet's new album ('Without You', 'Fire in the Hole', 'One I Want'), but, conspicuously, included nothing from the 'Van Hagar' years.

Released on 17 March, *Van Halen III* debuted at number 4 in the US, but failed to reach the UK Top 40, charting at number 43. By July, it had disappeared entirely from the *Billboard* 200; it would become the first Van Halen album not to reach platinum status. Unsurprisingly, when Eddie was interviewed for issue 11 of *The Inside*, he sounded thoroughly disenchanted.

'In LA, there's not one station that will play us,' he lamented. 'There's no AOR station, no adult-oriented rock station, that will play us. I'll be very, very surprised if they play us on Top 40 radio. A lot of radio stations, when they hear the name, they won't even give it a chance.

'I'll never forget hearing "You Really Got Me" at two o'clock in the morning, the very first time on the radio. I ran and woke up my mom and dad, going, "We're on the radio, we're on the radio!" It's like that every time. Except this time, it's like, the album's released, and . . . nothing. I have not yet heard anything on the radio. It's kinda depressing, you know? Like, "Wow."

'The new record is not a one-listen record, you know? There's a lot of depth to it, and a lot of diversity. To me, rock 'n' roll is freeform music, and it's there to take chances to not fit a mould or be trendy or this and that. So, no, it wasn't the right time with a brand-new singer to start experimenting and doing tripped-out stuff. But hey, it's rock and roll. Ask me if I'll do it again and I'll say yes. That's what rock and roll is all about to me.'

By all accounts, the *Van Halen III* tour did not disgrace the band's legacy. In Japan in October 1998 to promote his band Black Label Society's *Sonic Brew* album, Zakk Wylde caught up with Eddie in Tokyo, where Van Halen were booked to play three shows at the city's historic Budokan venue. He ended up partying with his hero into the wee small hours.

'Van Halen opened up with "Unchained", and Ed was just killing it,' Wylde recalls. 'He came up to my hotel room afterwards and he was playing my Les Paul, with the bullseye, and the guitar was hanging around his knees like Jimmy Page in 1975. He was playing every Led Zeppelin lick that he knew, from back when Van Halen played covers. It was insane. It was like he was seventeen again, playing for fun, and none of the music-industry bullshit mattered.'

• • • • •

Gary Cherone left Van Halen on 5 November 1999, after Van Halen Mk III took a collective decision to cease work on a new studio album. Ray Danniels terminated his own contract with the band shortly afterwards.

'It wasn't going in the right direction,' the singer admitted to *Rolling Stone*. 'Also, I wasn't in a great place mentally. I had some things going on in my personal life that affected me. When we broke up, it was mutual.

'I feel blessed to have been there.'

On the day of Cherone's exit from the band, Eddie phoned Mitch Malloy in tears. The pair had kept in touch, with Eddie even sending the singer money to help fund his solo recordings, a generous gesture Malloy hadn't forgotten. In the weeks that followed, a tearful Eddie would call Malloy on several more occasions, finally asking, 'Mitch, what do you think I should do?'

'I said, "You want my honest opinion?"' Malloy told *Rolling Stone*. 'He goes, "Of course I want your honest opinion. We're friends! I don't want you to bullshit me. That's why I like you, because you never bullshit me." And I said, "OK. Here's the thing, I think you need to get Dave back." And he just *lost* it. He went coo-coo crazy.

'I was just like, "Whoa! You asked my honest opinion, man." He was like, "Yeah, but I never thought you'd say that." And I was like, "Oh, I'm sorry. But that's how I feel. I think that that's the right thing for the band. I think that's what the fans want."'

10
DISTANCE

As New York Police Department patrolmen patiently shooed rubbernecking tourists from the MacDougal Street entrance to Café Wha?, one bemused local resident sidled over to a uniformed sergeant.

'So wait, the *actual* Van Halen is playing here tonight?'

When Interscope Records sent New York-based arts correspondents and music writers an invitation to a Van Halen media event being staged at Manny Roth's storied Greenwich Village club on 5 January 2012, the initial assumption was that the label was hosting a press conference to officially announce the release of a new Van Halen studio album, the group's first for Jimmy Iovine's label and their first with David Lee Roth since *1984*. When word leaked that the Californian quartet would actually be performing at the tiny 250-capacity basement venue, the scramble to secure guest-list spots was positively unseemly. By showtime, Cafe Wha? was packed tighter than a Katz's Deli pastrami sandwich.

'It's like climbing into a rocket in here, and it's a rocket that comes from way, way back in our past all the way into what the future is going to look like,' said David Lee Roth by way of an introduction. 'Welcome to Occupy Van Halen, ladies and gentlemen.'

If the 2012 version of 'Diamond' Dave, more Nintendo plumber than golden god in his brown Carhartt overalls and newsboy cap, lacked a little showbiz sparkle, the singer's shark-like smile and carnival-barker patter showed little sign of wear and tear.

'It took us fifty years to get this gig,' the singer jived, with a nod to his Uncle Manny. 'It was easier getting into the Rock and Roll Hall of Fame.'

Those close enough to the stage to read the thirteen song titles printed in black type on the set-list sheets taped to the amplifiers and floor would have been unsurprised to see a sum total of zero songs representing Van Halen's second and third acts, with Sammy Hagar and Gary Cherone. More surprisingly for an album-launch showcase, there appeared be no new songs listed either, with 'She's the Woman' the only title unfamiliar to anyone with a passing knowledge of the six Roth-era studio albums, dating back to the quartet's club days. But there would be time to ponder the significance of this at a later juncture, when not standing inches away from America's biggest hard-rock band playing a set of jukebox classics at jet-plane-landing volume.

'I told you we was comin' back!' drawled Roth. 'Say ya missed us! Say it like ya mean it!'

'Van Halen is still one of the most limber bands in hard rock, with a higher center of gravity than most,' wrote the scholarly Jon Pareles, reviewing the gig for the *New York Times*. 'Eddie Van Halen's guitar is in constant, multiple-personality dialogue with itself: riffing power chords and then replying with leads that wriggle from the whammy bar, scamper in notes tapped on the fingerboard or screech from a scrape up a string...As the band socked its riffs, and Eddie Van Halen filigreed them with virtuoso guitar, the songs were still testimonials to hyperactive teenage hormones and musicians who remember them.'

'Just to be clear: Van Halen is still awesome,' wrote Chuck Klosterman, author of the highly entertaining heavy-metal memoir *Fargo Rock City*, for *Grantland*. 'They were really, truly, absolutely incredible . . . Watching Eddie Van Halen play guitar is like watching the detonation of a nuclear bomb from inside the warhead.'

· · · · ·

David Lee Roth was back in Van Halen, unofficially at least, as early as spring 2000. A marriage of convenience in 1973, the re-coupling of rock's most voluble vocalist with its most gifted guitarist now seemed like a matter of necessity post-*Van Halen III*. In what appeared like a none-too-subtle ground-razing exercise ahead of relaunching the group, Warners reissued remastered editions of the six Roth-era albums only, and when *Spin* selected a Neil Zlozower photo of a decidedly underdressed Roth circa 1980 for the cover image of its October 2000 'The 100 Sleaziest Moments in Rock' issue, the timing seemed right for California's hard-raunch kings to strut back into the spotlight. But despite the quartet committing to tape three new songs Roth considered 'astonishing', business wrangling stalled momentum. And soon enough, Eddie had more pressing matters on his mind.

In January 2000, a routine dental check-up revealed irregular scar tissue on the guitarist's tongue, and he was referred to a specialist at UCLA Medical Center. A chunk of his tongue was subsequently removed and biopsied, the tests revealing that the lump was cancerous. Eddie suggested that the brass and copper guitar picks he held in his mouth may have conducted the electromagnetic energy radiated at 5150;

his doctors pointed out that chain-smoking since the age of twelve might just be more of a factor in his ill health. Eddie promised the doctors and his distraught wife that he'd quit. His willpower broke after about a month.

On 26 April 2001, Van Halen fans logging on to the band's official website were met with a message from the guitarist.

'I'm sorry for having waited so long to address this issue personally,' it began. 'But cancer can be a very unique and private matter to deal with. So, I think it's about time to tell you where I'm at. I was examined by three oncologists and three head & neck surgeons at Cedars-Sinai just before spring break and I was told that I'm healthier than ever and beating cancer. Although it's hard to say when, there's a good chance I will be cancer free in the near future. I just want to thank all of you for your concern and support.'

It would be a further thirteen months before the guitarist posted a follow-up message, informing fans on 9 May 2002 that he'd been given a '100% clean bill of health – from head to toe'. After expressing his gratitude for the 'good wishes and prayers' offered up on his behalf, Eddie ended his statement by saying, 'Now it's time to really get back to the music and the fun . . . so party on and you'll be hearing from us very soon.'

The following month, *People* magazine broke the news that Eddie and Valerie had separated.

'After 20 years, I was done making excuses for Ed and his reliance on the drugs and alcohol,' Valerie wrote in *Losing It*. 'I was done compromising my own life. I'd spent two decades telling myself that one day he'd get better. If it wasn't that, I was saying, "Poor guy, he's got such a big heart, but look at how much pain he's in." I had an endless supply of excuses. But . . . the well had run dry.'

Warners, too, decided to let Van Halen go, dissolving their record contract to end a twenty-three-year working relationship with the band. Amid this personal and professional up-heaval, one can only imagine how Eddie felt when, in April, David Lee Roth and Sammy Hagar announced a twenty-one-date summer co-headlining tour, which Hagar subsequent-ly admitted was at least partially motivated by the desire to 'piss off Van Halen and get the fans worked up'. The tour was launched under the billing 'Song for Song, the Heavyweight Champs of Rock and Roll', though fans would soon wittily dub it 'The Sans Halen Tour'. Entirely predictably, it would end in chaos, with cancelled shows, bitter mud-slinging from both parties, and Van Halen's reputation tramped deeper into the dirt by proxy.

Not that Eddie needed much assistance in this regard during this troubled time. In 2003, for reasons that are en-tirely unfathomable, the guitarist set up a jam with jock-metal stars Limp Bizkit, who had parted company with innovative guitarist Wes Borland around the same time as their third al-bum, *Chocolate Starfish and the Hot Dog Flavored Water*, passed the six-million sales mark in America. When an Interscope Records executive suggested that perhaps there might be mu-tual benefit in Eddie and Limp Bizkit frontman Fred Durst working together, Durst at least had the good grace to laugh off the idea, saying, 'That would be hilarious. The greatest gui-tar player ever jams with the worst band ever.' Eddie, however, gave the idea more weight than it merited. 'Fuck it, let's jam,' he reportedly told Durst.

The session, convened in a Hollywood Hills house where Limp Bizkit were holding auditions, did not go well, with Eddie apparently storming out when his new pals ignored his requests that they stop smoking weed in his presence. The following day, Eddie contacted Durst to ask that his gear be dropped back at 5150, but when twenty-four hours passed without a response from the singer, the guitarist resolved to be his own repo man.

The story of what happened next is recounted in photographer/ videographer Andrew Bennett's photo book *Eruption in the Canyon: 212 Days & Nights with the Genius of Eddie Van Halen*.

'Eddie once bought an assault vehicle from a military auction,' Bennett writes. 'It has a shine gun mount on the back and is not legal. Eddie drove that assault vehicle through LA, into Beverly Hills, then parked and left it running on the front lawn of the house Limp Bizkit was rehearsing in. He got out wearing no shirt, his hair in a Samurai bun on top of his head, his jeans held up with a strand of rope and combat boots held together by duct tape. And he had a gun in his hand.'

Bennett then recalled Eddie telling him, 'That asshole answered the door. I put my gun to that stupid fucking red hat of his, and I said, "Where's my shit, motherfucker?" That fucking guy just turned to one of his employees and starts yelling at him to grab my shit . . .'

. . . . .

On 31 December 2003, Alex Van Halen and his family accepted Sammy Hagar's offer to see in the New Year with him and his family at their home in Laguna Beach. Before midnight, Alex's phone rang, and he passed it across to Hagar, who recognised the voice on the line as belonging to a tired and emotional Eddie.

'Why did you quit the band?' the guitarist slurred.

For once, Hagar was lost for words.

Early in 2004, Warners proposed releasing a second Van Halen greatest hits collection, drawing exclusively from the Roth and Hagar years and to be titled *The Best of Both Worlds*. As discussions deepened, conversations between Hagar and the Van Halen brothers became more amicable, to the point where the idea of a reunion tour to tie in with the album release was mooted. Hagar was invited to 5150 for an exploratory meeting with Eddie and Alex. He recounted the events of the day in unflinching detail in his 2011 biography *Red: My Uncensored Life in Rock*, alarming all who read it.

'His marriage was over,' Hagar wrote. 'Valerie was gone. He finally invited me over to this giant, extravagant, sixteen-thousand-square-foot house that he and Valerie had built before she split. It looked like vampires lived there. There were bottles and cans all over the floor . . . There were spider webs everywhere . . . He was sleeping on the floor with a blanket and pillow. There was no food in the cupboards. I had never seen a dirtier place in my life.

'I hadn't seen him in a decade. He looked like he hadn't bathed in a week. He certainly hadn't changed his clothes in at least that long. He wasn't wearing a shirt. He had a giant overcoat and army pants, tattered and ripped at the cuffs, held up with a piece of rope. I'd never seen him so skinny in my life. He was missing a number of teeth and the ones he had left were black.'

'I got a lot of flak from hardcore Eddie fans for what I said about him in my book, but I was kind to the man,' Hagar told me in 2019. 'It was horrifying, reckless and brutal. When I first saw the mess of my man, I should have said, "Al, you know what, let's get together some other time, come back in a year." I seldom say I'd have made a different decision, but there I should have: I should have canned that whole tour.

'I wanted to do it for the fans, and I wanted to do it for me, because getting thrown out of a band like that, I had a little chip on my shoulder, I had a little attitude about that for a long time. There's always a little hurt inside that you carry. It's like getting dumped by your girlfriend – you always want either to have another shot at it or you want to find another girlfriend that's hotter so that you can shove it in her face. I was carrying some luggage, and I kinda thought if we did this tour, that'd get rid of that luggage and I can move on. Or I can stay in this band for ever, because it's great, and I love this band. I was hoping for closure, because I'd felt that the Van Halen I was a part of was poisoned. We didn't die of natural causes. But it was horrible, it was the worst thing that ever happened. That made Eddie so ugly in my heart and soul.'

With the release of *The Best of Both Worlds*, a thirty-six-track double album bolstered by three new Hagar-fronted songs – 'It's About Time', 'Up for Breakfast' and 'Learning to See' – set for 20 July 2004, the Van Halen Tour 2004 was booked to begin in Greensboro, North Carolina, on 11 June, running through to 19 November in Tucson, Arizona, taking in a total of eighty concerts. For reasons that were never fully explained, Eddie didn't want Michael Anthony involved in the tour and only authorised the bassist's participation after Anthony struck a deal with the band's new manager, Irving Azoff, to sign away all his rights to the Van Halen name and logo. For all the turbulence behind the curtains, the tour's opening night, in Sammy Hagar's opinion at least, was 'phenomenal'. From there things nose-dived almost immediately. There was a visible lack of chemistry between the musicians onstage, and Eddie's guitar-playing was so erratic that the band's own sound engineers often turned him down in the mix. From the outside, it seemed as if the whole endeavour might derail, with disastrous consequences, at any moment.

'It was a brutal experience,' says Hagar. 'There were nights I was embarrassed to be standing next to Eddie Van Halen, and I'm not saying that out of anger.

'I was looking on a website recently, and they wrote about that tour and said something like, "Everything that could have gone wrong, did . . . and worse!" It showed Eddie smashing up his guitar, and it churned my stomach seeing this. There's a clip of "It's About Time", and I was watching it, thinking, "It's about time Eddie learned this fucking song!" There were times when I couldn't even tell what song Eddie was playing. There's footage on YouTube where we're playing "Panama", and Al is yelling at Ed, while Ed is fiddling around trying to figure the damn song out. Al is looking at him, yelling, "Come on, Ed! Come on, Ed!" To have to go through that song after song, night after night . . .

'There were nights where we were good, there were nights where we were pretty damn good but not great, and there were nights where we were horrific.

'I was going to walk away halfway through the tour. We signed up for eighty shows, and I was going to walk away after forty. We had a real bad run-in after the fortieth show, where Eddie was trying to smash a window out of an airplane with a bottle of wine at 40,000 feet, and I was going, "Man, I'm done." I tried to quit, but the contract we had signed was not favourable for anyone to leave; basically, if you left, you had to compensate everyone else for the lack of finances they would have gotten, and that would have put anybody into bankruptcy. And then Eddie apologised, and even though his apology didn't mean anything to me, because he was so incapable of apologising and meaning it, and even though I knew the remaining shows would be brutal, I sucked it up. Michael Anthony and I would go into our dressing room at the arena and wait until we heard the first sound of Eddie's guitar onstage and then we'd go, "Well, he made it, let's go!" I always gave it 100 per cent, I'd never coast through a show, but it wasn't pleasant.

'Eddie's drinking didn't work for him any more, he could not play any more under the influence like he used to be able to do. It's a problem, and I saw it as a problem. I was going, "This is fucked up, I can't be around people like this." Because my father was such a bad alcoholic, my tolerance for alcoholics is pretty high: like, my father would be drunk and he'd still be nice to me, and I still felt like I was protected, and so it wasn't such an issue as it was to my mother, say. If someone can function, you can't really force your will upon them, but when they become [so drunk] that they can't do their job, or they can't be what they're supposed to be to you, then it's time to say, "Hey, hold it, you can't do that any more, and if you do, I'm outta here...'"

On 1 December, Alex Van Halen called Valerie Bertinelli to ask if she would participate in another intervention with Eddie. That plan, however, failed to materialise, partly because one week later, on 8 December, former Pantera guitarist Darrell 'Dimebag' Abbott, a lifelong Van Halen fan who'd befriended Eddie in recent months and hung out with his hero after the group's show in Lubbock, Texas, on 29 September, was shot dead on stage in Columbus, Ohio, while performing with his new band, Damageplan. At the invitation of Dimebag's widow, Rita Haney, Eddie spoke at the guitarist's memorial service and, in a sweet and touching tribute, placed the iconic yellow and black guitar he'd used on *Van Halen II* in the guitarist's coffin. But his erratic behaviour at the memorial service alarmed even close friends.

'I don't know what the hell happened to Ed,' commented Zakk Wylde, who downed shots with the guitarist during the ceremony to toast Dimebag's memory. 'He hasn't just gone off the deep end. He's living in Atlantis.'

'Ed's adrift right now,' David Lee Roth told *Classic Rock*'s James McNair. 'I think the Van Halens have lost their way . . . forgot why they originally do this. I don't think Eddie Van Halen has enjoyed more than 10 minutes of his success.'

Things would get stranger still. First came the news that Eddie was co-financing and writing music for a porn film, *Sacred Sin*, a production he likened to '*Braveheart* with a cum shot'.

Then it was revealed that the guitarist had given director Michael Ninn full access to his home as a location for filming. Eddie told the Adult Video News website that he was unconcerned about what anyone might think of this left-field collaboration: 'Michael Ninn is like a Spielberg to me,' he said, 'the imagery, the way he makes things look, just...sensual.'

On 8 September 2006, Eddie called in to 'shock jock' Howard Stern's radio show, ostensibly to promote the film, which he revealed would also be issued in a less-graphic, R-rated format, under the title *Rise*. The guitarist opened up a wide-ranging, and frequently jaw-dropping, twenty-five-minute conversation by casually downplaying the talents of Jimi Hendrix and Eric Clapton ('I hate to say it, but when he was a heroin addict he was good'), and went on to claim that he had beaten cancer 'without chemo or radiation'. When Stern pressed him as to exactly how he'd achieved this, Eddie replied, 'I did it in a way that is not exactly legal in this country,' and revealed that he had founded a pathology lab, McClain Laboratories, in Smithtown, Long Island, alongside Dr Steve McClain, with a view to curing cancer.

As his host sought to process this extraordinary revelation, the conversation switched to a discussion of Van Halen's future and Eddie's animosity towards former bandmates. Taking a swipe at Michael Anthony, aka 'Sauce Sobolewski', and Sammy Hagar, aka 'the Little Red Worm' – references, respectively, to the two musicians' hot sauce and tequila lines – Eddie said, 'They're out there billing themselves as the Other Half of Van Halen. My brother is the other half of Van Halen. They're out there selling hot sauce and tequila . . . and they're playing all my music'. He then announced that his fifteen-year-old son Wolfgang was the new bass player in Van Halen.

'My son is in, and Sauce Sobolewski can do whatever the hell he wants,' Eddie said.

Promising that Van Halen would soon be back in action, with Wolfgang dragging him and Alex along for the ride, Eddie promised, 'This kid is fucking *dangerous*. Fasten your seatbelt...'

'Wolfgang breathes new life into what we're doing,' he enthused to *Guitar World*. 'He brings youthfulness to something that's inherently youthful. He's only been playing bass for three months, but it's spooky. He's locked tight and puts an incredible spin on our shit. The kid is kicking my ass!'

Outside of the band's inner circle, photographer Ross Halfin was one of the first people to hear the new-look Van Halen. In a posting on his website on 13 December, Halfin revealed that he'd shot the band in Los Angeles and heard rehearsal tapes which he'd assumed were from 1978 but were actually only forty-eight hours old. 'It was jaw-droppingly amazing,' Halfin wrote, 'the band sounded untouchable. It was as exciting as the first time I saw them . . . Having Edward's son on bass has rejuvenated them.

'They will come back and destroy the world.'

On 2 February 2007, Eddie authorised the band's management to announce that Van Halen were back in business.

'In what is no doubt one of the most anticipated moments in rock and roll, Van Halen officially announces their 2007 North American tour,' the press statement read. 'The tour will mark the first time since 1984 that original Van Halen front man David Lee Roth will perform with Eddie and Alex Van Halen along with new bassist Wolfgang Van Halen for 40 shows this summer. Van Halen fans can look forward to legendary high intensity performances, featuring a set list of the most iconic hits ever produced by America's premiere rock band.

'Eddie Van Halen states, "I am very excited to get back to the core of what made Van Halen."'

For many fans, the excitement over Roth's return was weighed against outrage at the news that Michael Anthony had been ousted from the band. Eddie had been bemoaning Anthony's contributions to Van Halen since 1982, and the bassist had been forced to endure humiliation after humiliation at the guitarist's hands, from being coerced into signing away his publishing to being placed on a wage for the disastrous 2004 tour with Hagar. Even so, Anthony had no idea that he was now considered surplus to requirements.

'I found out about that tour like everybody else did – in the press,' he admitted. 'At that point, I kind of sighed and went, "Whatever. If this is what Eddie wants to do, he's going to do what he wants to do." If he wants me out of the band and for Wolfgang to play bass, what was I going to do about it?'

Given the chaos which surrounded the 2004 tour, the announcement of the reunion dates was met with a certain amount of scepticism . . . and within three weeks, *Rolling Stone* declared the just-announced tour 'Kaput'.

'The Van Halen tour has been "shut down",' the *LA Times* reported, 'according to a top official at Live Nation, the huge concert promoter that finally surrendered in the face of the chaos surrounding guitar hero Eddie Van Halen . . . Conversations with the business team behind the tour paint a picture of a rock star who is somewhere between Axl Rose and Michael Jackson on the music industry scale of eccentric recluses. The result is that the Van Halen venture imploded before take-off.'

'I cannot tell you how frustrating and completely nuts this has been,' a tour insider admitted.

On 8 March, Eddie confirmed the rumours in a statement on Van Halen's official website, revealing that he was returning to rehab.

'I have always and will always feel a responsibility to give you my best,' it read. 'At the moment, I do not feel that I can give you my best. That's why I have decided to enter a rehabilitation facility to work on myself, so that in the future I can deliver the 110% that I feel I owe you and want to give you. Some of the issues surrounding the 2007 Van Halen tour are within my ability to change and some are not. As far as my rehab is concerned, it is within my ability to change, and change for the better. I want you to know that is exactly what I am doing, so that I may continue to give you the very best I am capable of. I look forward to seeing you in the future better than ever and I thank you with all my heart. Love, Ed.'

One week later, on 12 March, Van Halen were inducted into the Rock and Roll Hall of Fame by the Guns N' Roses/Stone Temple Pilots alumni of hard rock 'supergroup' Velvet Revolver. Neither Roth nor the Van Halen brothers were in attendance to hear guitarist Slash hail Eddie as a 'guitar genius and innovator, God to fans and musicians alike'. In their absence, ex-members Sammy Hagar and Michael Anthony accepted the accolade.

Then, from the flames, a phoenix. On 13 August, Eddie, Alex, Wolfgang and David Lee Roth staged a press conference at the Four Seasons hotel in Los Angeles to announce a twenty-five-date arena tour, to commence on 27 September in Charlotte, North Carolina, wrapping up on 11 December in Calgary, Canada.

'This is the press conference that you probably never thought that you would see happen,' said Roth, by way of an introduction. 'Certainly not while we are all young, skinny and good-looking. Welcome, one and all.'

After introducing each of the band members in turn, Roth turned to embrace Eddie in a tight hug, and received a peck on the cheek from the guitarist in return.

'I got a new brother,' Eddie said, before Roth threw the floor open to any journalist with a question. Before long, a query was raised about Michael Anthony's absence, which Roth deflected by hailing the bassist as one of the band's 'great alumni . . . part of this band's history'.

'And as far as why Wolf is in the band, may I speak for you, Ed?' he continued. 'Tap me on the shoulder in the limo on the way home if I'm wrong here. But while we're at the top of our game, and we really are, I understand how he wanted to play with the boy because he is *amazing*, and you heard me say that. When you hear these vocals, when you hear what's going on in this rhythm section now, it is young, it is skinny, and it is fucking vicious. Get ready.'

When the subject of a potential new album was brought up, Eddie said, 'Just know this: we're a band, and we're gonna continue. A whole new beginning . . .'

As the press conference drew to a close, Matt Linus from *MTV News* posed a final question, referencing Eddie's March statement about entering rehab. 'You said you didn't feel like you were at your best,' he said, quoting the guitarist. 'Why'd you make that decision? And do you feel at your best right now?'

'None of us wanna give you less than our best,' Eddie replied. 'And we are at our best.'

Remarkably, they pulled it off, ultimately extending the trek through to June 2008 and playing a total of seventy-five arena shows. Performing for almost a million fans, the tour brought in $93 million, making it the highest-grossing tour in Van Halen's history.

As it drew to a close, Eddie was asked about the possibility of the quartet recording a new album. 'We'll cross that bridge when the tour is over,' he said.

In reality, the guitarist would spend the rest of the year almost catatonic at home, after being prescribed the anticonvulsant Klonopin to wean him off alcohol, and then antidepressants to wean him off Klonopin.

'All I wanted to do was stop drinking,' he complained. 'But instead I literally could not communicate. Yeah, I was gone. I don't know what dimension I went to, but I was not here. It was such a long process to come out of this. Just to be able to communicate, to talk, was a feat in itself. You know when you see homeless people and they're literally not here, you know? I laid on the couch for a year. Just watching *Law & Order*. I was always in the studio making music, and now, nothing.'

Better days lay ahead. On 27 June 2009, Eddie married his girlfriend of three years, publicist Janie Liszewski, in the garden of the couple's seven-acre estate. Alex Van Halen, an ordained minister, officiated at the twenty-minute, non-denominational ceremony, Wolfgang served as his father's best man, and Valerie Bertinelli was among the hundred invited guests in attendance. Liszewski walked down the aisle to a string-quartet version of Van Halen's 'When It's Love', and Eddie chose Joe Cocker's 'You Are So Beautiful' to soundtrack the newlyweds' first dance.

'For the first time in my life I really feel good,' Eddie told *Hustler* magazine. 'I don't really wanna get into the whole sobriety trip. But I'm just workin' on a lot of things to get better at being here in the moment and stay clear, ya know? It's a trip to look back and go, Fuck, I've been doing this for over 40 years. I'm lucky to be alive. I'm healthier and happier than I've ever been.

'Janie's a beautiful, sexy, sweet, strong and smart woman who loves me unconditionally. And, of course, vice versa...I have the most insanely gifted, talented, wonderful son (a direct gift from God), whom I love more than he'll ever know. My brother Alex, who I just love so fucking much, it makes me wanna cry out of joy that I'm so blessed to have him since the day I was born...What the fuck more could I ask for? I feel like my life is just beginning.'

It was Wolfgang who sowed the initial seeds for the first Van Halen studio album in over twenty years, urging his father and uncle to start jamming again, just for fun, for the simple pleasure of playing music for its own sake. This accomplished, the teen-ager encouraged the pair to revisit some old Van Halen demos to

see if the songs still connected and lit a fire within them. Within a matter of months, the trio – and a rejuvenated David Lee
Roth – had the skeleton of a twelfth Van Halen studio album.

'We went up to 5150 and started jamming,' Eddie recalled.
'When you walk into the studio there are endless shelves of recordings. I grabbed a bunch of random tapes and picked out
a few songs that I had known and liked. We started changing
them around and writing new parts for them. We recorded the
first demo of "She's the Woman" in August of 2009, and it felt
really awesome. It felt like classic Van Halen that was written
today. I sent Pro Tools files of recordings over to Dave, who
was working over at Henson Studios, where he likes to record,
which got him totally excited. He said, "Let's get going!" Working with Dave again was like we had never left each other.

'I was amazed how fresh some of the songs sounded,' he
admitted. 'I was going, "Did I really write that way back then?"
The biggest trip is that I wrote some of those songs when I was
still in high school and even junior high. A good idea is a good
idea no matter when you do it.

'[Originally] I didn't want to do something new because I
felt that even if we did, the fans wouldn't like it anyway. We just
snapped back and realized that, hey, we're doing this for us, too.
This is what we do.'

A Different Kind of Truth was released by Interscope on
7 February 2012. Largely composed of reworked versions of
Van Halen songs written between 1974 and 1977, the thir-
teen-track album had a fire, a focus and an exuberant sense of
energy and adventure that few could have envisaged hearing
from Van Halen in their fifth decade. Opener and lead-off single 'Tattoo' was a ballsy new take on club favourite 'Down in
Flames', while 'She's the Woman', first recorded on the 1977
Gene Simmons demo, featured new lyrics and a new mid-song
breakdown, with the original section having already been re-

appropriated for 'Mean Street'. The rollicking 'Bullethead' was originally written in Roth's basement, on the same afternoon in 1977 on which Eddie wrote 'Ain't Talkin' 'Bout Love', while the infectious 'Blood and Fire' was recognisable to hardcore fans as a retooled take on the instrumental 'Ripley', recorded for the soundtrack to Cameron Crowe's 1984 film *The Wild Life*. Of the newly written songs, the chugging, sassy 'You and Your Blues' had sweet vocal trade-offs and a skyscraper chorus, 'The Trouble with Never' was a classic old-school rocker, and the acoustic country-blues 'Stay Frosty' had warm, welcome echoes of 'Ice Cream Man'.

Exemplifying the overwhelmingly positive critical response to the album, *Rolling Stone*'s Rob Sheffield wrote: 'Van Halen's "Heard you missed us, we're back" album is not only the most long-awaited reunion joint in the history of reunion joints, it is – against all reasonable expectations – a real Van Halen album.' Debuting at number 2 on the *Billboard* chart, the album also broke the Top 10 in Japan, Germany, Australia and the UK, where, in debuting at number 6, it became the band's highest-ever-charting album.

In the week of the album's release, the quartet hosted a private show for media and music-industry VIPs at Hollywood's Henson Studios, performing a thirteen-song set which included live premieres for 'Tattoo' and 'The Trouble with Never'. Chris Epting, writing for *Noisecreep*, hailed the guitarist's performance as 'masterful'.

'His recent personal struggles seem to have been dealt with,' Epting observed. 'He looks a little heavier, but a lot healthier, and he played with the joy of a teenager, losing himself in the music while ripping off one ferocious solo after another. His trademark red and white guitar elicited all sorts of spacey moans, shrieks and rumbles. It was like seeing Eddie in one of Van Halen's classic '80s videos all over again.'

Beginning on 18 February at the KFC Yum! Center in Louisville, Kentucky, and running through to 26 June at the New Orleans Arena in Louisiana, the North American leg of the *A Different Kind of Truth* tour was an unqualified success, selling 448,506 tickets across forty-nine shows. Pearl Jam vocalist Eddie Vedder was among those in attendance at the quartet's gig at the Tacoma Dome in Washington on 5 May.

'I brought *Van Halen I* and *II* on eight-track, and that's what we cranked on the way to the Tacoma Dome,' Vedder later told Howard Stern. 'I was like, you know, "I'm going to take that in, because we might get to meet him, and I might even get him to sign this damn thing!" Sure enough, we did, and I was a little nervous, because if you are Eddie Van Halen, you could be a complete asshole and I would totally respect that. You could be however you want if you're Eddie Van Halen. It turned out that he was the sweetest, sweetest guy.

'I kind of sheepishly say, "Hey, Ed, would it be funny if I asked you to sign this thing?" He said, "Oh my God, look at that! Wolfie, come over here!" He said [to Wolfgang], "This is what we used to put out." He explained it. So I have this nice thing where he wrote, "To Eddie, from Eddie".'

Though a proposed thirty-date summer tour was cancelled – 'We bit off more than we could chew,' Eddie admitted to *USA Today* – the group returned to the road in the spring and summer of 2013, to perform in Australia and Japan, where a first live album with Roth, *Tokyo Dome Live in Concert*, was recorded on 21 June.

'There are mistakes,' Eddie admitted to *Guitar World*'s Chris Gill. 'But that's how it sounded that night, so we just left it . . . When you fix parts or mistakes, it's not a real live experience anymore.

'Van Halen has been aggressive since day one,' he said. 'The rawness of the recording adds to the power. There's this uncontrolled energy that exists in us that spills over the edges. It's never really right or perfect, but it creates tension. It's like, "Okay, who is going to blow it?" [laughs] When you keep waiting for someone to fuck up but no one does, it keeps you on the edge of your seat. It's just raw. It's the real thing.'

Beyond the commercial and critical success garnered by *A Different Kind of Truth*, Van Halen, now in their fifth decade, finally began to receive a measure of respect beyond the hard-rock community. In February 2011, the Smithsonian's National Museum of American History announced that it would be exhibiting Eddie's 'Frank 2' guitar as part of its Division of Culture and the Arts. Describing Eddie as 'a Dutch–American guitarist, keyboardist, songwriter, producer and self-taught inventor of guitar technology and technique', the museum stated that 'he is best known as the lead guitarist and co-founder of the hard-rock band Van Halen and recognized for his innovative performing and recording styles in blues-based rock, tapping, intense solos and high-frequency feedback'.

'The museum collects objects that are multidimensional, and this guitar reflects innovation, talent and influence,' said Brent D. Glass, the museum's director. 'The guitar moves the museum's instrument collections into more contemporary history.'

Four years later, in 2015, the guitarist was invited to the museum to be interviewed as part of its 'What It Means to Be American' series.

'What more could you ask for [than] to be recognized as being part of having contributed to change, you know?' Van Halen told *Billboard*. 'To be recognized as someone who has contributed to American music, especially being an immigrant, is a hell of an honor.'

Unrecognisable from the gaunt, broken figure Sammy Hagar described in *Red*, the guitarist looked handsome and healthy, and proved to be a charming, eloquent and insightful speaker, holding the sold-out audience enrapt throughout his conversation with music journalist Denise Quan. Asked for the secret of Van Halen's longevity, he shared a Dutch phrase, regularly employed by his father Jan, that translates as 'just keep pedalling'.

'I'm always pushing things past where [they're] supposed to be,' Eddie admitted. "When Spinal Tap was going to 11, I was going to 15.'

'Do you feel as though you're living the American Dream?' asked Quan.

'We came here with approximately $50 and a piano, and we didn't speak the language,' Eddie replied, looking out at his brother and son in the audience. 'Now look where we are. If that's not the American Dream, what is?'

• • • • •

In 2018, rumours began circulating that Van Halen were looking to put together a huge global stadium tour to bring their extraordinary career to a triumphant close. Within the music industry, word spread that superstar acts such as Metallica and Foo Fighters, stadium acts in their own right, were prepared to support the band on specific dates, as a mark of respect for Van Halen's game-changing contributions to the rock 'n' roll community. Sammy Hagar had his own take on how this might play out. Asked if there was any amount of money that would tempt him to reunite with the band, he replied, 'Oh, fuck, I would do it for free . . . if it was right, if it could be four grown-ups.

'If we could elevate ourselves out of the cesspool that we fell into, have a nice shower, put on some fresh clothes and go out and see who we are today, I would love to make a record with Eddie, Alex and Michael in a second,' he insisted. 'As far as a tour goes, I would only want to do it with Eddie, Alex, Michael and Dave. We'd call it The Best of Both Worlds and we'd take it somewhat chronologically, so Dave would come out and do, say, "You Really Got Me" and "Runnin' with the Devil", and then I'd come out, and I'd have to kill it, so I'd do "Why Can't This Be Love" and "Best of Both Worlds", and then he'd come back out again, and so on. It'd be for the Van Halen fans, and it'd be a way to go out on a good note. I don't know where everyone else's heads are at, but that's where mine's at.'

Whether or not Hagar's proposal was ever given serious consideration by the Van Halens or their manager Irving Azoff, the group soon had more pressing matters to consider. The first hint that unforeseen forces were conspiring to prevent a new Van Halen tour happening came in September 2019, when David Lee Roth declared, 'I think Van Halen's finished.'

During a radio interview promoting his scheduled 2020 solo residency in Las Vegas, Roth shrugged off a question about rumours of a full band tour, saying, 'It's been cancelled a number of times and I think Van Halen's finished and this is the next phase. I've inherited the band de facto – whatever that means. Van Halen isn't going to be coming back in the fashion that you know.

'That being said,' he added, 'Eddie Van Halen's got his own story to tell – it's not mine to tell.'

The singer compounded this comment by telling the *New York Times*, 'I don't know that Eddie Van Halen is ever really going to rally for the rigours of the road again,' prompting Wolfgang to respond, 'I don't really think that's up for him [Roth] to decide.'

This unusually terse reply from Eddie's always diplomatic, respectful son attracted a certain amount of attention. But it prepared no one for the news that Wolfgang would break on 6 October 2020.

'I can't believe I'm having to write this, but my father, Edward Lodewijk Van Halen, has lost his long and arduous battle with cancer this morning,' Wolfgang's statement began. 'He was the best father I could ever ask for. Every moment I've shared with him on and off stage was a gift. My heart is broken, and I don't think I'll ever fully recover from this loss. I love you so much, Pop.'

The shock news was met with a huge outpouring of grief from the rock community, and beyond. Sammy Hagar, who had recently reconciled with the guitarist, pronounced himself 'heartbroken and speechless'. Queen's Brian May said that the news had 'punched a big hole in my heart'.

'This wonderful man was way too young to be taken,' he wrote. 'What a talent – what a legacy – probably the most original and dazzling rock guitarist in history. I think of him as a boy – an innocent prodigy – always full of joy, always modest – and those truly magical fingers opened a door to a new kind of playing. I treasure the moments we shared.'

On Instagram, Guns N' Roses guitarist Slash posted a single black-and-white photograph of Van Halen with his self-made 'Frankenstrat' guitar and wrote 'RIP #EddieVanHalen'.

'I just heard about Eddie Van Halen and I feel terrible about it,' wrote Beach Boy Brian Wilson. 'Eddie was such a great guitarist and I remember how big Van Halen was, especially here in L.A. Love and Mercy to Eddie's family & friends.'

'I probably can't speak as well as others have spoken over the last 24 hours as to Ed's musical genius,' said Irving Azoff, 'but Ed the human being, especially as he had to come to grips with being human, really shined. He was a great father. You get this image of this bombastic, incredible, loud prodigy, but personally, he had a big heart.'

Having battled cancer himself in recent years, Tony Iommi's tribute to his old pal carried an added poignancy.

'I'm just devastated to hear the news of the passing of my dear friend Eddie Van Halen,' Iommi wrote. 'He fought a long and hard battle with his cancer right to the very end. Eddie was one of a very special kind of person, a really great friend. Rest In Peace my dear friend till we meet again.'

David Lee Roth reacted to the news by posting on his social media channels a black-and-white Robert Yager photograph of the guitarist and himself holding hands backstage before Van Halen's 2007 'comeback' tour opener, at the Bobcats Arena, in Charlotte, North Carolina. His caption read: 'What a Long Great Trip It's Been . . .'

As more details emerged, it was revealed that Eddie had passed away at the Providence St John's Health Center in Santa Monica, California, with his family by his side. His death certificate, issued by the Los Angeles Department of Public Health, cited his immediate cause of death as a cerebrovascular accident, or stroke, and listed several underlying causes, including pneumonia, the bone marrow disorder myelodysplastic syndrome and both lung and skin cancer.

'At the end of 2017, he was diagnosed with stage-four lung cancer and the doctors were like, "You have six weeks,"' Wolfgang later revealed to Howard Stern. 'And then he went to Germany. Whatever the fuck they do over there, it's amazing because I got three more years with him.

'Things started getting really bad at the beginning of 2019. He got in a motorcycle accident and he had a brain tumour. We took care of it, he got this crazy procedure and he was OK. But as time went on, shit kept stacking up and stacking up. It just never let up.'

On 16 November, Wolfgang released his own emotional tribute to his father, sharing the video for 'Distance', the debut single from his band Mammoth WVH, which featured archive home video footage of his mother and father. The song's lyrics, he explained, were written 'imagining what my life would be without him, and how terribly I'd miss him'.

'I never intended "Distance" to be the very first piece of music people would hear from me,' Wolfgang admitted, 'but I also thought my father would be here to celebrate its release. While the song is incredibly personal, I think anyone can relate to the idea of having a profound loss in their life. This is for him. I love and miss you, Pop.'

Speaking about the track to Lou Brutus of HardDrive Radio, Wolfgang also revealed that he'd played 'Distance' to his father before his passing.

'When I showed it to Dad for the first time, maybe it was out of pride or also just the song in general, he cried when he heard it,' Wolfgang said. 'And I don't think he was aware of the significance of it for me; he just understood it as a song about loss.'

That sense of loss permeated every obituary as writers paid their respects to Eddie's extraordinary talent and impact upon the music world. The *New York Times* hailed the sixty-five-year-old musician as 'the most influential guitarist of his generation'.

'Mr. Van Halen structured his solos the way Macy's choreographs its Independence Day fireworks shows: shooting off rockets of sound that seemed to explode in a shower of light and color,' wrote Jim Farber. 'His outpouring of riffs, runs and solos was hyperactive and athletic, joyous and wry, making deeper or darker emotions feel irrelevant.'

'When Jimi Hendrix died in 1970, there was this huge void. All of a sudden there was something missing in music,' says Jas Obrecht. 'During the '70s, we were all wondering who the new Hendrix would be, the next game-changer. Eddie was that guy.

'He was one of those transcendent people who changed music, like Jimi did. Eddie Van Halen may be the most sensitive male I've ever met, and his hands seemed to be hard-wired to his heart and soul. Music just flowed out of him.'

In one of his last major interviews, Eddie was asked if he had any advice for aspiring guitar players who might harbour dreams of emulating his achievements.

'Bottom line is, you've gotta love what you're doing,' he replied. 'There are no rules. You have 12 fucking notes . . . do whatever you want with them.'

· · · · ·

Wolfgang Van Halen was twelve years old when he asked his father for a guitar of his own. On Christmas Day, 2003, the youngster woke to discover that he'd been gifted a custom-striped 5150 Kramer, a back-up version of the model his father played in the video for 'Panama'. Inside the instrument's case, the boy found a Christmas card styled as a *Playboy* magazine cover, featuring a blonde Playmate spilling out of a carelessly buttoned Santa suit.

'Play, boy,' Wolfgang explained to *Classic Rock*, still tickled at the memory of decoding his father's tongue-in-cheek reference. 'He was really proud of that joke.'

'My dad wasn't the best teacher,' Wolfgang noted. 'He was, like . . . "Do this." And I was, like, Fuck you! I can't do that! You're Eddie Van Halen! How the hell do I do that?' [Laughs]

Despite this, Wolfgang learned fast, mastering not just guitar, but bass, drums and keyboards too. Consequently, his 2021 album, *Mammoth WVH*, titled in tribute to his father's teenage covers band, finds him playing every instrument and singing every note. Released on 11 June 2021, and drawing upon influences from Foo Fighters, Alter Bridge, Jimmy Eat World and Muse, it's a strong contender for the best modern rock album of the year. And while it's a collection which sees the thirty-year-old musician convincingly asserting his own personality, there are subtle nods to his heritage too, be that the use of the 'Sunday Afternoon in the Park' synth on album opener 'Mr. Ed' or the guitar solo on 'Mammoth' being tracked using his father's original 'Frankenstrat'.

'You feel the history,' Wolfgang admitted. 'It's kind of terrifying holding it.'

In truth, long before his death, Eddie Van Halen was excited to pass the torch to his boy.

'Wait 'til you hear his record,' he told interviewer Denise Quan during his 2015 'What It Means to Be American' talk, nodding towards his son. 'It blew my mind.'

'What advice did your father give you that you wanted to make sure Wolfie knew?' Quan asked the guitarist towards the end of the interview.

Eddie puffed out his cheeks and considered the question.

'The thing he always used to say to us, was that you can learn from everybody, what to do, and what not to do,' he replied.

'And, if you make a mistake, try to do it twice, and smile,' he added. 'That way people will think you meant it.'

SOURCES

All quotations are taken from interviews conducted by the author, except as noted below:

1 LITTLE DREAMER

I have to hand it: Keith Valcourt, 'Eddie Van Halen's Immigrant Take on American Rock, New Album and Concert Tour', *Washington Times*, 2 April 2015

He would just sit: Jas Obrecht, 'Young Wizard of Power Rock', *Guitar Player*, April 1980

It was important: Van Halen interviews, Interscope Records, 2012

She wore the pants: David Curcurito, 'Eddie Van Halen: The *Esquire* Interview', *Esquire*, 17 April 2012

For my dad, America: Mike Boehm, 'No Method to Their Madness', *Los Angeles Times*, 5 September 1991

We were two outcasts: David Wild, 'Eddie Van Halen: Balancing Act', *Rolling Stone*, 6 April 1995

I didn't give a shit: Steven Rosen, 'The Life and Times of Van Halen', *Guitar World*, July 1985

Alex and I went to: Wild, 'Eddie Van Halen'

I didn't even think about: Rosen, 'The Life and Times of Van Halen'

The first song I ever: Steve Baltin, 'Eddie Van Halen Dismisses Jimi Hendrix Comparisons', Spinner.com, 16 March 2009

Fuck the piano: Jas Obrecht, 'The Van Halen Tapes: Early Eddie 1978–1982', *Best of Guitar Player: Van Halen*, 1994

I plugged my normal guitar: Rosen, 'The Life and Times of Van Halen'

What attracted me: Brian Hiatt, 'Eddie Van Halen on His Guitar Heroes and How He Found His Sound', rollingstone.com, 6 October 2020

We would play: Chris Gill, 'Tony Iommi and Eddie Van Halen Discuss Their Careers, Friendship and the Past Three Decades of Our Favorite Instrument', *Guitar World*, 1 January 2010

My dad got me: Tom Beajour and Greg Di Benedetto, 'Eddie Van Halen Regains His Balance', *Guitar World*, February 1995

Welcome to the: Ian Christie, *Everybody Wants Some: The Van Halen Saga*, John Wiley & Sons, 2007

2 ERUPTION

I tripped on it: Rosen, 'The Life and Times of Van Halen'

When you hear: Joe Bosso, 'The Monster of Rock', *Guitar World*, February 1990

When you wanted to go: Steven Rosen, 'Van Halen: The True Beginnings', *Classic Rock*, December 2005

Everybody goes through: Debby Miller, 'Van Halen's Split Personality: How a Geek and a Physique Created Thud Rock's Most Successful Oddsemble', *Rolling Stone*, 21 June 1984

My brother would go: Billy Corgan, 'Billy Corgan Interviews Eddie Van Halen', *Guitar World*, April 1996

'*When we began playing*: Rosen, 'The Life and Times of Van Halen'

'*We used to play backyard*: Wild, 'Eddie Van Halen'

We asked him to learn: ibid.

The guy couldn't sing: Rosen, 'Van Halen: The True Beginnings'

It sounded like pure hell: ibid.

All the girls would go: Greg Renoff, quoting from an unpublished Steven Rosen interview with Rudy Leiren, *Van Halen Rising: How a Southern California Backyard Party Band Saved Heavy Metal*, ECW, 2015

It was never about: Wild, 'Eddie Van Halen'

At that time: Rosen, 'Van Halen: The True Beginnings'

When you graduate: Kristen Luna, *Spotlight*, 2015

My first encounter with Dave: ibid.

We would stumble: ibid.

They had more: Corey Seymour, '131 Totally Uncensored Minutes with David Lee Roth, from His New Tattoo Skin-Care Line to the Secret of Van Halen', Vogue.com, 11 December 2018

Everything with me: David Lee Roth, *Crazy from the Heat*, Ebury Press, 1997

I remember my parents: Jane Rocca, 'What I Know About Women', *Brisbane Times*, 7 April 2013

I saw lesbians: Roth, *Crazy from the Heat*

Music got cool: ibid.

I just wanted: staff writers, 'The World According to Dave', *The Inside*, Issue 6, Fall 1996

I used to love: author unknown, *Hit Parader*, year unknown

Eddie was kind of: James Parker, 'The Mad Genius of Eddie Van Halen', theatlantic.com, 9 October 2020

Every time we go: Charles M. Young, 'Van Halen', *Musician*, June 1984

You play all 20: Roth, *Crazy from the Heat*

So unanimously, in fact: ibid.

There was no room: Bosso, 'The Monster of Rock'

When we used to play: Gill, 'Tony Iommi and Eddie Van Halen Discuss Their Careers'

My mom's just going: Curcurito, 'Eddie Van Halen'

The first time we auditioned: Van Halen News Desk, 'Van Halen's Early Days at Gazzarri's – As Told by the Band, Bill Gazzarri, Rodney Bingenheimer, and Childhood Friends', vhnd.com, 11 April 2014

The first time we ever played: ibid.

We'd have meetings: Neil Zlozower, *Eddie Van Halen*, Chronicle Books, 2011

We did everything: Van Halen News Desk, 'Van Halen's Early Days at Gazzarri's'

Eddie was the quiet: Zlozower, *Eddie Van Halen*

We were jealous: Matt Blackett, 'George Lynch', *Guitar Player*, May 2009

We were playing parties: Wild, 'Eddie Van Halen'

I knew of Ed: Steve Rosen, 'Ace of Bass', *Guitar World*, May 1986

I remember standing: Miller, 'Van Halen's Split Personality'

I was nervous: Rosen, 'Ace of Bass'

It was just Edward and Alex: Rosen, 'Ace of Bass'

We met one day: *The Van Halen Story: The Early Years,* Passport International, 2003

Make sure people: Terry Atkinson, 'Breaking Out of Bar-Band Gigs', *Los Angeles Times*, 27 December 1977

We only had: James McNair, 'I'm the One', *Planet Rock*, June 2019

I'm changing my clothes: Jon Wiederhorn and Katherine Turman, *Louder Than Hell: The Definitive Oral History of Metal*, ItBooks, 2014

I actually died: ibid.

I was thinking: Steven Appleford, 'Kiss' Gene Simmons remembers a 21-year-old Eddie Van Halen: You Couldn't Believe Your Ears', *Los Angeles Times*, 7 October 2020

It was really depressing: *Guitar World* staff, 'Eddie Van Halen Goes Deep on the Playing and Tone Secrets Behind 10 Iconic Van Halen Tracks', *Guitar World*, December 1996

I didn't know: Roth, *Crazy from the Heat*

I went around back: Neil Zlozower, *Van Halen: A Visual History 1978–1984*, Chronicle Books, 2008

As I gave Dave: ibid.

If the term punk-rock: Richard Cromelin, 'Spreading Out from Punk-Rock', *Los Angeles Times*, 24 December 1976

When Van Halen came: Ted Templeman (as told to Greg Renoff), *Ted Templeman: A Platinum Producer's Life in Music*, ECW, 2020

We popped it: Chris Gill, 'Eddie Van Halen Revisits Van Halen's Landmark 1984 Album', *Guitar World*, February 2014

My mom just: Mike Boehm, 'No Method to Their Madness', *Los Angeles Times*, 5 September 1991

3 ON FIRE

It's like having a: Steven Rosen, 'California Dreamin'', *Van Halen: 40 Years of the Great American Rock Band*, Time Home Entertainment, 2012

They'd barely had: Dave Simmons, 'Tales from the Top: Van Halen's *Van Halen* (1978)', songwriter101.com, December 2013

Gene said, 'Here's what': *Guitar World* staff, 'Eddie Van Halen Goes Deep'

Van Halen is three: Steven Rosen, 'Eddie Van Halen – The 1978 Interview', loudersound.com, 6 October 2020

People always ask me: Unknown author, *Guitar World*, 1991

Donn Landee is such: ibid.

Sunset Sound's just a big room: Rosen, 'California Dreamin''

I knew he was: Kory Grow, 'Producer Ted Templeman Remembers Eddie Van Halen: He Wasn't Just a Shredder', *Rolling Stone*, 9 October 2020

They tried to make: Steven Rosen, 'Unchained Melodies', *Guitar World*, January 1997

We started in the: Scott Stephens, Robert Olshever and Murray Schwartz, 'Van Halen: Today LA, Tomorrow the Galaxy', *Raw Power*, October/November 1977

We celebrate all: Phast Phreddie Patterson, 'Van Halen's Back Door Rock 'n' Roll', *Waxpaper*, 1978

All we're trying: Rosen, 'California Dreamin''

Three months prior to the tour: Eddie Trunk, 'Sirius XM Trunk Nation with Eddie Trunk', 13 October 2020

Ed was the new: Matt Wardlaw, 'Journey's Neal Schon Recalls the Rise of Eddie Van Halen and the Birth of Don't Stop Believin'', ultimateclassicrock.com, 21 May 2012

The Shuffle had about: Mike Woods, 'An Insider's Look at Van Halen's Three Days in Madison', spectrumnews1.com, 9 October 2020

We're kicking some ass: Rosen, 'California Dreamin''

I don't want to be: Noel Monk, *Runnin' with the Devil: A Backstage Pass to the Wild Times, Loud Rock and the Down and Dirty Truth Behind the Making of Van Halen*, Dey Street Books, 2017

I realise I've let: Tony Stewart, 'Ozzy Osbourne – Beyond Black Sabbath', *NME*, 3 December 1977

We took shoe polish: Van Halen, 'The Van Halen Interview', Interscope Records, 2012

A gold record: McNair, 'I'm the One'

The pair of us watched: Brian May on BBC Radio 1, 10 October 2020

AC/DC was probably: Rosen, 'Unchained Melodies'

I bought the body: Jas Obrecht, 'Eddie Van Halen: A Legend Is Born', *Guitar Player*, November 1978

Frankenstrat . . . looked like: Brian Hiatt, 'Eddie Van Halen: The Joy and Pain of Rock's Last Guitar Superhero', rollingstone. com, 28 October 2020

I went to Ted: Van Halen, 'Van Halen: Interviews with the Band', Interscope Records, 2012

4 DANCE THE NIGHT AWAY

It's getting easier now: Sylvie Simmons, 'Van Halen', *Sounds*, 7 April 1979

I was feeling: *Guitar World* staff, 'Eddie Van Halen Goes Deep'

Ted seems pretty: Obrecht, 'The Van Halen Tapes'

To me, anything over 20: ibid.

He had a heavy: ibid.

It was a hell: ibid.

I think it's our: Steven Rosen, 'Third Power', *Van Halen: 40 Years of the Great American Rock Band*, Time Home Entertainment, 2012

That was one of: McNair, 'I'm the One'

Our stuff, to me: Obrecht, 'The Van Halen Tapes'

The Japanese have: McNair, 'I'm the One'

We put the poster: Dave DiMartino, 'Van Halen: Remnants of the Flesh Hangover', *Creem*, July 1980

I could honestly: Monk, *Runnin' with the Devil*

There would be, like: Johnny Black, 'Runnin' with the Devil', *Classic Rock*, April 2012

Van Halen was: Roth, *Crazy from the Heat*

I came backstage: ibid.

It was adjacent: Valerie Bertinelli, *Losing It – And Gaining My Life Back One Pound at a Time*, Free Press, 2008

After Edward dried: Monk, *Runnin' with the Devil*

It's definitely my: Obrecht, 'The Van Halen Tapes'

Everything was music: Greg Prato, *MTV Ruled the World: The Early Years of Music Video*, Greg Prato, 2011

We were punch-drunk: Bertinelli, *Losing It*

The guys didn't: Grow, 'Producer Ted Templeman Remembers Eddie Van Halen'

I swear to God: Monk, *Runnin' with the Devil*

I cringe at how: Bertinelli, *Losing It*

There I found: Monk, *Runnin' with the Devil*

5 LOSS OF CONTROL

Bottom line is: Monk, *Runnin' with the Devil*

I wrote a check: ibid.

I was angry: Corgan, 'Billy Corgan Interviews Eddie Van Halen'

I worked my ass: Steven Rosen, 'So This Is Love', *Van Halen: 40 Years of the Great American Rock Band*, Time Home Entertainment, 2012

Ed typically worked: Bertinelli, *Losing It*

I'm pretty much: Obrecht, 'The Van Halen Tapes'

He put tremendous: Bertinelli, *Losing It*

One of my biggest: McNair, 'I'm the One'

I had bought: ibid.

The truth is: Rosen, 'So This Is Love'

I wasn't very happy: Corgan, 'Billy Corgan Interviews Eddie Van Halen'

You cannot label: Rosen, 'So This Is Love'
A lot of people: Sylvie Simmons, 'Van Halen: The Philosophy of Diving Down', *Creem*, September 1982
He's on an ego: Obrecht, 'The Van Halen Tapes'
I hated every minute: Corgan, 'Billy Corgan Interviews Eddie Van Halen'
Michael left to go: Denise Quan, 'Eddie Van Halen Deconstructs his Collaboration on "Beat It"', CNN, 30 November 2012
It cooks! It smokes!: Obrecht, 'The Van Halen Tapes'
I remember that a teacher: Frank Meyer, 'Little Guitarist', *The Inside*, Issue 13

6 JUMP

The thing the Clash don't: Laura Canyon (aka Sylvie Simmons), 'Metal Daze', *Kerrang!*, 14–27 July 1983
This was not a good night: Monk, *Runnin' with the Devil*
This was Van Halen's audience: Canyon, 'Metal Daze'
Wait a minute: Templeman (as told to Greg Renoff), *Ted Templeman*
He drove down in: Grow, 'Producer Ted Templeman Remembers Eddie Van Halen'
It was the five o'clock: Lisa Robinson, 'David Lee Roth', *Rock Video Magazine*, July 1984
After a while: Templeman (as told to Greg Renoff), *Ted Templeman*
We were always disagreeing: McNair, 'I'm the One'
Nobody was happy: Gill, 'Eddie Van Halen revisits Van Halen's landmark 1984 album'
I'd made a little acoustic: Chris Bird, 'Brian May Pays Tribute to His Friend Eddie Van Halen: "I Miss His Presence in the World"', *Total Guitar*, 18 December 2020
I heard the guitar solo: Roth, *Crazy from the Heat*

What did Edward do: Miller, 'Van Halen's Split Personality'
I said to myself: Roth, *Crazy from the Heat*
The fun and camaraderie: Bertinelli, *Losing It*
Most heavy-metal bands: Miller, 'Van Halen's Split Personality'
We were all tired: Monk, *Runnin' with the Devil*

7   Love Walks In

It's just that: David Gans, 'What It Be, David Lee?', *Record*, April 1985
I'm not going solo: Ben Fong-Torres, 'David Lee Roth – Hyperactive, Irrepressible, Self-Satisfied', *San Francisco Chronicle*, 10 February 1985
Right now, in real life: Fong-Torres, 'David Lee Roth'
It's business conflicts: ibid.
We have a commitment: Gans, 'What It Be, David Lee?'
The chemistry had turned: Roth, *Crazy from the Heat*
He said, 'Look I gotta': Lyndsey Parker, 'Patty Smyth Talks Hiatus, McEnroe Marriage and How She Almost Became Van Halen's Singer: "I Went the Route I Was Supposed to Go"', Yahoo.com, 15 October 2020
He said, 'Wow, this could be': Rosen, 'On the Road', *Guitar World*, September 1986
These guys had cigarette butts: Dave Everley, 'Sammy Hagar interview: Diamond Dave, the Van Halens, and a Long Life in Rock', *Classic Rock*, 9 October 2019
Dave always hated Sammy: Rosen, 'On the Road'
We just cranked up: Everley, 'Sammy Hagar interview'
Sammy said, 'Mick, you and I': Paul Elliott, 'Van Halen: On 5150, Dave Lee Roth Was the Enemy of All Enemies', *Classic Rock*, March 2014
I've never heard anything: ibid.

8 Feels So Good

I don't know if: Rosen, 'On the Road'

I was able to push: Elliott, 'Van Halen'

He was just a great: Kory Grow, 'Foreigner's Mick Jones Remembers Racing Cars with Eddie Van Halen While Making 5150', *Rolling Stone*, 6 October 2020

We had a good time: ibid.

Every day seemed to become: Bertinelli, *Losing It*

The guys go on about: Dave DiMartino, 'David Lee Roth: Foul-Mouthed Reagan Shocks the World', *Creem*, June 1986

I said a few: David Fricke, 'Van Halen: Can This Be Love?', *Rolling Stone*, 3 July 1986

Now that they realise: DiMartino, 'David Lee Roth'

At first Sammy thought: Gene Stout, 'Van Halen: Aching but Sober', *Seattle Post Intelligencer*, 21 September 1995

I didn't drink to party: Chuck Klosterman, 'Eddie Van Halen on Surviving Addiction, Why He's Still Making Music, and What He Really Thinks of David Lee Roth', *Billboard*, 19 June 2015

Alcohol is funny: David Criblez, 'Lord of the Skins', *The Inside*, Issue 2, Summer 1995

Van Halen wanted to make: Steve Pond, 'Van Halen Feel the Burn', *Rolling Stone*, 14 July 1988

The way I look at it: ibid.

I just asked the guys: ibid.

9 Fire in the Hole

I had pneumonia: Rob Tannenbaum and Craig Marks, *I Want My MTV: The Uncensored Story of the Music Video Revolution*, Plume, 2011

Mo Ostin, the chairman: ibid.

I can always make: Jas Obrecht, 'Edward the 9th: Van Halen Finds the Big Vibe on for Unlawful Carnal Knowledge', *Guitar Player*, August 1991

It's really hard to: Sammy Hagar, *Red: My Uncensored Life in Rock*, It Books, 2011

Having a son is: Obrecht, 'Edward the 9th'

Sometimes I caught Ed: Bertinelli, *Losing It*

I fucked everything: Hagar, *Red*

It was just his: Wild, 'Eddie Van Halen'

When I walked up: www.vhlinks.com/vbforums/threads/2784-Nirvana-and-Van-Halen

Eddie went into this: Charles Cross, *Heavier Than Heaven*, Hyperion, 2001

Actually you can jam: ibid.

I was just shocked: www.vhlinks.com/vbforums/threads/2784-Nirvana-and-Van-Halen

He was like a: Roy Trakin, 'Difficult Years Give "Balance" to Van Halen's Newest Effort', spokesman.com, 24 January 1995

I was sitting around: Wild, 'Eddie Van Halen'

Sam was distant: excerpted from *Hits*, 15 June 1996, reported in *The Inside*, Issue 6, Fall 1996

Bruce just said: Tom Beaujour with Greg Di Benedetto, 'Cut and Dry', *Guitar World*, February 1995

I didn't drink: ibid.

I drink more when: ibid.

We'd been traveling: Dave Larsen, 'Van Halen "Gun Thing" Behind Him', sfgate.com, 24 April 1995

Just two weeks ago: ibid.

I understand him: excerpted from *Pollstar*, 15 June 1996, reported in *The Inside*, Issue 6, Fall 1996

Nobody ever talks: Roth, *Crazy from the Heat*

OK, you can't repeat: Brian Hiatt, 'Did Van Halen Have a Fourth Singer? Mitch Malloy Tells His Story', rollingstone.com, 10 February 2021

The door opened: ibid.

I jumped out: ibid.

We are not going: excerpt from *Pollstar*, 15 June 1996, reported in *The Inside*, Issue 6, Fall 1996

In LA, there's not: Doug Fox, 'Using the Gift', *The Inside*, Issue 11

I'll never forget: ibid.

The new record: ibid.

It wasn't going: Andy Greene, 'Gary Cherone Reflects on His Three-Year Stint in Van Halen', rollingstone.com, 10 February 2016

I said, "You want": Hiatt, 'Did Van Halen Have a Fourth Singer?'

10 DISTANCE

After 20 years: Bertinelli, *Losing It*

Eddie once bought: Andrew Bennett, *Eruption in the Canyon: 212 Days & Nights with the Genius of Eddie Van Halen*, Permuted Press, 2020

His marriage was over: Hagar, *Red*

Ed's adrift right now: McNair, 'I'm the One'

Wolfgang breathes new life: author unknown, *Guitar World*, December 2006

I found out: Joe Bosso, 'Michael Anthony: I Never Quit Van Halen', musicradar.com, 2 June 2009

All I wanted: Curcurito, 'Eddie Van Halen'

For the first time: author unknown, *Hustler*, April 2009

We went up to 5150: Chris Gill, 'Interview: Eddie Van Halen Talks a Different Kind of Truth', *Guitar World*, August 2012

I was amazed: ibid.

I didn't want to: ibid.

There are mistakes: Chris Gill, 'Eddie Van Halen Discusses Tokyo Dome Live in Concert, Van Halen's First Official Live Record with David Lee Roth', *Guitar World*, 23 April 2015

Bottom line is: Stuart Williams, 'There are no rules', musicradar. com, 2016

Play, boy: Dave Ling, 'Into The Spotlight', *Classic Rock*, July 2021

My dad wasn't: ibid.

You feel the history: Jonny Scaramanga, 'And The Cradle Will Rock…' *Total Guitar*, June 2021

BIBLIOGRAPHY

Before listing the key texts which have sought to document and dissect the Van Halen story across the past five decades, it would be doing readers a disservice not to single out for recommendation the outstanding *Van Halen Rising*, published by ECW Press in 2015 and referenced earlier in these pages as the definitive early-years Van Halen biography. Written by Greg Renoff, it's a forensically researched, illuminating and evocative account of the group's formative years, a work of such magnitude that, quite truthfully, the prospect of following in its wake caused this writer such anxiety that it delayed the publication of the book you're now holding by six whole years. Every Van Halen fan should seek it out forthwith.

Massive credit is also due to Steven Rosen and Jas Obrecht, two writers Eddie Van Halen trusted more than any other, whose classic interviews with the guitarist, for *Guitar World* and *Guitar Player* respectively, will forever be religious texts for Van Halen disciples.

Bertinelli, Valerie, *Losing It – And Gaining My Life Back One Pound at a Time* (Free Press, 2008)

Christie, Ian, *Everybody Wants Some: The Van Halen Saga* (John Wiley & Sons, 2007)

Dodds, Kevin, *Eddie Van Halen: A Definitive Biography* (iUniverse, 2011)

Hagar, Sammy, *Red: My Uncensored Life in Rock* (It Books, 2011)

Konow, David, *Bang Your Head: The Rise and Fall of Heavy Metal* (Plexus, 2002)

Monk, Noel, *Runnin' with the Devil: A Backstage Pass to the Wild Times, Loud Rock and the Down and Dirty Truth Behind the Making of Van Halen* (Dey Street Books, 2017)

Renoff, Greg, *Van Halen Rising: How a Southern California Backyard Party Band Saved Heavy Metal* (ECW, 2015)

Roth, David Lee, *Crazy from the Heat* (Ebury Press, 1997)

Scanlan, John, *Van Halen: Exuberant California, Zen Rock 'n' Roll* (Reaktion Books, 2012)

Tannenbaum, Rob and Marks, Craig, *I Want My MTV: The Uncensored Story of the Music Video Revolution* (Plume, 2011)

Templeman, Ted (as told to Greg Renoff), *Ted Templeman: A Platinum Producer's Life in Music* (ECW, 2020)

Wiederhorn, Jon and Turman, Katherine, *Louder Than Hell: The Definitive Oral History of Metal* (It Books, 2014)

Wiley, Elizabeth *Could This Be Magic: Van Halen Before 1978* (Trafford, 2012)

Zlozower, Neil, *Eddie Van Halen* (Chronicle Books, 2011)

Zlozower, Neil, *Van Halen: A Visual History 1978–1984* (Chronicle Books, 2007)

In addition, the following publications proved invaluable in researching this book: *Billboard*, *Classic Rock*, *Creem*, *Esquire*, *Guitar Player*, *Guitar World*, *The Inside*, *Kerrang!*, the *New Musical Express*, *Planet Rock*, *Record Mirror*, *Rolling Stone*, *Sounds*, the *Los Angeles Times*, the *New York Times* and the incomparable Van Halen News Desk site, vhnd.com.

ACKNOWLEDGMENTS

This book would not exist were it not for the invaluable support, guidance and expertise of Sabrina Choo at Jigsaw Complete, Anne Owen, Paul Baillie-Lane, Mark Bolland, Dan Papps and Hannah Marshall at Faber, Daniel Oertel at Ullstein, Jacob Hoye at Permuted Press, Andrea Shallcross at Hachette Book Group, Nicki Kennedy and May Wall at ILA, Ian Bahrami, Luke Bird, Matt Turner and my much-valued agent Matthew Hamilton at the Hamilton Agency (UK).

Respect and gratitude to Geezer Butler, Ian Danter, Malcolm Dome, Elliott Gilbert, Scott Gorham, Lynore Grace, Lizzie Grey (RIP), Sammy Hagar, Ross Halfin, the fabulous Catherine 'English Cathy' Hutchin-Harris, Tony Iommi, Mark Kendall, Greg Magie, Brian May, Bob Nalbandian, Jas Obrecht, Ozzy Osbourne, Joe Perry, Michael Schenker, Gene Simmons, Paul Stanley, Liz Wiley, Nancy Wilson, Zakk Wylde and Neil Zlozower for insights and interviews.

Sincere thanks, and in some instances, equally sincere apologies, to the brilliant Briony Edwards and all at *Louder*, Sam Coare and all at *Kerrang!*, Pat Gilbert, Mark Blake and Russell Moorcroft at *Planet Rock* (RIP), Siân Llewellyn and all at *Classic*

Rock, Merlin Alderslade and all at *Metal Hammer*, Jenny Bulley and all at *Mojo*, plus word-bothering brothers-in-arms Ian Winwood, Dave Everley, Simon Young, James McNair, Paul 'Gooner' Elliott and the ever-inspirational Phil Alexander.

Special thanks to Angus Denvir for introducing me to Van Halen in 1981, and to Angus Cargill, my superb editor at Faber & Faber, for his peerless craft, priceless guidance and boundless patience.

The first draft of this book was initially due to be with Faber & Faber on 31 March 2015. In reality, the final chapter was filed on 1 April 2021. Much has occurred in the six years that separate these dates – most significantly, in terms of the story presented here, the death, on 6 October 2020, of Edward Van Halen. Condolences to those that loved him most.

To Patricia and Joe Corrigan, sorry I didn't get to say goodbye. Rest in peace together.

And finally, endless love to my own family – Hiroko, Yuki and Tyler – and the extended Brannigan and Kato families.

ABOUT THE AUTHOR

London-based Irish writer and journalist Paul Brannigan has two books due for publication in 2021—a fully updated and revised 10th anniversary edition of his 2011 *Sunday Times* bestseller *This Is a Call: The Life and Times of Dave Grohl*, set for publication via HarperCollins on September 2, and a revealing new biography of legendary, much-missed guitar god, Eddie Van Halen, scheduled for publication via Faber & Faber (UK, September 23), Permuted Press (US, December 14), and Ullstein (GER, August 30). Brannigan is a former editor of *Kerrang!* and *Planet Rock* magazine, and a contributor to *Mojo*, *Classic Rock*, and *Kerrang!*